Montgomery's
Auditing
Eleventh Edition
1993–94 Cumulative Supplement

Montgomery's
Auditing
Eleventh Edition
1993–94 Cumulative Supplement

Vincent M. O'Reilly, CPA
**Chief Operating Officer,
Coopers & Lybrand**

Patrick J. McDonnell, CPA
**Vice Chairman, Business Assurance,
Coopers & Lybrand**

James S. Gerson, CPA
Director, Audit Policy, Coopers & Lybrand

Henry R. Jaenicke, Ph.D., CPA
**C. D. Clarkson Professor of Accounting,
College of Business and Administration,
Drexel University**

John Wiley & Sons, Inc.
New York • Chichester • Brisbane • Toronto • Singapore

SUBSCRIPTION NOTICE

In recognition of the importance of preserving what has been written, it is a policy of John Wiley & Sons, Inc., to have books of enduring value published in the United States printed on acid-free paper, and we exert our best efforts to that end.

Material from Statements on Standards for Consulting Services, Statements on Auditing Standards, Statements on Standards for Attestation Engagements, and Statements of Position, copyright © 1990–1993 by American Institute of Certified Public Accountants, Inc., is reprinted with permission.

Library of Congress Cataloging-in-Publication Data

Montgomery, Robert Hiester, 1872–1953.
  Montgomery's Auditing.
  Includes index.
  1. Auditing. I. O'Reilly, Vincent M.   II. Title.
III. Title: Auditing.
HF5667.M7   1990   657'.45   84-27103
ISBN 0-471-50522-6
ISBN 0-471-59241-2 (Supplement)

Printed in the United States of America
10 9 8 7 6 5 4 3 2 1

Preface

The business environment in the 1990s is more fast-paced than ever before, affecting all aspects of the economy. All enterprises, whether in the public or the private sector and regardless of industry, are subject to volatile economic forces as well as to new legislation reaching into unprecedented areas. As clients adapt to these changing conditions, the audit environment also changes, necessitating that practitioners keep up-to-date with developments on various fronts.

This environment calls for increased professional standards and guidance. It also leads to increased reflection about and study of the theory and practice of auditing. This Supplement, then, updates the eleventh edition of *Montgomery's Auditing*, published early in 1990, for legislative, regulatory, and professional developments through June 30, 1993. It presents the authors' current thinking and insights about material discussed in the main volume, as well as coverage of relevant events that have occurred since the main volume was published. To facilitate its use in conjunction with the main volume, this Supplement contains a cumulative index that includes all entries in the main volume plus new entries (page numbers preceded by "S").

We acknowledge with thanks the permission granted to us by the American Institute of Certified Public Accountants to quote or paraphrase passages from its publications. Copies of the complete documents can be obtained directly from the Institute.

This Supplement represents the efforts and ideas of many people. The following individuals, presently or formerly associated with Coopers & Lybrand, contributed to various portions of the book: Martin Abrahams, James B. Alfano, Christy P. Armstrong, George R. Auxier, John T. Baily, Alan M. Bangser, Clark L. Bernard, Bhaskar H. Bhave, Colin Blair, Donald E. Brooks, Robert A. Brown, Stephen P. Bucalo, John Tobin Buckley, Clark Chandler, Michael J. Cuddy, William E. Decker, Jr., Robert L. DeNormandie, Raymond L. Dever, Nelson W. Dittmar, Jr., Richard D. Dole, Alan L. Earhart, Richard W. Ellis, W. Larry Farmer, Robert J. Faulk, Joseph B. Feiten, Cynthia L. Feldmann, Gary G. Flori, Michael J. Ford, Robert T. Forrester, John J. Gillen, Michael P. Glinsky, Richard A. Gnospelius, Lynford E. Graham, Jr., Delaine H. Gruber, Bjorn Hanson, John M. Hollenbeck, Normandie R. Holmes, Robin M. Honig, Sheryl A. Huffaker, William

L. Jennings, Keith F. Jensen, Sandra L. Johnson, Phyllis M. Jones, Douglas M. Keeslar, Curtis J. Klement, Cheryl H. Lippert, Stephen J. Lis, Rocco J. Maggiotto, Ronald T. Maheu, Michael A. McBride, John H. McCarthy, Joel W. Meyerson, David L. Millstein, Nicholas G. Moore, Ronald J. Murray, Joel S. Osnoss, Dennis E. Peavey, Susan C. Rector, Walter G. Ricciardi, Laura A. Ring, Michael A. Rogge, Henry J. Schultzel, Larry P. Schumann, H. Lin Shiau, Glenn A. Shively, Richard M. Steinberg, Joel Tancer, Kim D. Thorpe, Allison Thrush, Stanley B. Tulin, Lynn E. Turner, Robert W. Uek, Kenneth D. Williams, and Linda J. Worthylake.

We owe a special acknowledgment to A. J. Lorie, partner at Coopers & Lybrand, for his invaluable assistance in thoughtfully and carefully reviewing the manuscript. Our thanks also go to Myra D. Cleary, senior editor of this work. To all the above-named individuals, and any who were inadvertently omitted, go not only our thanks, but also the usual absolution from blame for errors and omissions.

V.M.O.
P.J.M.
J.S.G.
H.R.J.

Cumulative Supplement Contents

Note to the Reader: Materials new to or modified in *this* Supplement are indicated by an asterisk (*) in the left margin of the contents and throughout the Supplement. Sections not in the main volume are indicated by a (New) after the title.

Chapter 25   Compliance Auditing   149

Chapter 26   Auditing Banks   165

Chapter 27   Auditing Colleges, Universities, and Independent Schools   177

Chapter 28   Auditing Construction Companies   183

Chapter 29   Auditing Emerging Businesses   185

Chapter 30   Auditing Health Care Institutions   191

1

An Overview of Auditing

* **p. 20.** *Add at end of chapter:*

An Overview of Current Developments

The main volume noted the principal ways through which the auditing profession has sought to narrow the expectation gap. This section summarizes a few of the more significant events affecting the expectation gap that have taken place since the eleventh edition was published, including events that are still unfolding as this Supplement is being written. (Many of the matters discussed in this section are elaborated on in greater detail later in this Supplement.)

Strengthening Public Trust in Financial Reporting. In June 1993, the AICPA Board of Directors announced a series of proposals to increase the usefulness of financial reporting, improve the prevention and detection of fraud, ensure auditor independence and objectivity, strengthen the profession's system of self-regulation, and reform the liability system. Titled *Meeting the Financial Reporting Needs of the Future: A Public Commitment from the Accounting Profession,* the document also endorsed and incorporated recommendations from the Special Report by the Public Oversight Board (POB), *In the Public Interest: Issues Confronting the Accounting Profession,* published in March 1993.

Making Financial Reporting More Useful. The AICPA created a Special Committee on Financial Reporting in 1991 to determine the type of information that users will need in the years ahead. That committee is expected to issue its report in 1994. In addressing users' more immediate needs, the AICPA (1) urged the Accounting Standards Executive Committee (AcSEC) to complete work on its proposal to require financial statement disclosure of significant

1

risks and uncertainties (see the discussion in Chapter 21A of this Supplement); (2) called for mandatory management reporting on the effectiveness of internal control over financial reporting, accompanied by an auditor's report on management's assertions (see below and Chapter 23 of this Supplement); and (3) proposed that the SEC require audit committees to include a statement in the annual report describing their responsibilities and how they were met.

Improving Fraud Prevention and Detection.   The AICPA and the six largest accounting firms had previously supported proposed federal legislation, known as the Financial Fraud Detection and Disclosure Act, that would identify auditor performance and reporting responsibilities related to fraudulent financial reporting (see the discussion below and in Chapter 4 of this Supplement). The AICPA also suggested ways to enhance the auditor's fraud-detection capabilities and committed the accounting profession to establishing "a systematic process for reviewing past cases of fraud to learn how the financial statements were manipulated, how detection was initially avoided, what audit procedures did detect or might have detected the illegality, and how audits can be changed to prevent a reoccurrence."

Ensuring Auditor Independence and Objectivity.   The AICPA, noting that "a few recent high-profile financial scandals have . . . called auditors' independence into question," recommended that the SEC and other regulators impose a one-year waiting period before a public company could hire the audit partner who previously served it. The AICPA also endorsed the proposal made by the POB, and others before it, that public companies should be required to have audit committees and that those committees should be charged with specific responsibilities (see the discussion in Chapter 3 of the main volume).

Strengthening the Self-Regulatory System.   Chapter 3 of the main volume describes the profession's self-disciplinary mechanism for individuals who are AICPA members. Under present practices, disciplining of alleged wrongdoers must await the conclusion of any related litigation. In its June 1993 statement, the AICPA recommended eliminating that constraint, provided that a mechanism was created to insulate the disciplinary system and the civil liability system from each other. The AICPA also endorsed the POB's proposals for expanding the responsibilities of firms, the peer review process, and the SECPS Quality Control Inquiry Committee (see Chapter 3 of the main volume) with respect to investigating and learning from alleged audit failures.

Reforming the Civil Liability System.   For several years, the major accounting firms have expressed concern over a joint and several liability standard that can result in the full monetary loss suffered by investors and creditors being borne by the auditing firm, which may be a relatively minor participant in fraudulent financial reporting. (See the discussion on page 104 of the main volume.) Accountants are also concerned about a number of other aspects of the present legal system, namely, that it may not ensure that those who are defrauded receive the compensation they deserve; may discourage the disclosure of useful financial information; may provide disincentives for innocent defendants to vindicate themselves at trial; and may provide incentives for attorneys to profit by pursuing plainly meritless cases. In addition, there are restrictions under state law governing the way CPA firms can be organized that give each partner in a firm unlimited liability for the actions of every other partner and of every employee. (See also the discussion on form of practice in Chapter 3 of this Supplement.)

The June 1993 statement by the AICPA, echoing the March 1993 Special Report of the POB, noted the consequences of the present liability system, as follows:

> For fear of unreasonable liability, auditors are reluctant to introduce innovations that the financial markets urgently need, such as assurance on forward-looking financial data. Some firms are refusing to audit smaller, high-risk companies; often, these are high-technology companies whose success is vital to the nation's economic growth and competitiveness. Moreover, accountants' liability exposure damages the profession's ability to attract and retain highly qualified people, which has an adverse impact upon the profession's ability to serve American business and the investing public.

In response, the major firms, the POB, and the AICPA have all called for adoption of a proportionate liability standard, which would hold a defendant responsible solely for his or her actions and not the harm caused by others. Those groups also have pressed for legislation that would permit practice in a corporate form that would limit the liability of individual auditor/shareholders to the amount of their investment in their firms. In addition, there are those who advocate the establishment of safeguards against frivolous lawsuits, for example, through higher standards of evidence for determining culpability and revised guidelines for awarding of attorney fees. At the time of this writing, legislation is under consideration in a bill before Congress (H.R. 417), entitled the Securities Private Enforcement Reform Act, that addresses many of the concerns noted above.

Auditor "Whistleblowing."   One of the more significant demands on the profession is for it to accept expanded responsibilities for publicly reporting instances of clients' noncompliance with laws and regulations—commonly referred to as "whistleblowing." As detailed in Chapter 4 of this Supplement, both the AICPA and the six largest accounting firms have endorsed the concept of a statutory requirement for the auditor to notify the SEC of possible illegal acts by clients if management and the board of directors, after having been informed of such acts by the auditor, fail to take timely and appropriate remedial action, and fail to notify the SEC of that inaction. At the time of this writing, legislation to enforce this requirement has been introduced in both houses of Congress but has not been enacted.

Professional auditing standards presently limit the auditor's whistleblowing responsibilities to disclosure to the SEC if an auditor withdraws from an engagement with a client subject to the federal securities laws because the client has failed to take the appropriate remedial action in the face of an irregularity or illegal act and the client has reported an auditor change on Form 8-K. As discussed in Chapter 23 of this Supplement, Statement on Auditing Standards (SAS) No. 71, *Interim Financial Information,* which was issued in May 1992, also requires an auditor to consider resigning from the engagement if, as a result of assisting the client in the preparation of the interim information or performing any review procedures, he or she becomes aware of a probable material misstatement in interim financial information and the client does not respond appropriately when notified of the misstatement.

Auditor resistance to direct reporting of noncompliance results principally from a belief that management—when it becomes aware of an irregularity or illegal act—should be given the opportunity to exercise its responsibility to take appropriate action or to disclose that it has failed to do so. The proposed legislation discussed above accommodates this concern. Also, there are concerns that allegations of illegalities might in retrospect be unfounded but public disclosure of them may still cause harm to the client.

Reporting on Internal Control.   Another contentious area where an expectation gap continues to exist involves public reporting on an entity's internal controls. As discussed in Chapter 23 of the main volume and this Supplement, several study groups and professional organizations have recommended that enterprise management issue a report to shareholders that would include an assessment of the entity's internal control structure. The Commission on Auditors' Responsibilities (Cohen Commission) and the National Committee on Fraudulent Financial Reporting (Treadway Commission) recommended auditor association with management's report, as did the 1993 Special Report of the Public Oversight Board and the 1993 proposal by the AICPA Board of Directors.

In 1988, the SEC issued proposed rules that would require registrants to include a report of management's responsibilities for internal controls in annual reports to shareholders and annual filings with the SEC. The proposed rules did not include explicit auditor reporting on internal controls or management's report thereon, but they did require the auditor to consider the requirements of SAS No. 8, *Other Information in Documents Containing Audited Financial Statements.* Many reservations were expressed about the proposed rules, and the SEC withdrew the proposed rules in April 1992.

One potential impediment to management reporting on internal control—the absence of established criteria for evaluating internal controls—has been removed. In September 1992, the Committee of Sponsoring Organizations of the Treadway Commission (COSO) issued its report entitled *Internal Control—Integrated Framework,* authored by Coopers & Lybrand, which set forth such criteria. Concurrent with that endeavor, the Auditing Standards Board developed guidance for performing and reporting on engagements to attest to management's report on internal controls. (See Chapter 24 of this Supplement.) A common thread woven through the profession's positions both on reporting on internal control and on whistleblowing is that the responsibilities of the auditor and of enterprise management are clearly delineated: Enterprise management is the asserter; the CPA reports on management's assertions.

There are some who contend that existing laws such as the Foreign Corrupt Practices Act (see page 210 of the main volume) and the 1933 and 1934 Securities Acts provide for adequate sanctions and accountability for internal controls and financial reporting for all SEC registrants. Additionally, they point to the COSO report as a private-sector initiative that will bring about improvement in the internal control area and further encourage voluntary reporting by management.

They note that there may be significant costs, particularly to smaller entities, of engaging auditors to attest to management reports on internal control, and question whether the benefits to users outweigh those costs. Accordingly, they oppose any legislative or regulatory attempts to mandate management reporting on internal control and accompanying auditor attestation.

In May 1993, however, the Federal Deposit Insurance Corporation issued a rule to implement the Federal Deposit Insurance Corporation Improvement Act of 1991 (FDICIA) that would require managements of insured depository institutions with $500 million or more in total assets to report on internal controls over financial reporting (as defined in the rule) and obtain auditor attestations to those reports. The rule also includes provisions with respect to annual audits, the composition of audit committees, reporting on compliance with certain laws and regulations, and other matters. FDICIA is discussed in more detail in Chapter 26 of this Supplement.

Accounting Profession's Position on Proposals to Legislate Auditing Requirements.   The major accounting firms and the AICPA have set forth what they believe are fundamental principles that should be incorporated in any legislation mandating new auditing and accounting requirements. A summary of these principles follows:

- The integrity of generally accepted auditing standards and generally accepted accounting principles should be maintained, and setting of these standards should be preserved in the private sector. If regulators need additional financial information, the information should be provided separately from the general-purpose financial statements.
- If management is required to report on matters such as the effectiveness of internal controls, the report should be accompanied by an accountant's attestation thereon, setting forth the accountant's responsibility.
- Any requirement for an accountant to report events to a third party should be preceded by a requirement that management first report the events. Only upon failure of such management reporting would an accountant be required to make such a report.
- Assurances sought on matters beyond those provided by an audit of the financial statements and report on internal controls (e.g., assurances concerning compliance with specified laws and regulations) should be accomplished through the following framework:
  - • The matter should be within the accountant's competence.
  - • The matter should be one for which criteria can be developed and permit reasonably consistent determinations.
  - • The requirement should be precise enough to permit an objective evaluation.
  - • The accountant's report should be in the form of procedures and findings whenever an agreed-upon procedures attest engagement is performed.
  - • Regulators should be required to give adequate consideration to the costs and benefits of implementing any changes.

Other Developments.   Other recent developments related to the public's expectations of auditors, and the chapter in this Supplement in which they are discussed, are

- In late 1990, the 75-year-old accounting firm of Laventhol & Horwath, besieged by lawsuits and indebtedness, entered bankruptcy (Chapter 4).
- The past several years have seen a heightened concern over both accounting and auditing aspects of environmental liabilities. The FASB's Emerging Issues Task Force has addressed a number of accounting issues related to accounting for environmental costs, and the SEC has expressed concerns over the adequacy of disclosures, in the Management Discussion and Analysis section of 10-K filings, of potential liabilities for environmental clean-up costs (Chapter 16).
- In 1990, the AICPA began issuing a series of "Audit Risk Alerts" covering economic, regulatory, and professional developments that could affect the auditor's assessment of inherent risk conditions (see Chapter 6 of the main volume) in specific industries. (Similar matters are discussed in the specialized industry chapters of this Supplement.)
- Accounting standard setters and regulators continue to devote significant resources to measurement and disclosure issues related to financial instruments in general and to how they are accounted for and disclosed by financial institutions in particular. For example, since the publication of the main volume, the FASB has issued the following Statements of Financial Accounting Standards:

No.	Date Issued	Title	Supplement Chapter No.
105	March 1990	*Disclosure of Information about Financial Instruments with Off-Balance Sheet Risk and Financial Instruments with Concentrations of Credit Risk*	21A
107	December 1991	*Disclosures about Fair Value of Financial Instruments*	21A
114	May 1993	*Accounting by Creditors for Impairment of a Loan*	26
115	May 1993	*Accounting for Certain Investments in Debt and Equity Securities*	17

- Accounting standard setters are imposing increasing requirements on preparers to present information based on measurements that are subject to a wide range of values. Those measurements frequently involve estimates whose accuracy depends on future events and developments—sometimes referred to as "soft" information. Certain components of the FASB Statements noted above contain such requirements. Other examples can be found in FASB Statement No. 106, *Employers' Accounting for Postretirement Benefits Other Than Pensions,* FASB Statement No. 112, *Employers' Accounting for Postemployment Benefits,* FASB Statement No. 109, *Accounting for Income Taxes,* and the exposure draft of the AICPA Statement of Position on disclosure of risks and uncertainties, discussed in Chapters 16, 19, and 21A of this Supplement.

2

The Organization and Structure of the Auditing Profession

The Organization of the Auditing Profession

* **p. 30.** *Add at bottom of page:*

Pages 30 and 31 of the main volume discuss the structure of the American Institute of Certified Public Accountants (AICPA) and its senior technical committees. In late 1991, the Management Advisory Services Executive Committee changed its name to the Management Consulting Services Executive Committee.

The Personal Financial Planning Executive Committee is one of the senior committees of the AICPA authorized to issue public statements. In November 1992, the AICPA issued Statement on Responsibilities in Personal Financial Planning Practice (SRPFP) No. 1, *Basic Personal Financial Planning Engagement Functions and Responsibilities,* which provides guidance for CPAs who offer personal financial planning (PFP) services. (This series of statements does not constitute enforceable standards under the AICPA Code of Professional Conduct.)

SRPFP No. 1 establishes the scope of PFP and delineates the CPA's responsibilities in defining the objectives of an engagement, planning the work, developing and communicating recommendations, helping the client in implementing decisions, monitoring the client's achievement of objectives, and updating objectives.

In May 1993, two additional proposed SRPFPs were issued for exposure. The first, *Working With Other Advisers,* would provide guidance for CPAs in interacting with other advisers, including using the advice of others and referring a client to other advisers. The proposed statement covers engagement scope limitations, selecting other advisers, using advice provided by others, and recommending advisers to clients. The exposure draft recommends that CPAs disclose limitations on the scope of engagements.

The second exposure draft, *Implementation Engagement Functions and Responsibilities*, establishes the scope of implementation engagements as assisting clients in taking action on planning decisions developed during a basic personal financial planning engagement, as described in SRPFP No. 1. The exposure draft provides guidance on planning, communicating with clients, establishing selection criteria, participating in the selection process, and implementing planning decisions made by others. The proposed SRPFP recommends that CPAs disclose limitations imposed on information used or work performed in developing recommendations.

* **p. 31.** *Replace first paragraph under the figure with the following:*

In addition, the AICPA has four voluntary member sections that individuals with special interests may join: tax, personal financial planning, management consulting services, and information technology. (There is also a Division for CPA Firms, composed of an SEC Practice Section and a Private Companies Practice Section, that CPA firms may join. The Division for CPA Firms is discussed in Chapter 3.) Non-CPAs employed by CPA firms and meeting other eligibility requirements may join one or more of the AICPA's member sections, but not the AICPA itself, as Section Associates and receive the same member section benefits as CPA members. Effective August 1993, individuals who have passed the Uniform CPA Examination, but have not received their CPA certificates because they have not completed their experience requirements, may join an AICPA Associate section.

Professional Standards and Standard-Setting Bodies

* **p. 35.** *Replace third full paragraph with:*

International Auditing Standards.   The desirability of developing more uniform auditing standards and practices worldwide has long been recognized and is gaining increasingly greater support as international business continues to expand. Efforts to promote international uniformity in auditing standards were formally initiated in 1977, when representatives of approximately 50 countries, including the United States, established the International Federation of Accountants (IFAC). The broad objectives of IFAC, as stated in paragraph 2 of its Constitution, are "the development and enhancement of a coordinated worldwide accountancy profession with harmonized standards." IFAC's efforts are directed toward developing international technical, ethical, and educational guidelines for auditors, and reciprocal recognition of practitioners' qualifications.

Responsibility for developing and issuing exposure drafts and standards on generally accepted auditing practices and audit reports is vested in IFAC's International Auditing Practices Committee (IAPC); through June 1993 it has issued 30 International Standards on Auditing (ISAs; previously called International Auditing Guidelines), plus four others in its series entitled International Standards on Auditing/Related Services, all of which are codified in AU Section 8000 of *AICPA Professional Standards.* (The "related services" addressed by the standards are compilations and reviews.) In addition, nine proposed ISAs have been exposed for comment, including two of three planned distributions of what IAPC is calling its "Codification Exposure Drafts," which are the result of a decision to consolidate and codify the ISAs to facilitate their usefulness.

For the most part, the provisions of the standards coincide closely with comparable U.S. standards for audits, compilations, and reviews. Although the standards are not authoritative in the United States and are not covered by the AICPA Code of Professional Conduct, if a standard is intended to be issued that would deviate significantly from U.S. standards, the AICPA's Auditing Standards Board or Accounting and Review Services Committee considers ways of resolving the differences. In addition, the IAPC has issued six International Statements on Auditing, which are intended to assist auditors in implementing the provisions of certain ISAs. This series of statements, which are codified in AU Section 10,000 of *AICPA Professional Standards,* does not have the same authority as the ISAs.

In 1990, IFAC issued "Guideline on Ethics for the Accountancy Profession," which revised and codified its previous ethics pronouncements, consisting of a Statement of Principles, a series of notes explaining the intentions underlying the principles, guidance on implementing ethical standards, and guidelines for formulating ethical requirements. In issuing ethics guidelines, IFAC recognizes that implementation is affected by the legal, social, and economic conditions prevailing in individual countries. Nevertheless, the "Guideline on Ethics" was designed to serve as a prototype for an international code of business ethics.

In October 1992, the International Organization of Securities Commissions (IOSCO) approved a resolution to recognize the ISAs for use in multinational reporting. In recommending that the IOSCO membership take that step, key members of IOSCO's Technical Committee, which reviewed the standards, concluded that they "represent a comprehensive set of auditing standards and that audits conducted in accordance with these standards could be relied upon by securities regulatory authorities for multinational reporting purposes." IOSCO has more than 100 members.

* **p. 37.** *Replace section* **Standards for MAS Practice** *(including Figure 2.2) with:*

Standards for MCS Services.   In late 1991, the AICPA's Management Consulting Services Executive Committee withdrew Statement on Standards for Management Advisory Services (SSMAS) Nos. 1, 2, and 3 and issued the first of a new series of statements entitled Statements on Standards for Consulting Services (SSCS). SSCS No. 1 encompasses a broader range of professional services than was previously covered by the SSMASs. SSCS No. 1 defines the following types of consulting services: consultations, advisory services, implementation services, transaction services, staff and other support services, and product services. It also establishes general standards for consulting services, which consist of the general standards in Rule 201 of the AICPA Code of Professional Conduct plus additional standards that address the distinctive characteristics of consulting services. The latter standards are established under Rule 202 of the Code of Professional Conduct. The standards applicable to consulting services, adapted from *AICPA Professional Standards* CS Sections 100.06 and .07, are summarized in Figure 2.2.

Figure 2.2   Standards for Consulting Practice

General Standards:

Professional competence. Undertake only those professional services that the member or the member's firm can reasonably expect to be completed with professional competence.

Due professional care. Exercise due professional care in the performance of professional services.

Planning and supervision. Adequately plan and supervise the performance of professional services.

Sufficient relevant data. Obtain sufficient relevant data to afford a reasonable basis for conclusions or recommendations in relation to any professional services performed.

General Standards for Consulting Services:

Client interest. Serve the client interest by seeking to accomplish the objectives established by the understanding with the client while maintaining integrity and objectivity.

Understanding with client. Establish with the client a written or oral understanding about the responsibilities of the parties and the nature, scope, and limitations of services to be performed, and modify the understanding if circumstances require a significant change during the engagement.

Communication with client. Inform the client of (*a*) conflicts of interest that may occur pursuant to interpretations of Rule 102 of the Code of Professional Conduct, (*b*) significant reservations concerning the scope or benefits of the engagement, and (*c*) significant engagement findings or events.

Source: AICPA Professional Standards CS Sections 100.06 and .07.

SSCS No. 1 states that the independence rules of the AICPA, state boards of accountancy, state CPA societies, and other regulatory agencies relating to the performance of attest services may prohibit the performance of certain consulting services for attest clients. In general, however, performing consulting services for an attest client would not, in itself, impair independence.

3

Auditing Standards and Professional Conduct

THE AICPA CODE OF PROFESSIONAL CONDUCT

Independence, Integrity, and Objectivity

* **p. 53.** *Add after carryover paragraph:*

In November 1991, the AICPA Professional Ethics Executive Committee issued revisions of Interpretation 101-1, which is quoted on page 52 of the main volume, and Interpretation 101-5, "Loans from Financial Institution Clients and Related Terminology." The revisions prohibit CPAs from having a loan to or from a client, with the exception of the following types of personal loans from financial institutions: (a) automobile loans and leases collateralized by the automobile, (b) loans of the surrender value under terms of an insurance policy, (c) borrowings fully collateralized by cash deposits at the same financial institution (e.g., "passbook loans"), and (d) credit cards and cash advances on checking accounts with an aggregate balance not paid currently of $5,000 or less. Also permitted are home mortgages, other secured loans (for which the value of the collateral must at all times exceed the balance of the loan), and loans not material to the CPA's net worth that (a) existed as of January 1, 1992, (b) were obtained before the lending financial institution become a client requiring independence, (c) were obtained from a financial institution for which independence was not required and were later sold to a client for which independence is required, or (d) were obtained from a firm's financial institution client requiring independence by a borrower before he or she became a member with respect to such client. Permitted loans must be kept current as to all terms and must have been obtained under the financial institution's normal lending procedures, terms, and requirements.

* **p. 54.**   *Replace subsection* **Independence and Attest Engagements** *with:*

Independence and Attest Engagements.   Statement on Standards for Attestation Engagements, *Attestation Standards* (AT Section 100.22–.24), requires members to be independent in performing engagements covered by that Statement. In February 1990, the Professional Ethics Executive Committee issued Interpretation 101-11 (ET Section 101.13) to provide guidance regarding independence for attest engagements not covered by Statements on Auditing Standards, Statements on Standards for Accounting and Review Services, or Statements on Standards for Accountants' Services on Prospective Financial Information.

The Interpretation is noteworthy in that it proscribes specified relationships with both the subject matter of the assertion and the asserter, and provides guidance or examples for each situation. However, the prohibited relationships apply only to the attest engagement team (which is precisely defined in the Interpretation) and their families, to partners or proprietors (and their families) located in an office performing a significant part of the attest engagement, and to certain individuals whose relationships with the subject matter or asserter are known to members of the engagement team. In contrast, prohibited relationships in audit engagements apply to all members of the engagement team, all partners or proprietors in the accounting firm, and all managerial employees in an office that participates in a significant portion of the engagement. A major reason for the difference is that many attest engagements result in client relationships that are only temporary, rather than ongoing, as is usually the case, for example, with audit engagements.

p. 55.   *Add after last paragraph:*
Ethics Ruling No. 52, dealing with unpaid fees (ET Section 191.103–.104), was revised in November 1990, as follows:

> Independence of the member's firm is considered to be impaired if, when the report on the client's current year is issued, fees remain unpaid, whether billed or unbilled, for professional services provided more than one year prior to the date of the report. Such amounts assume the characteristics of a loan within the meaning of Rule 101 and its interpretations.
>
> This ruling does not apply to fees outstanding from a client in bankruptcy.

* **p. 56.**   *Add after subsection* **Conflicts of Interest:**

Members Other Than in Public Practice.   In May 1993, the Professional Ethics Executive Committee issued three proposed interpretations relating to members in industry. Two of the proposed interpretations are under Rule 102 and would clarify that the requirements of that rule regarding integrity and objectivity apply to all AICPA members performing professional services. The first proposed interpretation concerns a member's obligations to an employer's external accountant; the second deals with circumstances where a member has a disagreement with a supervisor regarding the preparation of financial statements or the recording of transactions. In the latter instance, members would be required to take certain steps to ensure that the situation did not constitute a subordination of judgment, which is prohibited by Rule 102. The third proposed interpretation, this one under Rule 203, would emphasize a member's responsibility for the preparation of financial statements in conformity with GAAP. The Professional Ethics Executive Committee and other AICPA divisions are currently considering proposals that would clarify the obligations under the Code of Professional Conduct of other categories of AICPA members who are not in public practice.

Responsibilities to Clients

* **p. 58.** *Replace first paragraph with:*
A fundamental responsibility of the CPA concerns the confidentiality of client information. Rule 301, as revised in January 1992, states that "a member in public practice shall not disclose any confidential client information without the specific consent of the client."[1] A major reason for revising the rule was to clarify that members may disclose certain information to the AICPA ethics division and state boards, or in connection with a practice monitoring program, but may not volunteer confidential client information to government agencies.

p. 60. *Add after fourth paragraph:*
Ethics Interpretation 301-3, "Confidential Information and the Purchase, Sale, or Merger of a Practice" (ET Section 301.04), was issued in February 1990 to clarify that Rule 301 does not prohibit the review of a CPA's professional practice in conjunction with a prospective purchase, sale, or merger. The Interpretation states that the CPA must take precautions to prevent the disclosure of any client information obtained by the reviewer, since such information is considered to be confidential.

On a related matter, several state licensing authorities have concluded that a peer review of an accounting firm, in which engagement documentation is reviewed by another accounting firm, violates client confidentiality. In response, some accounting firms are asking clients for advance approval for review of information by another firm; the request is sometimes made in the engagement letter.

* In 1992, the AICPA membership voted to amend Rule 301 to clarify that CPAs could file complaints with state societies or boards of accountancy without violating client confidentiality, even if the complaint necessitates disclosing confidential client information without the specific consent of the client. The intent of the Rule, however, is not to permit CPAs to inform on their clients to regulatory agencies, such as the IRS.

---

[1] Rule 301, as revised, states that "this rule shall not be construed (1) to relieve a member of his or her professional obligations under rules 202 and 203, (2) to affect in any way the member's obligation to comply with a validly issued and enforceable subpoena or summons, or to prohibit a member's compliance with applicable laws and government regulations, (3) to prohibit review of a member's professional practice under AICPA or state CPA society or Board of Accountancy authorization, or (4) to preclude a member from initiating a complaint with, or responding to any inquiry made by, the ethics division or trial board of the Institute or a duly constituted investigative or disciplinary body of a state CPA society or Board of Accountancy."

Other Responsibilities and Practices

* **p. 61.** *Add item 5 to list:*

> 5. Failure to follow requirements (e.g., established standards, guides, rules, and regulations) of governmental or regulatory agencies in performing attest or similar services.

pp. 61–63. *Replace from* **Form of Practice and Name and Ownership of Practice Units** *up to* **AICPA–FTC Consent Agreement** *with:*

* **Form of Organization and Name.** In November 1991, the AICPA voted overwhelmingly in favor of revising Rule 505 to remove the restrictions on the form of a CPA's practice. Previously, Rule 505 restricted the form of practice to a proprietorship, partnership, or professional corporation. In the latter case, the corporation had to conform with characteristics stipulated by the Institute. Rule 505 now allows CPAs to practice public accounting in any organizational form permitted by state law or regulation, including a general corporation. A major reason underlying the change is a belief that the previous rule restricted CPAs in limiting their individual liability exposure and their flexibility in responding to a dynamic business environment.

* Rule 505 was revised previously to eliminate a prohibition against using a firm name that included a fictitious name or indicated specialization. The prohibition against fictitious names was removed because it was vulnerable to restraint of trade allegations and was inconsistent with the rule on advertising and solicitation, which prohibits only claims that are false, misleading, or deceptive. Since a member may advertise a specialty, there is no reason a firm should not be allowed to do so in its name, provided the false, misleading, or deceptive test is met.

* Rule 505 now reads as follows:

> A member may practice public accounting only in a form of organization permitted by state law or regulation whose characteristics conform to resolutions of Council.

> A member shall not practice public accounting under a firm name that is misleading. Names of one or more past owners may be included in the firm name of a successor organization. Also, an owner surviving the death or withdrawal of all other owners may continue to practice under a name which includes the name of past owners for up to two years after becoming a sole practitioner.

> A firm may not designate itself as "Members of the American Institute of Certified Public Accountants" unless all of its owners are members of the Institute.

* Appendix B to the Code contains a resolution of AICPA Council that specifies the characteristics that an entity (other than a proprietorship or partnership) must have to comply with Rule 505. That resolution restricts ownership of an entity to persons engaged in the practice of public accounting, and is intended to make an entity's owners subject to the Institute's technical, ethical, and practice-monitoring requirements and its self-regulatory and disciplinary processes.

*   The issue of ownership of CPA firms involves complex economic and social considerations. One aspect of the question has been settled by the revision of Rule 505 to allow CPAs to choose the form of organization in which to practice. Critics of the previous rule argued that it unfairly restricted CPAs in their professional practice by preventing them from limiting their personal liability exposure and from practicing across state lines. Another significant aspect of the issue remains to be debated: the issue of who should be allowed to own CPA firms. As noted earlier, Appendix B to the Code presently restricts ownership of firms to CPAs. However, that restriction has been the subject of recent debate within the profession. Many CPA firms are concerned in particular that the restriction on ownership of CPA firms constrains them in attracting and retaining non-CPAs with the specialized skills needed in today's complex auditing environment.

*   In March 1993, Interpretations 505-1 and 505-2 were revised to conform to the revised Rule 505.

Marketing Professional Services

Until the late 1970s, the AICPA code of ethics prohibited members from advertising and using all forms of direct solicitation, including competitive bidding. CPAs marketed their services by performing quality work and relying on word of mouth to inform potential clients about their professional qualifications. Changes made to the code of ethics, as explained on page 63 of the main volume, removed many of those prohibitions.

The Rules of the AICPA Code of Professional Conduct, as revised to reflect the final order issued by the Federal Trade Commission (FTC) in 1990, discussed later in this chapter of the Supplement, presently address the marketing of professional services in four ways. Rule 302 prohibits performing services for certain attest clients, and preparing tax returns for any client, on a contingent fee basis; Rule 503 restricts paying commissions to or receiving commissions from a client when the CPA also performs certain attest services for that client; Rule 503 also requires disclosure of the acceptance or payment of referral fees and of permitted commissions; and Rule 502 sets restraints on advertising and solicitation.

Contingent Fees, Commissions, and Referral Fees.   Rule 302—Contingent Fees—and Rule 503—Commissions and Referral Fees—were recently revised as a result of the FTC order issued pursuant to the 1990 consent agreement between the AICPA and the FTC. As revised, Rule 302 prohibits CPAs from performing any professional services for, or receiving, a contingent fee, if the CPA performs any of the following services for the client:

- An audit or review of financial statements.
- A compilation of financial statements, when a third party can reasonably be expected to use the financial statements, and the compilation report does not disclose a lack of independence.
- An examination of prospective financial information.

The AICPA–FTC consent agreement defines the above services as attest services. As used in the consent agreement, "attest services" do not include all the types of services described as attest services in the accounting and auditing literature. Excluded from the definition would be compilations of financial statements intended for management's use only or that disclose a lack of independence, services involving prospective financial information other than an examination, and any service covered solely by the Statements on Standards for Attestation Engagements.

Rule 302 also prohibits CPAs from preparing original tax returns for any client on a contingent fee basis. This is also generally true for preparing amended returns.

For purposes of Rule 302, fees are not considered contingent if they are fixed by courts or other public authorities or, in tax matters, if they are determined based on the results of judicial proceedings or the findings of government agencies.

An Interpretation under Rule 302, issued concurrently with the Rule, defines certain terms in the provisions of the Rule dealing with tax matters and provides examples of tax services that would and would not be permitted. Among the services for which contingent fees would be permitted are

- Representing a client in an examination by a revenue agent.
- Filing an amended tax return claiming either a refund based on an issue that is the subject of a test case involving a different taxpayer or a refund greater than the threshold for review by the appropriate taxing authority.
- Requesting consideration by a taxing authority of a reduction in the assessed value of property.
- Representing a client in connection with obtaining a private letter ruling or influencing the drafting of a regulation or statute.

Rule 503 prohibits CPAs from accepting commissions for recommending or referring a product or service to a client, or recommending or referring a product or service to be supplied by a client, when the CPA performs "attest services" for that client, as that term is defined in the AICPA–FTC consent agreement and explained previously. The Rule also requires that permitted commissions be disclosed to the party to whom the CPA recommends or refers a product or service to which the commission relates. Further, the acceptance of a referral fee for recommending or referring a potential client to a CPA or the payment of a referral fee to obtain a client must be disclosed to the client.

Under new Rules 302 and 503, a CPA is precluded from performing attest services (as defined above) for a client during the period in which the CPA is engaged to render or performs services for a contingent fee or a commission, or receives a contingent fee or a commission. Further, a CPA may not provide the defined attest services if the engagement, performance, or receipt occurred during any period covered by the historical financial statements. For example, if a CPA was asked in February 1994 to audit financial statements as of December 31, 1991, 1992, and 1993, he or she could not accept the engagement if he or she had performed services for a contingent fee, or had received a contingent fee, during any of the years 1991, 1992, or 1993, or in the period from February 1994 until the issuance date of the audit report. This prohibition would apply even if the CPA, at the time of performing services or of receiving a contingent fee or commission, had no reason to expect to be asked to perform the audit.

p. 65. *Add after carryover paragraph:*

Final FTC Order.   On August 3, 1990, the Federal Trade Commission issued a final order pursuant to its March 1989 consent agreement with the AICPA, which is discussed in Chapter 3 of the main volume. Under the terms of the agreement and the final order, the AICPA may continue to prohibit members from accepting contingent fees or commissions for services performed for attest clients[5.1] and to require members to disclose to clients referral fees and commissions received. The final order contains some modifications of the consent agreement, most notably a provision allowing the AICPA to continue to prohibit members from accepting contingent fees for preparing tax returns or refund claims. The final order also allows the AICPA to continue to prohibit members from providing attest services to clients from whom they received contingent fees in connection with the performance of nonattest professional services, during both the period of the attest services engagement and the period covered by any historical financial statements involved in such attest services.

The final order provides that the AICPA may not interfere with members' accepting contingent fees from nonattest clients (except as noted above), accepting disclosed commissions relating to nonattest clients, paying or accepting disclosed referral fees, engaging in advertising and solicitation, and using trade names (unless advertising, solicitation, and the use of trade names are considered by the AICPA to be false or deceptive). As a result of the FTC agreement and order, the AICPA has changed its Rules relating to contingent fees, commissions and refer-
* ral fees, and form of name. The new Rules are discussed earlier in this chapter of the Supplement. In other respects, the AICPA's Rules were not inconsistent with the FTC order.

The practical effect of the FTC order will be mitigated by the fact that many state societies of CPAs and state boards of accountancy proscribe CPAs from accepting commissions and contingent fees in any circumstances. In most instances those prohibitions are in the form of rules, but several states have enacted statutes banning CPAs from accepting commissions and contingent fees. In those states, and any others that might enact similar statutes, the FTC would have to prevail in a court of law to enforce its order.

[5.1] As used here, "attest client" refers to a client for whom the services defined in the consent agreement as "attest services" are performed. Those services are specified earlier in this chapter; they do not include all the services described as attest services in the professional literature.

4

Professional Responsibility and Legal Liability

AUDITORS' PROFESSIONAL RESPONSIBILITY

Responsibility for Detecting Misstatements

* **p. 94.** *Add after second full paragraph:*

Distinguishing between illegal acts that have a direct and material effect on financial statements and illegal acts whose financial statement effect is indirect can be difficult. Although SAS No. 54 gives examples of both types of illegal acts, it does not provide explicit guidance on determining which category an illegal act falls into. Direct-effect illegal acts relate to violations of laws and regulations that affect a line-item financial statement amount. An example of such laws and regulations is the tax code provisions that determine how an entity's tax liability is measured and presented in its financial statements. In contrast, failure to comply with tax code provisions relating to the filing of information has only an indirect effect on financial statements, namely, the requirement to disclose the contingent liability for tax penalties. Another example of a direct-effect illegal act would be violations of state usury laws when related regulations provide for the remedy of refunding excess interest charged. Still other examples of direct-effect illegal acts are cited in SAS No. 68, *Compliance Auditing Applicable to Governmental Entities and Other Recipients of Governmental Assistance* (AU Section 801), discussed in Chapter 25 of this Supplement.

Early in 1993, bills with identical provisions and known as the Financial Fraud Detection and Disclosure Act were introduced in both houses of Congress. The bills, which have the support of the AICPA and the six largest accounting firms, require auditors of public companies to notify the SEC of material illegal acts when a company's management and board of directors have failed to take timely and appropriate remedial action and have failed to comply with a requirement to notify the SEC of such inaction. (See the more detailed discussion below under "Auditor 'Whistleblowing.'") The bills also require the auditor to use procedures in accordance with generally accepted auditing standards (as may be modified or supplemented by the SEC) that would provide reasonable assurance of detecting illegal acts that have a direct and material effect on a company's financial statements. The bills would thereby codify into law the requirements of SAS No. 54. They would also codify into law current professional requirements that the auditor identify related party transactions that either are material to the financial statements or require disclosure (see Chapter 6 of the main volume), and that the auditor evaluate whether there is substantial doubt about the entity's ability to continue as a going concern over the ensuing fiscal year (see Chapter 22 of the main volume).

* **p. 96.**   *Add after carryover paragraph:*

Auditor "Whistleblowing."   In large part because of the savings and loan crisis and other business failures, Congress and regulators have become increasingly concerned about auditors' responsibilities with respect to their clients' compliance with laws and regulations and about how instances of noncompliance are reported. As a result, some regulators and legislators are demanding that more direct reporting responsibilities be placed on auditors. The auditing profession has resisted proposals that would require direct reporting to regulators, principally out of a belief that the correction of illegalities and reporting on them are the responsibility of management. The profession does not, by and large, seem to have the same concern about requirements to report to regulators matters that auditors communicated to management or the board but were not acted on or reported by management or the board in accordance with applicable statutory requirements.

The reporting requirements of the proposed Financial Fraud Detection and Disclosure Act, other aspects of which were discussed above, are consistent with the latter reporting framework and accordingly have the support of the AICPA and the six largest accounting firms. As proposed, the Act requires that if the auditor determines it is likely that an illegal act has occurred, he or she would be required to

- Determine and consider the possible effect of the illegal act on the company's financial statements, including any monetary fines, penalties, or damages; and
- As soon as practicable, inform the appropriate level of the company's management and ensure that the audit committee (or board of directors in the absence of an audit committee) is informed of the illegal act, unless the illegal act is clearly inconsequential.

The auditor would be required to go further and report, as soon as practicable, his or her conclusions directly to the company's board of directors in circumstances where

- The illegal act has a material effect on the financial statements;
- Senior management has not taken, and the board of directors have not caused senior management to take, timely and appropriate remedial action with respect to the illegal act; and
- The failure to take remedial action is reasonably expected to warrant departure from a standard auditor's report or the auditor's resignation.

On receipt of such a report by the board of directors, the company is required to notify the SEC within one business day, with a copy of the notification sent to the auditor. If the auditor fails to receive such a notice within one day, he or she should either

- Furnish the SEC with a copy of his or her report on the next business day following the failure to receive notice; or
- Resign from the engagement and furnish the SEC with a copy of his or her report within one business day.

With respect to the report made to the SEC, the bill provides that no auditor will be held liable in a private action for any finding, conclusion, or statement made pursuant to the direct reporting provisions of the bill. Willful violations, however, are subject to SEC civil action.

As noted later in this chapter of the Supplement, auditors' whistleblowing obligation has been rejected by the courts in recent cases. In one case, the court indicated the adverse effects that whistleblowing could have on the client–auditor relationship and on the free exchange of information.

AUDITORS' LEGAL LIABILITY

The Litigation Explosion

* **p. 101.** *Add after third full paragraph:*

Jury awards against accounting firms reached new highs in 1992. One firm was hit with a $338 million award over an allegedly faulty audit of a bank; the verdict, however, was set aside by the trial judge. In another case, investors in a bankrupt company were able to obtain a jury award of $26 million in compensatory and $200 million in punitive damages against the company's former auditors. The matter was subsequently settled out of court for an undisclosed amount after the court set aside the verdict. The year 1992 was also marked by extremely large settlements, as illustrated by an accounting firm's $400 million settlement with federal banking regulators arising out of services performed for savings and loan institutions. In 1992 the amount paid by the six largest accounting firms in self-protection costs, including insurance premiums, legal fees, and awards and settlements, increased to $598 million, or 10.9 percent of accounting and audit revenues nationwide. That amount was up from $477 million, or 9 percent, in 1991, and $404 million, or 7.7 percent, in 1990.

p. 102.   *Add after carryover paragraph:*

The effect the litigation explosion may have on an accounting firm was dramatically illustrated when Laventhol & Horwath, a 75-year-old firm with 50 offices and $345.2 million in revenue in fiscal 1990, filed for bankruptcy on November 21, 1990. Laventhol's failure was attributed to litigation problems, including 110 lawsuits pending at the time of bankruptcy and settlements in the amount of $30 million and $13 million in late 1989 and early 1990, which wiped out the firm's insurance coverage.

Civil Liability to Third Parties Under Common Law

* **p. 110.   *Replace first full paragraph through first two sentences of first paragraph on page 111:***

In 1992, *International Mortgage* (discussed on p. 109 of the main volume) was overruled by the supreme court of California, which held in *Bily* v. *Arthur Young*[26.1] that in professional negligence cases, an accounting firm is liable only to its clients and not to third parties, such as investors or lenders, unless the third party can establish fraud or negligent misrepresentation. The court's rationale for adopting a new precedent was the prevention of liability out of proportion to fault. With this decision, which represented a significant victory for the accounting profession, California moved away from the foreseeability test, adopted by only a minority of the states, which would expose accountants to the broadest universe of potential claimants in professional negligence actions.

Since 1987 no additional states have adopted the foreseeability test. Additional states that decided to continue adhering to the *Ultramares* view are Alabama,[26.2] Alaska,[26.3] Maryland,[26.4] and Montana.[26.5] In addition to California, the following states adopted the Restatement approach: Florida,[26.6] Louisiana,[26.7] and West Virginia.[26.8]

At the time of this writing, the following jurisdictions, in addition to those cited above and on pages 109 and 110 of the main volume, appear to be adhering to the *Ultramares* rule: Arkansas,[26.9] Delaware,[26.10] Indiana,[26.11] Kansas,[26.12] and Pennsylvania.[26.13] The following jurisdictions are apparently following the

---

[26.1] 834 P.2d 745 (Cal. 1992).

[26.2] *Colonial Bank* v. *Ridley & Schweigert,* 551 So.2d 390 (Ala. 1989).

[26.3] *Selden* v. *Burnett,* 754 P.2d 256 (Alaska 1988).

[26.4] *Tischler* v. *Baltimore Bancorp,* 801 F. Supp. 1493 (D. Md. 1992).

[26.5] *Thayer* v. *Hicks,* 793 P.2d 784 (Mont. 1990).

[26.6] *First Florida Bank* v. *Max Mitchell & Co.,* 558 So. 2d 9 (Fla. 1990).

[26.7] *First National Bank of Commerce* v. *Monco Agency, Inc.,* 911 F.2d 1053 (5th Cir. 1990).

[26.8] *First National Bank* v. *Crawford,* 386 S.E.2d 310 (W. Va. 1989).

[26.9] *Robertson* v. *White,* 633 F. Supp. 954 (W.D. Ark. 1986).

[26.10] *McLean* v. *Alexander,* 599 F.2d 1190 (3d Cir. 1979).

[26.11] *Toro Co.* v. *Krouse, Kern & Co.,* 827 F.2d 155 (7th Cir. 1987).

[26.12] *Nortek, Inc.* v. *Alexander Grant & Co.,* 532 F.2d 1013 (10th Cir. 1974), *cert. denied,* 429 U.S. 1042 (1977).

[26.13] *Hartford Accident & Indemnity Co.* v. *Parente, Randolph, Orlando, Carey & Associates,* 642 F. Supp. 38 (M.D. Pa. 1985); *Pennine Resources, Inc.* v. *Dorwart Andrew & Co.,* 639 F. Supp. 1071 (E.D. Pa. 1986).

Restatement approach: Georgia,[26.14] Hawaii,[26.15] Iowa,[26.16] Minnesota,[26.17] Missouri,[26.18] New Hampshire,[26.19] New Mexico,[26.20] North Carolina,[26.21] Ohio,[26.22] Tennessee,[26.23] Texas,[26.24] and Washington.[26.25] The only court to join New Jersey and Wisconsin was the supreme court of Mississippi in 1987.[26.26] In that case the accountant provided a copy of the financial statements to a third party.

An interesting development on this issue occurred in 1987, when the Illinois legislature enacted a statute that codified the *Ultramares* rule.[26.27] Arkansas, Kansas, and Utah have since enacted similar statutes.[26.28]

Civil Liability to Third Parties Under the Federal Securities Acts

p. 116. *Add after third full paragraph:*

The expansive view of aiding and abetting liability expressed in the *Roberts* case by the U.S. Court of Appeals for the Ninth Circuit has been rejected by certain other courts. See, for example, *Latigo Ventures* v. *Laventhol & Horwath.*[54.1] In *Latigo Ventures*, investors claimed that the accounting firm should have disclosed the company's losses that occurred after it issued its report to investors. The Seventh Circuit ruled that accountants have no obligation to "blow the whistle" for the protection of investors every time they discover that a client is in financial difficulty.

More recently, in *DiLeo* v. *Ernst & Young*,[54.2] the Seventh Circuit reaffirmed its rejection of a duty to "blow the whistle" and suggested that implying such a duty would destroy the relationship of trust between accountant and client and reduce the free and full exchange of information. The *DiLeo* case arose out of the failure of Continental Illinois Bank. The thrust of the complaint was that the accountants failed to require the bank to increase its loan loss reserves quickly enough as the

---

[26.14] *Badische Corp.* v. *Caylor*, 257 Ga. 131 (1987).

[26.15] *Chun* v. *Park*, 51 Haw. 462 (1969).

[26.16] *Pahre* v. *Auditor*, 422 N.W. 2d 178 (Iowa 1988).

[26.17] *Bonhiver* v. *Graff*, 311 Minn. 111 (1976).

[26.18] *Lindner Fund* v. *Abney*, 770 S.W.2d 437 (Mo. App. 1989); *Aluma Craft Mfg. Co.* v. *Elmer Fox & Co.*, 493 S.W.2d 378 (Mo. App. 1973).

[26.19] *Spherex, Inc.* v. *Alexander Grant & Co.*, 122 N.H. 898 (1982).

[26.20] *Stotlar* v. *Hester*, 92 N.M. 26 (Ct. App. 1978).

[26.21] *Raritan River Steel Co.* v. *Cherry, Bekaert & Holland*, 332 N.C. 200 (1988).

[26.22] *BancOhio National Bank* v. *Schiesswohl*, 515 N.E.2d 997 (Ohio 1986).

[26.23] *Stinson* v. *Brand*, 738 S.W.2d 186 (Tenn. 1987).

[26.24] *Blue Bell, Inc.* v. *Peat, Marwick, Mitchell & Co.*, 715 S.W.2d 408 (Tex. Ct. App. Dallas 1986); *Shatterproof Glass Corp.* v. *James*, 466 S.W.2d 873 (Tex. Civ. App. 1971).

[26.25] *Haberman* v. *WPPSS*, 109 Wash. 2d 107 (1987).

[26.26] *Touche Ross & Company* v. *Commercial Union Insurance Co.*, 514 So.2d 315 (Miss. 1987).

[26.27] Ill. Rev. Stat. ch. 111 ¶5535.1 (1987).

[26.28] Ark. Stat. Ann. § 16-114-302 (Supp. 1987); Kan. Stat. Ann. § 1-402 (Supp. 1988); Utah Code Ann. § 58-26-12 (Supp. 1990).

[54.1] 876 F.2d 1322 (7th Cir. 1989).

[54.2] 901 F.2d 624 (7th Cir.), *cert. denied*, 111 S.Ct. 347 (1990).

bank's financial condition deteriorated. The court rejected the argument that favorable financial statements closely followed by financial difficulties were evidence of fraud, and stressed that the accountants would have nothing to gain by participating in a fraud with the bank. The court concluded that "fees for two years audits could not approach the losses [the accounting firm] would suffer from a perception that it would muffle a client's fraud."

RICO

* **p. 117.** *Delete last sentence of carryover paragraph and replace with:*
In March 1993, however, the Supreme Court[56.1] limited the liability of outside professionals, such as accountants, under RICO in ruling that in order to be liable one must participate in the operation or management of the enterprise itself; mere association through the provision of accounting or auditing services is not sufficient.

Other SEC Sanctions

p. 118. *Add after second full paragraph:*
The Securities Enforcement Remedies and Penny Stock Reform Act of 1990 substantially increased the SEC's enforcement powers and remedies. The Act empowers the SEC to issue "cease-and-desist" orders requiring compliance with the securities laws and possibly requiring a party to take affirmative action to avert future violations. Prior to the Act, the SEC was required to seek such relief as a party in federal court. The Act also authorizes the SEC to obtain monetary penalties in civil actions in federal court and in certain administrative proceedings of up to $500,000 for each violation.

* **p. 119.** *Add after carryover paragraph:*
In a significant victory for the accounting profession, a federal court entered a judgment in favor of an accounting firm[65.1] in an SEC injunctive action for alleged violations of the antifraud provisions of the securities acts. The court handed down a highly stringent rule of liability. In order for the SEC to get an injunction against an accounting firm, the SEC must prove that the accounting firm's procedures were so deficient that the audit amounted to no audit at all or that the accounting judgments made were such that no reasonable accountant would have made the same decisions if confronted with the same facts.

* **p. 120.** *Delete last sentence of first full paragraph and replace with:*
The SEC's view was reinforced in August 1992 when it used its Rule 2(e) authority to bar two auditors accused of having negligently conducted an audit from appearing before the Commission for two years.[65.2]

[56.1] *Reves* v. *Ernst & Young,* 113 S.Ct. 1163.

[65.1] *SEC* v. *Price Waterhouse,* 797 F. Supp. 1217 (S.D.N.Y. 1992).

[65.2] Accounting and Auditing Enforcement Release No. 412 (Aug. 26, 1992).

5

The Audit Process

AUDIT EVIDENCE AND AUDIT TESTS

Types of Evidence

* **p. 135.** *Add to end of subsection* **Confirmation:**

In November 1991, the ASB issued SAS No. 67, *The Confirmation Process* (AU Section 330), which provides guidance on using confirmations in an audit. Most of the discussion in the SAS applies to the confirmation process generally, that is, it is not limited to any particular financial statement item. Two paragraphs specifically address the confirmation of receivables. SAS No. 67 superseded paragraphs 3 through 8 of Section 331 of SAS No. 1 (AU Section 331.03–.08) and the portion of paragraph 1 of Section 331 that deals with confirming receivables. The general guidance in the SAS is discussed briefly in Chapter 9 of this Supplement; a more detailed description of confirmation of receivables is presented in Chapter 12 of this Supplement.

THE STEPS IN AN AUDIT

Obtaining and Documenting Information About the Client

p. 150. *Add after second paragraph:*

In 1990, the AICPA's Control Risk Audit Guide Task Force issued an audit guide to SAS No. 55, *Consideration of the Internal Control Structure in a Financial Statement Audit* (AU Section 319), that illustrates the application of the provisions of the SAS. The guide refers to the activities described on pages 147–149 in the main volume as constituting the development of the preliminary audit strategy.

The guide emphasizes that the preliminary audit strategy is not a detailed audit plan, but preliminary judgments about the approach to the audit. Those judgments, which will be revised as necessary as the audit work proceeds, form the basis for the auditor's initial consideration of which of two audit strategies will be followed: performing tests of controls to reduce the amount of assurance needed from substantive tests, or performing primarily substantive tests. The extent of the understanding of the control structure needed varies depending on which of the strategies is planned.

6

Audit Risk, Materiality, and Engagement Strategy

PLANNING AND CONTROLLING THE AUDIT

Using the Work of Internal Auditors

p. 180. *Replace second full paragraph through end of section with:*

SAS No. 65, *The Auditor's Consideration of the Internal Audit Function in an Audit of Financial Statements* (AU Section 332), which was issued in May 1991 and superseded SAS No. 9, specifies that as part of obtaining an understanding of the control structure, the external auditor should obtain an understanding of the internal audit function sufficient to identify those internal audit activities that are relevant to planning the audit. The auditor can ordinarily obtain the necessary understanding through inquiries of appropriate management and internal audit personnel. Principal areas of inquiry should include

- The charter, mission statement, or similar directive from management or the board of directors, and the goals and objectives established for the internal audit function.
- The level or position of the person or persons within the organization to whom the internal audit function reports, for instance, whether there is access to the board of directors or audit committee.
- The specific responsibilities assigned to the internal auditors.
- Whether the internal audit function adheres to the standards developed for the professional practice of internal auditing by the Institute of Internal Auditors.

- The internal audit plan, including the nature, timing, and extent of work.
- The extent, if any, to which the internal auditors' access to records, documentation, and personnel is restricted.

If the external auditor determines that internal audit activities are not relevant to the financial statement audit, no further consideration of the function is required. However, if the internal audit activities are relevant to the audit, and it is efficient to consider the work of the internal auditors, the external auditor should

- Assess the competence and objectivity of the internal audit function.
- Determine the effect of internal audit work on the audit strategy.
- Consider the extent of the effect of internal audit work on the external auditor's procedures.
- Evaluate and test the effectiveness of the internal auditors' work.

In assessing the competence and objectivity of the internal audit function, the external auditor should consider information obtained or updated from prior years and from discussions with management, as well as the results of any recent external review of the internal audit function. The following factors are relevant to an assessment of competence:

- Education level and professional experience. For example, if the circumstances require tests of general computer control procedures, the internal auditors should have an adequate knowledge of computer audit techniques.
- Professional certification of internal auditors and requirements for continuing education.
- Internal audit policies, programs, and procedures.
- Practices regarding assignment of internal auditors. For example, internal auditors may possess different types of skills, which should be consistent with the work assigned to personnel.
- Supervision and review of internal auditors' activities. For example, the work carried out by the internal auditors should be supervised by senior internal audit personnel.
- Quality of working paper documentation, including the adequacy of the evidence of the work done by internal audit.
- Quality of reports and recommendations, and the nature and frequency of, and response to, reports issued by internal audit.
- Hiring, training, performance evaluation, and consultation practices of internal audit.

Even though internal auditors are not independent of the organization, they should maintain objectivity. When assessing objectivity, the external auditor should pay particular attention to the nature of internal audit work in areas that are sensitive or entail a high level of subjective judgment. The need for objectivity is critical in such areas. Factors that should be considered are policies prohibiting internal auditors from auditing areas where there may be a conflict of interests and the organizational status of the internal audit function.

If the external auditor determines that the competence and objectivity of the internal audit function are sufficient, he or she should then consider how the internal auditors' work may affect such audit areas as obtaining an understanding of the internal control structure, assessing risk, and performing substantive procedures. The internal auditors may perform procedures in all those areas that will provide useful information to the external auditor. In many organizations, the internal auditors review, assess, and monitor internal control structure policies and procedures; the results of that work may be useful to the external auditor in gathering information about the design of the control structure and about whether policies and procedures have been placed in operation. The external auditor may also consider the internal auditors' work in assessing the risk of material misstatement at both the financial statement level and the account balance or class-of-transactions level. That work may consist of assessing the control environment and accounting system at selected locations, or of tests of control procedures directed at specific financial statement assertions. The external auditor may be able to reduce the number of locations at which he or she performs auditing procedures or to change the nature, timing, and extent of testing relating to a particular audit objective. Finally, the internal auditors may perform procedures that provide direct evidence about specific account balances and that the external auditor may consider in restricting detection risk for relevant audit objectives.

When considering the extent to which internal audit work may affect the procedures that the external auditor would otherwise need to perform, the auditor should keep the following in mind:

- Evidence obtained through the auditor's direct personal knowledge, including physical examination, observation, computation, and inspection, is generally more persuasive than information obtained indirectly.
- The responsibility to report on the financial statements is solely the external auditor's and cannot be shared with internal audit.
- Judgments on the assessment of inherent and control risks, materiality, sufficiency of testing, and evaluation of significant accounting estimates must be those of the external auditor.

In determining the extent of the effect of internal audit work, the external auditor considers the risk of material misstatement of financial statement amounts. The auditor also considers the materiality of financial statement amounts and the degree of subjectivity involved in evaluating the audit evidence supporting the assertions. As the materiality of the financial statement amounts increases and either the risk of material misstatement or the degree of subjectivity increases, the external auditor's need to perform his or her own audit tests increases. Conversely, as these factors decrease, the need for the external auditor to perform his or her own tests decreases.

For example, if the risk of material misstatement is assessed as low, the external auditor may decide, after considering the results of internal audit work, that additional testing is not necessary. On the other hand, for significant accounts or assertions where the risk of material misstatement or the degree of subjectivity is high, the external auditor should not use the work of internal audit without directly performing sufficient additional procedures to reduce audit risk to an acceptable level. Examples of assertions that might require direct testing by the external auditor are those relating to valuations based on accounting estimates and to the existence and disclosure of uncertainties, subsequent events, and related party transactions.

The external auditor should evaluate and test the effectiveness of internal audit work that will affect the nature, timing, and extent of auditing procedures. The extent of the evaluation and testing procedures is a matter of professional judgment, based on the extent of the effect of internal audit work on the audit. The auditor may wish to consider whether the

- Scope of internal audit work is appropriate to meet the objectives.
- The internal audit programs are adequate.
- Working papers adequately document the work performed.
- Conclusions are appropriate in the circumstances.
- Reports are consistent with the results of the work performed.
- Supervision and review within internal audit appear to have been appropriately carried out.

The external auditor should test the work of internal audit by either reperforming some tests of controls, transactions, or balances examined by the internal auditors or by testing similar controls, transactions, or balances not actually examined by internal audit. The external auditor should compare the results of his or her tests with the results of the internal auditors' work.

Whether or not the external auditor believes that internal audit activities are relevant to the audit, liaison with internal audit is generally desirable to keep the auditor informed of developments that may have audit implications. Liaison with internal audit also is important in terms of meeting client expectations and enhancing client relationships.

If the external auditor determines that internal audit is performing relevant audit work that is expected to have an effect on his or her procedures, the two auditor groups should coordinate their work. Techniques that may be useful in coordinating audit work include

1. Holding regularly scheduled coordination meetings.
2. Preparing integrated audit testing plans.
3. Sharing some of the more complex (as opposed to routine) audit tasks.
4. Reviewing internal audit programs before the internal audit work is performed.
5. Exchanging audit reports.
6. Discussing possible accounting and auditing issues.
7. Making joint presentations to the audit committee or board of directors.
8. Providing internal audit with audit software and training.

Because the auditing techniques used by internal and external auditors are often similar, the external auditor can sometimes use audit documentation prepared by internal audit rather than prepare the data independently. For example, flowcharts and systems documentation prepared by internal audit may also serve the external auditor's purposes, especially when they follow standard formats. To facilitate coordination and integration of audit efforts, it may be beneficial for the two auditor groups to create and maintain a common user file of permanent working papers.

The effectiveness of coordination with internal audit is enhanced if it takes place before internal audit finalizes its plans for the year, since the external auditor must assume responsibility for the overall scope of the audit, including determining the effect of internal audit work on the audit strategy. This effectiveness may be impeded if the planning by internal audit precedes the external auditor's planning. For example, internal audit may develop its annual plan based on the client's fiscal year, whereas the external auditor generally determines the audit strategy after the year has commenced. In this case, internal audit might be encouraged to use a planning cycle that coincides with, or follows, the external audit planning cycle; this could involve using a planning year other than the entity's fiscal year (e.g., a July 1–June 30 planning year for a calendar-year client).

Using the Work of a Specialist

* **p. 183.** *Delete last sentence of first paragraph and add:*
In April 1993, the Auditing Standards Board issued an exposure draft of a proposed Statement on Auditing Standards, *Using the Work of a Specialist,* that, if adopted, would supersede SAS No. 11. The exposure draft notes that "when a specialist does not have a relationship with the client, the specialist's work will ordinarily provide the auditor with greater assurance of reliability." The draft provides guidance when such a relationship exists.

The exposure draft amplifies SAS No. 11 by specifying that the work or findings of the specialist should not be referenced in the auditor's report unless, as a result of the specialist's report or findings, the auditor decides to add explanatory language to the standard report or depart from an unqualified opinion. Such reference to and identification of the specialist may be made if the auditor believes it will enable users to better understand the reason for the explanatory language or the departure from an unqualified opinion.

* **p. 184.** *Replace section* Using a Report on Internal Control at a Service Organization *with the following:*

Using a Report on the Processing of Transactions by a Service Organization

A client may use a service organization, such as a data processing center, to record certain transactions, process data, or even execute transactions and maintain the related accounting records and assets, such as securities. Transactions may flow through an accounting system that is, wholly or partially, separate from the client's organization, and the auditor may find it necessary or efficient in understanding and assessing the client's internal control structure to consider procedures performed at the service organization. To do that, the auditor may obtain a report prepared by the service organization's auditor covering the processing of transactions at the service organization.

SAS No. 70, *Reports on the Processing of Transactions by Service Organizations* (AU Section 324), which was issued in April 1992 and superseded SAS No. 44, provides guidance on the factors an auditor should consider when auditing the financial statements of an entity that uses a service organization to process certain transactions.

The auditor should consider the effect of the service organization on the client's internal control structure and the availability of evidence to obtain the necessary understanding of the control structure to plan the audit, assess control risk, and perform substantive tests. SAS No. 70 provides guidance on the auditor's use of either of the two reports (described next) that may be provided by service organization auditors. In deciding to obtain a report from a service organization's auditor, the auditor considers both the nature of the procedures the service organization provides and their relationship to the client's internal control structure. The decision to use a report on the service organization's processing of transactions, along with appropriate inquiries and other steps necessary to implement that decision, should be made during the planning phase of the audit.

The requirements of SAS No. 70 are applicable when the client uses a service organization in connection with executing transactions and maintaining the related accountability, or recording transactions and processing related data. In the latter situation, the auditor often considers it necessary, in order to obtain a sufficient understanding of the flow of transactions to plan the audit, to obtain a service organization's auditor's *report on policies and procedures placed in operation.* This report contains a description of the service organization's policies and procedures that may be relevant to a user organization's internal control structure, states whether such policies and procedures have been placed in operation as of a specific date, and states whether they are suitably designed to achieve specified control objectives.

When the service organization executes transactions and maintains the related accountability, the accounting and control procedures that are essential to achieving one or more of the client's control objectives will most likely be located in whole or in part at the service organization. Assuming the auditor seeks to assess control risk at below maximum, he or she will find it necessary to obtain a *report on policies and procedures placed in operation and tests of operating effectiveness.* This report includes all of the items contained in the report described in the previous paragraph, and in addition states whether the control structure policies and procedures that were tested were operating with sufficient effectiveness to provide reasonable, but not absolute, assurance that the related control objectives were achieved during the period specified.

SAS No. 70 also provides guidance on the responsibilities of an auditor who issues a report on the processing of transactions by a service organization for use by other auditors. (See Chapter 23 of this Supplement for further discussion.)

7

The Internal Control Structure

* p. 212. *Add new sections at end of chapter:*

INTERNAL CONTROL—INTEGRATED FRAMEWORK (NEW)

Concern on the part of regulators and others about management's responsibility for internal control, especially with respect to the reliability of financial reporting, has continued to increase, as has the diversity of definitions and concepts used by various interested parties. This led to a recommendation in the 1987 report of the National Commission on Fraudulent Financial Reporting, commonly referred to as the Treadway Commission, that its sponsoring organizations—the American Accounting Association, the American Institute of Certified Public Accountants, the Financial Executives Institute, the Institute of Internal Auditors, and the Institute of Management Accountants (formerly the National Association of Accountants)—work together to integrate the various internal control concepts and definitions, and to develop a common reference point for considering internal control. It was suggested that this guidance would help public companies improve their internal control systems.

The Committee of Sponsoring Organizations of the Treadway Commission (COSO) was formed to support implementation of the Treadway Commission recommendations. COSO then commissioned Coopers & Lybrand to conduct a study to develop practical, broadly accepted criteria for establishing internal control and evaluating its effectiveness. Their report, *Internal Control—Integrated Framework* (the COSO Report) was issued in September 1992.

The COSO Report had two objectives.

1. To establish a common definition of internal control that would serve the needs of different parties.

2. To provide a standard against which business and other entities—large or small, in the public or private sector, for profit or not—could assess their control systems and determine how to improve them.

In the report, internal control is defined as

A process, effected by an entity's board of directors, management and other personnel, designed to provide reasonable assurance regarding the achievement of objectives in the following categories:

- Effectiveness and efficiency of operations.
- Reliability of financial reporting.
- Compliance with applicable laws and regulations.

This definition is broad, covering operations and compliance controls as well as financial reporting controls. The report acknowledges that these categories are distinct but overlapping and are designed to meet the different needs of the various parties to whom the report applies—senior management, board members, independent accountants, internal auditors, other business personnel, legislators and regulators, and educators. This broad definition can be narrowed to focus on a specific aspect of internal control, such as financial reporting controls. This is consistent with the definition of internal control relevant to the independent auditor's responsibility, as described in SAS No. 55, which notes that policies and procedures are relevant to an audit of an entity's financial statements when they "pertain to the entity's ability to record, process, summarize, and report financial data consistent with the assertions embodied in the financial statements" (AU Section 319.06).

Internal Control—Integrated Framework also describes five interrelated components that constitute internal control. These components are the control environment, risk assessment, control activities, information and communication, and monitoring. The report also states that the functioning of these components serves as criteria for an effective internal control system, and as the basis for an entity's assessment of the effectiveness of its internal control over financial reporting and for an accountant's attestation report on a management report on such an assessment. Attestation reports on management assertions about internal control are discussed in Chapter 24 of this Supplement.

The Auditing Standards Board has established a task force to reconcile SAS No. 55 to the COSO Report. In addition to making necessary revisions to SAS No. 55, the task force will also consider whether revisions to other related professional standards are necessary.

FEDERAL SENTENCING GUIDELINES
FOR ORGANIZATIONS (NEW)

In late 1991, the United States Sentencing Commission issued Federal Sentencing Guidelines (the Guidelines) for judges to use in sentencing organizations convicted for crimes committed by their employees and agents, even if the organization was unaware of, or did not approve, an illegal act. The Guidelines affect all organizations and cover violations of federal employment, antitrust, securities, and contract laws, as well as crimes such as wire and mail fraud, commercial bribery, money laundering, and kickbacks.

Under the Guidelines, guilty organizations face fines that can reach hundreds of millions of dollars, depending on the severity of the crime and the culpability of the organization. Fines can be greatly reduced, however, if the organization shows that it had established an "effective program to prevent and detect violations of law" prior to the occurrence of an illegal act. A business is considered to have an effective program if it has exercised due diligence in seeking to prevent and detect criminal conduct. The Guidelines list the following seven steps that demonstrate the exercise of due diligence by an organization:

1. Establishing compliance standards and procedures for employees and other agents that are reasonably capable of reducing the potential of criminal conduct.

2. Assigning to specific, high-level individual(s) within the organization the overall responsibility for overseeing compliance with the established standards and procedures.

3. Using due care not to delegate substantial discretionary authority to individuals whom the organization knows (or should know) have a propensity to engage in illegal activities.

4. Taking steps to communicate the compliance standards and procedures effectively to all employees and agents (e.g., by requiring participation in training programs and by disseminating publications that explain in a practical manner what is required).

5. Taking reasonable steps to achieve compliance with its standards. These steps may include the use of monitoring or auditing systems designed to detect criminal conduct and implementing and publicizing a reporting system for employees and agents to report criminal conduct by others within the organization without fear of retribution.

6. Enforcing the standards consistently through appropriate disciplinary mechanisms, including, as appropriate, discipline of individuals responsible for the failure to detect an offense.

7. Taking all reasonable steps, after the detection of an offense, to respond appropriately and to prevent future similar offenses.

These steps include many of the control procedures described in Chapter 7 of the main volume, as well as the components of internal control as set forth in the COSO Report described earlier. That report, with its guidance on evaluating an organization's compliance with relevant laws and regulations, can provide an appropriate methodology for determining if an organization has an effective program to prevent and detect violations of law.

8

Assessing Inherent and Control Risk

p. 215. *Add after fourth paragraph:*

In 1990, the AICPA's Control Risk Audit Guide Task Force issued an audit guide to SAS No. 55, *Consideration of the Internal Control Structure in a Financial Statement Audit* (AU Section 319), to illustrate how auditors might apply the provisions of the SAS. The guide presents illustrations of the audits of three hypothetical companies—a small owner-managed business, a growing nonpublic company with multiple locations, and a large public company—and indicates the audit strategy that might be used for each company, including obtaining the necessary understanding of the control structure, assessing control risk, documenting the procedures performed, and designing substantive tests. The guide includes examples of various forms of documentation—narratives, flowcharts, and questionnaires—that can be used in recording the understanding of the control structure and assessment of control risk in the different audit strategies appropriate for the three types of organizations described in the guide.

OBTAINING AN UNDERSTANDING OF THE CONTROL STRUCTURE ELEMENTS

p. 219. *Add at beginning of second paragraph of section:*

In 1990, the AICPA's Control Risk Audit Guide Task Force issued an audit guide to SAS No. 55, *Consideration of the Internal Control Structure in a Financial Statement Audit* (AU Section 319), to illustrate how auditors might apply the provisions of the SAS in gaining and documenting a "sufficient" understanding of the elements of the control structure to plan the audit.

9

Controlling Detection Risk: Substantive Tests

DESIGNING AND PERFORMING SUBSTANTIVE TESTS

Tests of Details and Their Relationship to Audit Objectives

p. 265. *Replace second and third full paragraphs with:*

Confirmation consists of obtaining and evaluating a direct communication from a third party in response to a request for information about a specific item affecting one or more financial statement assertions. As noted in Chapter 5 of the main volume, evidence obtained from sources independent of the client usually is more reliable than that from parties within the client's organization. Thus, if the auditor seeks greater assurance about a financial statement assertion from substantive tests, for example, because the assessed levels of inherent and control risk are high or because a transaction is unusual or complex, he or she is likely to request confirmations from outside parties instead of or in addition to testing documents or making inquiries of client personnel. Although confirmations may provide assurance relating to any of the audit objectives, they do not address all objectives equally well. In general, and depending on their design, confirmation tends to be more effective in providing evidence about existence, rights and obligations, and, to a somewhat lesser extent, accuracy and cutoff than about valuation and completeness.

Confirmation requests should be tailored to specific audit objectives, client circumstances, information sought, and respondents. In designing confirmation requests, the auditor should consider the types of information respondents can be expected to be able to confirm, which is largely a function of their accounting and information systems. For example, a customer may not be able to confirm the total balance owed, but may be able to confirm individual transactions. To determine what information is relevant to the purpose of the confirmation, the auditor needs to understand the client's transactions; often details of transactions can be confirmed in addition to amounts. Confirmation requests should be directed to individuals who are believed to be knowledgeable about the specific items to be confirmed. For instance, an auditor seeking to confirm the terms of and balances outstanding under a major contract between the client and a supplier might address the confirmation request to the executive handling the client's account.

12

Auditing the Revenue Cycle

DETERMINING THE AUDIT STRATEGY

Audit Objectives

p. 384. *Add as third item under* **Presentation and Disclosure**:

- Concentrations of credit risk arising from accounts receivable are disclosed, as required by Statement of Financial Accounting Standards No. 105, *Disclosure of Information about Financial Instruments with Off-Balance-Sheet Risk and Financial Instruments with Concentrations of Credit Risk,* issued in March 1990.

SUBSTANTIVE TESTS

Accounts Receivable

p. 396. *Replace from subsection* **Confirming Accounts Receivable** *through second full paragraph on page 403 with:*

Confirming Accounts Receivable.   One of the most widely used substantive tests for determining the existence and, to a lesser extent, the accuracy of accounts receivable is direct communication by the auditor with customers, commonly referred to as "confirmation." Confirmation by the auditor of individual sales transactions or accounts receivable balances by direct communication with customers is one of only a few procedures that are designated as "generally accepted auditing procedures."

*   Confirmation of receivables has been required by the profession since 1939, when Statement on Auditing Procedure No. 1 was adopted by the AICPA as a direct result of the McKesson & Robbins fraud. In the intervening years, confirmation of receivables has been the subject of extensive authoritative and other professional pronouncements, the most recent of which is SAS No. 67, *The Confirmation Process* (AU Section 330). SAS No. 67—the first authoritative professional pronouncement to provide guidance on using and evaluating confirmations generally—retains the designation of confirmation as a generally accepted auditing procedure; states that there is a presumption that, in the absence of a limited number of circumstances (noted below), the auditor will request confirmations of receivables; and requires documentation of a decision not to request confirmations. Confirmations are not required if accounts receivable are immaterial, if the confirmation procedure would not be effective, or if the auditor's combined assessed level of inherent and control risk is low (and the assessed level, in conjunction with the evidence expected to be provided by analytical procedures or other substantive tests of details, is sufficient to reduce audit risk to an acceptably low level for applicable financial statement assertions). The assertion most directly addressed by confirmation is existence, so that it is unlikely that an auditor would be able to justify not confirming receivables if the assessed level of risk was other than low for the existence assertion.

As noted in Chapter 9 of this Supplement, however, while confirmation produces evidence about the existence and (to some extent) the accuracy of accounts receivable, other procedures are needed to establish their collectibility. The most direct evidence regarding collectibility of receivables is subsequent customer payments. Those payments also provide reliable evidence about existence and accuracy, because it is highly unlikely that a customer will pay a balance that is not owed or is overstated. Only the accuracy of the date the sale took place is not substantiated by a subsequent customer payment. Confirmation may, however, reveal the improper application of customer payments to older, disputed invoices, perhaps to conceal an unfavorable aging schedule. In practice, the auditor often uses a combination of confirmation, examination of subsequent customer payments, and other procedures to test the existence and accuracy of accounts receivable.

The auditor must make a decision regarding the confirmation date. If there was no deadline for the client to issue financial statements, confirming at year-end would be most effective. In today's business environment, however, there is usually a deadline, and accordingly the auditor often confirms receivables (and performs many other auditing procedures as well) at an earlier date. If early substantive testing is done, the auditor will need evidence that the risk of material misstatement occurring is sufficiently low during the intervening period, as discussed in Chapter 9 of the main volume.

Substantive tests sometimes provide evidence about control structure policies and procedures, if errors or irregularities disclosed by those tests are investigated and found to result from a control deficiency or breakdown. Specifically, confirmation procedures may provide evidence of control structure effectiveness with respect to the revenue cycle. Many auditors consider receivable confirmations as a source of evidence about the effectiveness of the control structure as well as a source of evidence about the existence and accuracy of accounts receivable.

Confirmation Procedures

Before selecting accounts for confirmation, the auditor should be sure the accounts receivable trial balance reconciles to the related control account. Normally the client routinely compares general ledger control account balances with the totals of individual accounts receivable, investigates discrepancies between the two, and makes appropriate adjustments. The auditor should compare the accounts receivable trial balance with the general ledger account and test the arithmetical accuracy of the trial balance (which is often done using audit software) or should test general control procedures for evidence that the trial balance is mathematically accurate. Reasons for recurring discrepancies between the control account and subsidiary ledger should be investigated.

The following paragraphs describe the procedures involved in confirming receivables.

Selecting Accounts for Confirmation.   Depending on the audit testing plan and the results of tests of controls, the auditor should decide whether all or only part of the accounts should be confirmed and, if the latter, the basis for selecting them. Chapter 10 of the main volume discusses various methods of sample selection. The selection should exclude debtors from whom replies to requests for confirmation cannot reasonably be expected, such as certain governmental agencies, foreign concerns, and some large industrial and commercial enterprises that use an open invoice or decentralized accounts payable processing system that makes confirmation impracticable.

The auditor should consider confirming accounts that appear unusual. Accounts with zero or credit balances should also be considered for confirmation. A credit balance suggests the possibility of an incorrect entry, especially if control structure policies and procedures are not effective.

Accounts and notes receivable that have been discounted or pledged should be confirmed with lenders, so that any unrecorded liability or contingency will be brought to the auditor's attention. This procedure helps the auditor achieve the audit objectives of rights and obligations, and presentation and disclosure. Confirming receivables with parties that they have been discounted or pledged with does not preclude an auditor from requesting confirmation from the debtors as well, particularly if the client is responsible for collections. (See Chapter 20 of this Supplement for a discussion of confirming contingent liabilities with financial institutions.)

To preserve the integrity of the confirmation process, the auditor should control the selection, preparation, mailing, and return of the confirmations. If the client does not wish statements or confirmation requests to be sent to certain debtors, the auditor should be satisfied that there is an adequate reason before agreeing to omit them. If such accounts are material, the auditor should use alternative procedures to test their existence and accuracy. If the results of the alternative procedures are satisfactory, the client's request not to confirm directly would not be considered a scope limitation (discussed in Chapter 22 of the main volume).

In determining the sample size and selecting the specific accounts to be confirmed, the auditor should follow the guidance provided in Chapter 10 of the main volume. Guidance for extrapolating confirmation results to a conclusion about the total accounts receivable balance, where appropriate, is also presented in that chapter.

Replies to confirmation requests are sometimes difficult to obtain if a debtor's accounts payable processing is decentralized or uses an open invoice system, which is increasingly the case in a number of governmental departments and agencies as well as many large industrial and commercial enterprises. In an open invoice system, the debtor processes invoices individually and does not summarize them by vendor. Therefore, the debtor can identify whether or not an individual invoice has been paid, but cannot determine the total amount owed to any particular vendor. In many instances, however, such difficulties can be overcome, for example, by supplying details of the balance to be confirmed, such as invoice dates, number (including customer purchase order number), and amounts, or by confirming specific transactions rather than an account balance. In addition, respondents that cannot confirm balances of installment loans may be able to confirm the original loan amounts, the amount of their payments, and other terms of their loans.

The auditor can often make effective use of a client's computerized accounts receivable system. Sample selection can be programmed and the files of detail accounts searched automatically, lists and analyses can be prepared, and the confirmation requests can be printed. General-purpose computer programs designed to aid in the confirmation process are available and are discussed in Chapter 11 of the main volume.

Designing the Confirmation Request.   Confirmation requests may be made by means of sticker or rubber stamp affixed to customer statements or by a separate letter; the letter form may be used if statements are not ordinarily sent at the time confirmations are requested or if statements are not mailed to customers. It should be noted that the request is worded as coming from the client. Even though the auditor drafts the request, prepares it, and selects the accounts, all confirmation requests should be made in the client's name because the relationship exists between client and customer (or client and creditor, when liabilities are being confirmed).

Positive vs. Negative Forms.   There are two types of confirmation request—the positive form and the negative form. The positive form either states the information about which confirmation is requested and asks the respondent to indicate agreement or nonagreement, or requests the recipient to fill in the information. (The type of positive form in which the recipient is asked to fill in the information, called a blank form, may provide greater assurance about the information confirmed, but may also generate lower response rates.) The negative form of confirmation requests a response only if the recipient disagrees with the information provided.

Positive confirmations may be used for all accounts, a sample of accounts, or selected accounts, such as those with larger balances, those representing unusual or isolated transactions, or others for which an auditor needs greater assurance of existence and accuracy. The positive form of confirmation is called for if there are indications that a substantial number of accounts may be in dispute or inaccurate or if the individual receivable balances are unusually large or arise from sales to a few major customers. Obtaining and evaluating positive confirmations constitutes a substantive test of details of transactions and balances, and provides direct evidence about one or more financial statement assertions.

Experience has shown that a form of positive request, whether made by letter or a sticker affixed to the statement, that requires a minimum of effort on the part of the recipient produces more responses. The letter form, illustrated in Figure 12.3 in the main volume, is designed so that, when the amount shown agrees with the debtor's records, the individual need only sign in the space provided and return the letter in the envelope enclosed with the request.

If statements of account prepared by the client are to be used for positive confirmation requests, they may be sent in duplicate, with an appropriately worded request (often imprinted on the statement) that the debtor acknowledge the correctness of the statement by returning the duplicate, duly signed, directly to the auditor. A variation is the use of a monthly statement in which the balance and the name of the debtor appear in two places, separated by perforations. One part may be torn off, signed by the debtor, and returned directly to the auditor. Replies to positive requests may be facilitated if the auditor furnishes the details of the individual items included in the balances, usually by providing a copy of the client's detailed customer statement. That may be particularly helpful if the debtor's accounting system does not readily permit identification of account balances.

Positive confirmations provide audit evidence only when responses are received. Second requests, and sometimes third requests by registered mail, should be sent to parties from whom replies were not received. SAS No. 67 requires the auditor to apply alternative procedures to accounts for which responses to positive confirmation requests were not received, unless considering them as 100 percent misstatements would not affect the auditor's decision about the receivables balance and provided that he or she has not identified unusual qualitative factors or systematic attributes related to the nonresponses. The particular alternative procedures to be applied would vary with the circumstances and might include examination of subsequent receipts, shipping documents, or other records to provide evidence of existence and accuracy, and examination of correspondence from third parties and other documentation to support the rights and obligations objective.

The negative form of confirmation is most frequently used for clients with a large number of low-value balances, as may occur in certain specialized industries, for example, financial institutions, utilities, and retail operations. Unreturned negative confirmations do not provide explicit evidence that the intended party received the request and determined that the information was correct. Accordingly, negative confirmations should be used only when the risk of material misstatement has been assessed as low. Unreturned negative confirmations can, however, provide indirect evidence supporting a belief that receivables are not materially misstated, if the auditor has sent out a large number of confirmations drawn from a large population and none or only a few are returned. Evidence provided by nonresponses to negative confirmation requests selected from a large population is similar to evidence from an analytical procedure that does not indicate a departure from the auditor's expectations.

The auditor should consider the audit effect of information contained on returned negative confirmations, which may provide direct evidence about financial statement assertions. Negative confirmations may generate responses indicating misstatements, especially if such misstatements are widespread in a large population and if requests are sent to a large proportion of the population. In those circumstances, negative confirmations may identify an unanticipated problem and thereby assist the auditor in assessing conclusions already reached and in determining whether additional evidence is needed. In this respect also, negative confirmations function similarly to analytical procedures used as substantive tests.

Negative confirmation requests may be returned by the post office with the notation "addressee unknown." Such requests may raise questions about the existence of the third parties and thus point out an unexpected problem. The auditor should follow up on such situations to determine the underlying cause, in much the same way as he or she would respond to an analytical procedure that indicated a problem where none was expected.

Because negative confirmations do not provide evidence that unreturned requests were received by the intended parties and reviewed by them, misstatements detected by evaluating returned confirmations cannot be projected to the entire population and cannot be used as a basis for determining the dollar amount of misstatement in the account as a whole. Responses indicating misstatements require the performance of additional tests of details to determine the nature and amount of misstatement in the account.

Processing Confirmation Requests.   After selecting the accounts for confirmation, the auditor should observe the procedures that follow in processing the requests, regardless of their form.

- Names, addresses, and amounts shown on statements of accounts selected for confirmation or on the confirmation letter should be compared with the debtors' accounts and reviewed for reasonableness.
- The auditor should maintain control over confirmations until they are mailed; this does not preclude obtaining assistance from appropriate client personnel, under the auditor's supervision.
- Requests for confirmation, together with postage-paid return envelopes addressed to the auditor, should be mailed in envelopes showing the auditor's address as the return address. If the client objects to using the auditor's address, returns may be addressed to the client at a post office box controlled by the auditor; the post office should be directed to forward mail to the auditor after the box is surrendered.
- All requests should be mailed by the auditor; the client's mail room may be used for mechanical processing under the control of the auditor, who should deposit the completed requests at the post office.
- Undelivered requests returned by the post office should be investigated, corrected addresses obtained, and the requests remailed by the auditor.

The purpose of those procedures is not so much to protect against possible fraud on the part of the client (although that possibility is clearly implied) as to preserve the integrity of the confirmation procedure. The audit evidence obtained from confirmation is less reliable if there is the possibility of accidental or purposeful interference with direct communication with debtors; the auditor should take all reasonable steps to minimize that possibility.

Respondents may use nontraditional media in replying to confirmation requests, such as electronic or facsimile responses, or may respond orally. In these circumstances, the auditor may need additional evidence to support a conclusion that the confirmations are reliable. For example, it is difficult to determine the source of facsimile responses; therefore, the auditor should consider steps such as calling the purported respondent to substantiate the source and contents of the confirmation and requesting the respondent to mail the original confirmation directly to the auditor. Oral confirmations should be documented in the working papers; if the information confirmed orally is significant, the auditor should request that it be provided directly to him or her in writing.

It is impracticable for an auditor to determine the genuineness or authenticity of signatures on replies to confirmation requests. If the client has appropriate control structure policies and procedures, particularly with respect to the acceptance of customer orders, and if the auditor has considered the reasonableness of the addresses on the confirmations, signature authenticity is usually not a concern. If, however, the auditor has determined that the risk of material misstatement in a particular customer account is high, the client should be asked to request an officer of the debtor to sign the confirmation reply. The auditor may then wish to communicate with that officer by telephone or other means to corroborate the authenticity of the confirmation.

Evaluating the Results of Confirmation Procedures.   Exceptions disclosed by the confirmation process should be carefully scrutinized. The auditor should evaluate all exceptions and decide whether they represent isolated situations or indicate a pattern of disputed sales or payments involving more than one customer. Debtors' responses indicating that payments were sent but not recorded by the client may signal misappropriations of cash and "lapping" of receivables (see Chapter 12 of the main volume). If so, the situation should be thoroughly investigated to determine the amount of the misappropriation, and receivables should be reduced (since the client received the payment) and a loss recorded in the amount of the misappropriation. In addition, the auditor should bring the matter to management's attention and should consider its effect on other auditing procedures.

In many instances, differences reported by debtors on accounts receivable confirmation requests do not have audit significance. Those differences are generally the result of either payments in transit at the confirmation date or delays in recording goods received by the debtor. The auditor should corroborate debtor assertions involving those kinds of differences by examining the cash receipts records and remittance advices for debtor payments received after the confirmation date to determine that the payments were for receivables existing at the confirmation date, and by examining bills of lading or other evidence of shipment. (Differences that are appropriately reconciled in this manner are not exceptions.) Those procedures are often performed on a sample basis. Other reported exceptions, usually involving small amounts, may result from disputes over allowances, discounts, shipping charges, or returned merchandise. These exceptions are usually neither material in amount nor indicative of serious deficiencies in the control structure. After the auditor has made a copy or other record for control purposes, investigation of replies may properly be turned over to a responsible client employee whose regular responsibilities do not involve cash, receivables, or credit functions. The auditor should review the employee's findings and, if considered necessary, perform additional procedures to substantiate the balance.

The auditor should evaluate all the evidence provided by the confirmations and any alternative procedures performed and determine whether sufficient evidence has been obtained for all applicable audit objectives. In making that evaluation, the auditor should consider the reliability of the evidence gathered; the nature of any exceptions, including their implications (both quantitative and qualitative); the evidence provided by other procedures; and whether additional evidence is needed. If the evidence provided by confirmations and other procedures is not sufficient, the auditor should request additional confirmations or extend other tests of details or analytical procedures.

15

Auditing Cash and Cash Equivalents

SUBSTANTIVE TESTS

p. 491. *Replace section* Confirming Bank Balances and Other Information *with:*

Confirming Account Balance Information with Financial Institutions

Account Balances.   An auditor often confirms account balances (both loan balances and deposit accounts) at year-end by direct correspondence with financial institutions, regardless of whether all year-end bank reconciliations are reviewed or tested. This may include accounts closed during the year. Requests to financial institutions for confirmation of both deposit and loan account balances should be made using the Standard Form to Confirm Account Balance Information with Financial Institutions, which was approved by the AICPA, the American Bankers Association, and the Bank Administration Institute in 1990. The form is shown in Figure S15.1.

The original and duplicate of the confirmation form are mailed to the financial institution; one copy is signed by the institution and returned to the auditor and the other is retained by the institution. The confirmation procedure can be expedited if the financial institution receives the confirmation form before the confirmation date and at least two weeks before a reply is required. The exact name and number of the accounts to be confirmed should be prelisted on the form.

In the past, other transactions and arrangements with financial institutions, including contingent liabilities, compensating balances, and lines of credit, were

Figure S15.1   Standard Financial Institution Confirmation Form

STANDARD FORM TO CONFIRM ACCOUNT
BALANCE INFORMATION WITH FINANCIAL INSTITUTIONS

ORIGINAL
To be mailed to accountant

CUSTOMER NAME

We have provided to our accountants the following information as of

the close of business on _____ , 19____ ,
regarding our deposit and loan balances. Please confirm the accuracy
of the information, noting any exceptions to the information provided.
If the balances have been left blank, please complete this form by
furnishing the balance in the appropriate space below.* Although we
do not request nor expect you to conduct a comprehensive, detailed
search of your records, if during the process of completing this confirmation additional information about other deposit and loan accounts
we may have with you comes to your attention, please include such
information below. Please use the enclosed envelope to return the
form directly to our accountants.

Financial [   ]
Institution's
Name and
Address

[   ]

1.   At the close of business on the date listed above, our records indicated the following deposit balance(s):

ACCOUNT NAME	ACCOUNT NO.	INTEREST RATE	BALANCE*

2.   We were directly liable to the financial institution for loans at the close of business on the date listed above as follows:

ACCOUNT NO./ DESCRIPTION	BALANCE*	DATE DUE	INTEREST RATE	DATE THROUGH WHICH INTEREST IS PAID	DESCRIPTION OF COLLATERAL

_____   _____
(Customer's Authorized Signature)   (Date)

The information presented above by the customer is in agreement with our records. Although we have not conducted a
comprehensive, detailed search of our records, no other deposit or loan accounts have come to our attention except as noted below.

_____   _____
(Financial Institution Authorized Signature)   (Date)

_____
(Title)

EXCEPTIONS AND/OR COMMENTS

Please return this form directly to our accountants: [   ]

* Ordinarily, balances are intentionally left blank if they are not
available at the time the form is prepared.   [   ]

Approved 1990 by American Bankers Association, American Institute of Certified Public Accountants and Bank Administration   D451 5951
Institute. Additional forms available from: AICPA—Order Department, P.O. Box 1003, NY NY 10108-1003

also confirmed using the same form that was used to confirm account balances. With the increase in the number and variety of services provided by financial institutions and the number of different people in positions to confirm various items, combining requests for confirmation of different items on one form became impractical. As a result, the AICPA Auditing Standards Division developed three illustrative letters for use in confirming transactions other than account balances. Those letters are discussed and illustrated in Chapter 20 of this Supplement. Using the revised standard confirmation form for account balances and the letter form of confirmation for other transactions with financial institutions will enable the auditor to direct requests for specific information to the appropriate recipients.

16

Auditing Prepaid Expenses, Accrued Liabilities, and Risk Management

SUBSTANTIVE TESTS

Substantive Tests of Specific Accounts

p. 513. *Add after first full paragraph:*

* **Environmental Liabilities (New).**   A large number of companies in a wide variety of industries are affected by environmental laws and regulations—primarily the Resource Conservation and Recovery Act of 1976 (RCRA) and the Comprehensive Environmental Response, Compensation and Liability Act of 1980 (CERCLA, also known as Superfund)—governing waste management and hazardous waste disposal, respectively. To date, the EPA has identified approximately 30,000 polluted sites, the most seriously contaminated of which are graded for their toxicity and danger to the public. The EPA also may initiate clean-up efforts at the sites and may seek to recover any related costs from companies that are determined to have contributed to the pollution. The most polluted sites—currently 1,200—are placed on a National Priority List (NPL). The EPA has estimated that clean-up might cost an average of $25 million per site, with the most troublesome sites costing more than $1 billion to remediate. Fewer than 60 sites have been cleaned up since the inception of Superfund in 1980.

Through the Superfund legislation, the Environmental Protection Agency (EPA) is empowered to seek recovery from any entity (commonly referred to as a potentially responsible party, or PRP) that ever owned or operated a contaminated site or generated or transported hazardous materials to a site. Clean-up costs of Superfund sites represent a potentially significant liability for companies in industries such as chemicals, primary metals, electroplating, textiles, petroleum refining, rubber, and plastics. Banks, insurers, and real estate developers may also be at risk in their dealings with manufacturers and their contaminated properties. Subsequent owners as well as parent companies of PRPs may be potentially liable for clean-up costs.

In identifying a hazardous waste site, the EPA determines the people or companies that have some connection with the property. For the 1,200 sites on the NPL, over 15,000 PRPs have been named. Under Superfund, PRPs can be held responsible for remediation costs for any one of five reasons.

1. They may be the current owners or operators of the property,
2. They may have been owners or operators of the property at the time the hazardous substances were deposited,
3. They may be, or may have been, the generators of the hazardous substances deposited at the property,
4. They may have been transporters of the hazardous substances to the property, or
5. They may have been the persons who arranged for treatment or disposal of an enterprise's hazardous substances at another enterprise's facility.

If the parties originally responsible for the contamination are financially insolvent or no longer exist, the responsibility falls on the sequential successors in the chain of title to the related property, which could be the present or former property owner, even if that party had no part in contaminating the site.

The EPA on occasion requires payment of *response* costs, which are costs incurred by the government in overseeing and studying remediation, as well as legal fees expended. In addition to remediation and response costs, any responsible party may also be liable for natural resource *damages* up to a maximum of $50 million per release of hazardous substances. These damage assessments are considered payment for pollution that cannot be remediated. The EPA has rarely assessed damages, but the potential cost if it does could be sizable.

A number of publicly held companies have announced significant income statement charges for environmental clean-up costs. The list of companies recording and disclosing these charges is expected to grow, as government authorities continue to evaluate hazardous waste sites, and as companies complete their cost estimates and engineering studies related to environmental clean-up. In addition, a number of lawsuits have been filed in which shareholders claim to have been financially damaged by corporations that failed to disclose environmental problems. As a result, companies are under pressure to take a hard and realistic look at their properties for potential exposure.

Accounting Implications.   Accounting for potential environmental liabilities is governed principally by Statement of Financial Accounting Standards (SFAS) No. 5, *Accounting for Contingencies* (Accounting Standards Section C59), discussed in Chapter 21 of the main volume. The Emerging Issues Task Force

(EITF) of the Financial Accounting Standards Board also provided guidance for determining whether to capitalize environmental expenditures or to charge them to current operations. In 1990, the EITF concluded that environmental contamination treatment costs should be charged to income unless they are considered recoverable from revenues to be generated from future operations and meet certain other criteria. If the costs incurred result in the extension of the life of the property, increase its capacity or improve its safety, reduce the possibility of future contamination, or are incurred in preparing the property for sale, they may be capitalized.

Establishing environmental estimates is a difficult process for companies for a number of reasons, including

- The time period required for clean-up is likely to extend over several years.
- Regulatory clean-up standards are constantly changing so that they may become more stringent with the passage of time.
- Clean-up technologies are still evolving.
- Various alternative remediation techniques exist.
- The existence, participation, and financial viability of other PRPs are difficult to determine.
- Insurance coverage is unclear.

Financial management must assess potential environmental clean-up costs by collecting all available pertinent information and developing a sensible range of estimates. Following FASB Interpretation No. 14, the most probable amount in this range should be accrued. If no amount is most likely, the minimum amount in the range should be accrued.

In calculating environmental accruals, companies should consider recoveries in measuring the amount of a probable loss. Recoveries may include insurance proceeds, proceeds from the sale of the property after remediation, or contributions from other responsible parties. In 1993, the EITF concluded that an environmental liability should be evaluated independently from any potential claim for recovery and that the loss arising from the recognition of an environmental liability should be reduced only when it is probable that a claim for recovery will be realized. In a number of instances, it may be difficult to conclude that insurance proceeds are probable of realization, as insurance companies have resisted paying claims related to environmental remediation. (They take the position that their comprehensive liability policies cover only sudden and accidental events, such as the $470 million judgment resulting from the lethal gas leak from Union Carbide's plant in Bhopal, India in 1984.)

The EITF also concluded in 1993 that discounting environmental liabilities for clean-up of a specific site to reflect the time value of money is allowed, but not required, only if the aggregate amount of the obligation and the amount and timing of the cash payments for that site are fixed or reliably determinable. Any asset that is recognized relating to recovery of a portion or all of a liability that is measured on a discounted basis also should be discounted. If the effect of discounting is material, the financial statements should disclose the undiscounted amounts of the liability and any related recovery, and the discount rate used. If only a range of possible losses from the environmental liability can be estimated and no amount within that range is a better estimate of the liability than any other amount within that range, discounting would not be appropriate because the aggregate obligation for the liability is not fixed or reliably determinable.

SEC Requirements.   The Securities and Exchange Commission has taken an increasingly influential role in requiring publicly held companies to disclose environmental clean-up costs. In recognition of potential liabilities, in 1989 the SEC issued Financial Reporting Release No. 36, which calls for disclosure of possible Superfund exposure. The SEC stated that a company designated as a PRP should disclose, if practicable, the quantified potential exposure, if material, in the MD&A section of the annual report. The SEC uses the EPA's list of PRPs during its review of registration statements and quarterly and annual reports to ensure that disclosures are made as required.

In June 1993, the SEC issued Staff Accounting Bulletin No. 92 (SAB 92), which provides guidance regarding accounting and disclosure of loss contingencies, including the following:

- *Insurance recoveries.* A claim for insurance recovery that is probable of realization ordinarily should not be offset against a probable contingent liability on the balance sheet.
- *Joint and several liability.* If a company is jointly and severally liable with respect to a contaminated site, but there is a reasonable basis for apportionment of costs among responsible parties, the company normally is not required to recognize a liability for costs apportioned to other responsible parties. However, if it is probable that other responsible parties will not fully pay costs apportioned to them, the company must recognize a liability in the amount that it expects to be required to pay.
- *Uncertainties inherent in estimates and assumptions.* Management of companies with environmental exposures is often reluctant to record liabilities unless they can be estimated with a high degree of accuracy. FASB Interpretation No. 14 and other related pronouncements set forth guidelines that require the recording of a liability even though the amount cannot be precisely estimated. SAB 92 further emphasizes that, in the absence of significant uncertainties, a company may not delay the recognition of a contingent liability until a single amount, as opposed to a range, can be estimated.

  Further, the SEC staff has indicated its belief that information necessary to support a reasonable estimate or range of loss may be available prior to the performance of a detailed remediation study. According to the staff, in measuring its environmental liability, a company should consider available evidence, including the company's prior experience in remediation of contaminated sites, other companies' clean-up experience, and data released by the EPA or other organizations. Even though the company may not have determined a specific remediation strategy, estimates of the costs associated with the various alternative remediation strategies being considered for a site may be available. While the range of costs associated with the alternatives might be broad, the SEC staff believes that it is unlikely that the minimum cost would be zero.

- *Financial statement disclosures.* The SEC staff has indicated that the disclosures of product and environmental liabilities should be more detailed than typical SFAS No. 5 disclosures. Factors such as the nature and terms of cost-sharing arrangements and the time frame over which the accrued or presently unrecognized amounts may be paid, may be required to be disclosed under SAB 92.

Auditing Environmental Costs. When performing risk assessment activities, auditors should consider the possibility of material environmental liabilities and should plan the audit accordingly. When assessing inherent risks, auditors should take into account the company's industry, which may be particularly susceptible to environmental issues; the nature of its operations and manufacturing or other processes; and real estate holdings that may represent environmental risks. Auditors should discuss with company management the steps they have taken to identify all exposures to environmental risks.

If a company has established an estimate for an environmental liability, the auditor needs to determine the reasonableness of the estimate. This involves gaining an understanding of the method management used to develop the estimate, which in turn requires that the auditor become familiar with the remediation process used or planned for cleaning up contaminated areas. This understanding will help the auditor select the appropriate procedures for evaluating the reasonableness of management's estimate.

According to SAS No. 57, *Auditing Accounting Estimates* (AU Section 342), when auditing environmental liability estimates, auditors should use one or a combination of the following approaches:

- Review and test the process used by management to develop the estimate.
- Develop an independent expectation of the estimate to corroborate the reasonableness of management's estimate.
- Review subsequent events or transactions occurring prior to completion of field work.

Typically, auditors use the first approach for an estimate of environmental clean-up costs. In reviewing and testing management's estimating process, the auditor should consider the following procedures specific to environmental costs, in addition to those used for auditing accounting estimates in general:

- Understand management's process for developing its estimate.
- Obtain the supporting detail for the estimate and review the underlying assumptions.
- Ensure that the estimate includes costs for all phases of remediation.
- Review the assumptions surrounding third-party involvement (such as other PRPs and insurance coverage).
- If necessary, review the remediation process and cost estimates with independent engineers and evaluate the credentials of the engineers.

Other Postretirement Benefit Obligations. SFAS No. 106, *Employers' Accounting for Postretirement Benefits Other Than Pensions* (Accounting Standards Section P40), was issued in December 1990 and became effective generally in 1993. Its provisions are similar in many respects to those of SFAS No. 87, *Employers' Accounting for Pensions* (Accounting Standards Section P16) and SFAS No. 88, *Employers' Accounting for Settlements and Curtailments of Defined Benefit Pension Plans and for Termination Benefits* (Accounting Standards Section P16). SFAS No. 106, however, addresses matters unique to nonpension postretirement benefits and provides recognition, measurement, and disclosure requirements related to those benefits.[1.1]

As SFAS No. 106 notes, "to the extent the promise to provide pension benefits and the promise to provide postretirement benefits are similar, the provisions of this Statement are similar to those prescribed by Statements 87 and 88; different accounting treatment is prescribed only when the Board has concluded that there is a compelling reason for different treatment." Thus, auditing procedures for postretirement benefit costs and obligations are similar to those for pension costs and obligations, although there are some distinctions.

Accounting for the Substantive Plan.   SFAS No. 106 requires that the accounting reflect the substantive terms of the postretirement benefit plan as understood by the employer and its employees. The substantive plan, however, may not be reflected in the terms described in the written plan. For example, a past practice of regularly increasing benefits or changing the cost-sharing provisions of the plan (e.g., deductibles, coinsurance provisions, or retiree contributions) may indicate that the substantive plan differs from the written plan.

An employer's cost-sharing policy will constitute the cost-sharing provisions of the substantive plan if either of the following conditions exist:

- The employer has a past practice of either (1) maintaining a consistent level of cost sharing with its retirees or (2) consistently increasing or decreasing its share of the cost of benefits by changing retirees' or active plan participants' contributions, deductibles, coinsurance provisions, out-of-pocket limitations, and so forth, in accordance with the employer's established cost-sharing policy.
- The employer has the ability, and has communicated to affected plan participants its intent, to institute different cost-sharing provisions at a specified time or when certain conditions exist (e.g., when health care cost increases exceed a certain level).

SFAS No. 106 provides little guidance as to what constitutes a past practice of consistently maintaining or changing the cost-sharing provisions.

In reviewing the employer's determination of the substantive plan, the auditor might, in addition to reading the plan document and its amendments and the actuary's report, perform a variety of procedures, including making inquiries of management and reviewing past changes to cost-sharing provisions and communications to employees and retirees.

Actuarial Assumptions.   SFAS No. 106 describes a number of actuarial assumptions that should be considered in measuring an employer's postretirement health care obligation. These include assumptions commonly associated with

---

[1.1] While SFAS No. 106 applies to all health and welfare postretirement benefits other than pensions, its main focus is on retiree health benefits because of their high cost and complexity of measurement.

calculations of pension obligations, as well as assumptions unique to postretirement health care benefits. Certain assumptions used in measuring pension obligations, however, such as mortality, retirement ages, turnover, and dependency status, may have a more significant effect when used to measure health care benefit obligations.

Measuring the obligation for postretirement health care benefits requires employers to make assumptions about the amount and timing of benefits expected to be paid in the future. In estimating the amount of future payments, employers need to consider various factors, including historical claims cost by age, health care cost trend rates, and medical coverage to be provided by governmental authorities and others. Since many of the calculations required by SFAS No. 106 are actuarial calculations, in auditing these amounts the auditor applies the provisions of SAS No. 11, *Using the Work of a Specialist* (AU Section 336). Auditing these amounts is similar to auditing accrued pension costs, as discussed on pages 510 and 511 of the main volume. In circumstances in which the auditor's testing of actuarial assumptions calls for corresponding directly with the actuary, the auditor may choose to use a standard confirmation request letter developed by the AICPA.[1,2]

Although the scope of SFAS No. 106 encompasses postretirement benefits other than health care, this letter was designed for postretirement health care benefits. Letters to actuaries, if any, that value other postretirement benefits, such as life insurance, tuition, legal services, and day care and housing subsidies, should be appropriately modified.

Much of the information used by the actuary to measure the obligation is often maintained and provided by the employer or by a third-party administrator (TPA). Such information includes historical claims cost and participants' age, sex, and dates of birth and hire. The auditor can usually test much of this information in conjunction with the testing required when auditing the pension plan obligation, except for historical claims cost, which will usually be the subject of separate audit focus.

In some circumstances, the claims cost experience of other employers— derived from data maintained by insurers, actuarial firms, or benefit consultants and adjusted as necessary for differing demographics—can be used to develop relevant cost information. If such third-party data is used, the auditor should consider its reasonableness and relevance to the employer's circumstances.

Employers often have information on net claims paid rather than on gross eligible charges. SFAS No. 106 allows calculations based on net claims cost, provided such amounts are appropriately adjusted to reflect the plan's cost-sharing provisions.

*   ***Materiality Considerations.***   In many circumstances, the same auditor audits the financial statements of both the employer company and the related health and welfare benefit plan. When designing the nature, extent, and timing

---

[1,2] This letter appeared in the November 1992 *Journal of Accountancy,* pp. 93–98. It has been reproduced in Richard M. Steinberg, Ronald J. Murray, and Harold Dankner, *Pensions and Other Employee Benefits: A Financial Reporting and ERISA Compliance Guide,* 4th ed. (New York: John Wiley & Sons, 1993), pp. 390–395.

of auditing procedures for financial statement amounts recorded in accordance with SFAS No. 106, the auditor should not only base materiality judgments on the employer's financial statements, but also consider expected materiality to the plan's financial statements. Under SOP 92-6, *Accounting and Reporting by Health and Welfare Benefit Plans,* the plan's financial statements reflect SFAS No. 106 amounts. Considering plan materiality when auditing the employer's financial statements can help avoid later adjustments to SFAS No. 106 amounts in the plan's financial statements, resulting in potential differences between the employer's and the plan's statements.

Disclosures and Reports.   If adoption of SFAS No. 106 has a material effect on an employer's financial statements, the auditor's report in the year of adoption should make reference to the accounting change. The effective date of SFAS No. 106 is generally 1993, but is 1995 for foreign plans and private company plans with no more than 500 plan participants. If a company adopts the provisions of SFAS No. 106 in different years for different plans, references to the accounting change may be required in each year. Until they adopt SFAS No. 106, public companies are required to comply with SEC Staff Accounting Bulletin No. 74 (SAB 74), *Disclosure of the Impact That Recently Issued Accounting Standards Will Have on the Financial Statements of the Registrant When Adopted in a Future Period.* SAB 74 requires disclosure of the anticipated effects, if they are known, on financial position and results of operations of adopting a new standard. If the effects are not known, other disclosures are required. The auditor should ascertain whether the financial statements contain the appropriate disclosures.

* **Postemployment Benefit Obligations (New).**   SFAS No. 112, *Employers' Accounting for Postemployment Benefits* (Accounting Standards Section P32), was issued to provide standards for accounting for and reporting the estimated cost of benefits provided by an employer to former or inactive employees after employment but before retirement (postemployment benefits). It amends SFAS Nos. 5 and 43, and becomes effective for fiscal years beginning after December 15, 1993.

Types of Postemployment Benefits Offered by Employers.   Employers may offer a variety of benefits to former or inactive employees after employment but before retirement, and to such employees' beneficiaries and covered dependents. Inactive employees are those who are not currently rendering service to the employer but have not been terminated, such as those who have been laid off or those on disability leave, regardless of whether they are expected to return to active status.

These benefits may include, but are not limited to, salary continuation, supplemental unemployment benefits, severance benefits, disability-related benefits (including worker's compensation), job training and counseling, and continuation of benefits such as health care and life insurance. Such benefits may be paid in cash or in kind, immediately upon cessation of active employment or over a specified period of time.

The auditor needs to gain an understanding of the benefits the company offers and how they are accounted for. In particular, the auditor should ascertain whether management has appropriately identified benefits to which SFAS

No. 112 applies. This determination can be difficult at times. For instance, some employers consider permanently disabled employees to be retired at the date of disability and therefore include certain benefits under their pension plan (accounted for under SFAS No. 87) and include health care benefits under their postretirement medical plan (accounted for under SFAS No. 106). Other employers do not consider a permanently disabled employee to be retired when he or she becomes disabled.

Accounting Requirements. SFAS No. 112 requires recognition of postemployment costs on an accrual basis. Under the statement, employers should recognize the obligation to provide postemployment benefits in accordance with SFAS No. 43, *Accounting for Compensated Absences* (Accounting Standards Section C44), if:

- The obligation is attributable to employees' services already rendered,
- Employees' rights to the benefits accumulate over time,
- Payment of the benefits is probable, and
- The amount of the benefits can be reasonably estimated.

If these four conditions are not met, the employer should account for postemployment benefits when it is probable that a liability has been incurred and the amount can be reasonably estimated, in accordance with SFAS No. 5, *Accounting for Contingencies*. If an obligation for postemployment benefits is not accrued in accordance with SFAS No. 5 or No. 43 only because the amount cannot be reasonably estimated, the financial statements are required to disclose that fact.

SFAS No. 112 provides little guidance or examples for determining whether the criteria in SFAS No. 43 or No. 5 apply to a particular benefit program. In many circumstances, the auditor will need to evaluate and review documentation supporting the policies and intent of management's plans. For instance, when assessing whether payment of benefits for severance and layoff benefits under SFAS No. 43 is probable, the auditor may review company memoranda or minutes of meetings that substantiate management's plans for workforce reductions.

The statement also contains little specific guidance on measuring postemployment obligations and expense. However, it does indicate that discounting is permitted (but not required). It also suggests that employers may look to SFAS Nos. 87 and 106 for guidance on measurement issues to the extent that similar issues apply to postretirement and postemployment benefits, although delayed recognition of the transition obligation would not be appropriate for postemployment benefits.

Auditing Postemployment Benefits. In many respects, the procedures for auditing employee postemployment benefit costs and obligations are similar to those for auditing postretirement benefits under SFAS No. 106, including reviewing the appropriateness of actuarial assumptions about the amount and timing of benefits, and personnel data, such as the employer's records of employees' salaries and employment terms. Auditing procedures should therefore be coordinated with work performed in connection with auditing postretirement benefits or, in some circumstances, auditing pension benefits.

CONSIDERING THE CLIENT'S RISK MANAGEMENT

* **p. 515.** *Add at end of chapter:*

Auditing Self-Insurance Arrangements (New)

Pages 513 to 515 of the main volume discuss how clients manage risk, including the use of methods of risk management in which the enterprise retains some part of the risk (commonly called self-insurance). When auditing companies using such self-insurance methods, the auditor should consider factors such as the following:

- Types of insurance policies in force.
- Actual or potential uninsured loss exposure from claims that could be filed after the expiration of a claims-made policy.
- Cancellation of any significant policies previously in force.
- Purchase of new policies with terms that are significantly different from previous policies (e.g., deductibles).
- Whether the company changed the form of its insurance policies from occurrence to claims-made or from guaranteed costs to retrospectively rated.
- Whether any prior insurers are insolvent, in rehabilitation, or of questionable solvency.

If the company has some form of self-insurance, the auditor will want to ensure that the liability for self-insurance claims is properly reported in the balance sheet. This includes determining whether all liabilities for self-insured occurrences through the balance sheet date have been considered. When an estimated accrual is made for the amount of a probable loss, the accrued amount should be the most likely amount in a range. If no amount in the range is more likely than any other, the minimum amount should be accrued. If the amount of the loss cannot be reasonably estimated, the nature of the contingency should be disclosed. The program of self-insurance coverage and the basis for any loss accruals should also be adequately disclosed in the financial statements.

When auditing companies with self-insurance liabilities, auditors should consider performing the following procedures:

- Review the amount of insurance coverage, if any, the type of coverage (claims-made or occurrence), the deductible provisions, and other relevant factors to determine the level of risk that is retained by the entity. Consider the financial viability of the insurance carrier.
- Test the accuracy and completeness of the company's incident reporting and monitoring system.
- Review and test the method of estimating incurred but not reported (IBNR) claims.
- Review actuarial reports used to estimate the liability for self-insurance claims, including the IBNR claims. Determine the extent of reliance on

actuaries in accordance with SAS No. 11, *Using the Work of a Specialist* (AU Section 336).

- Determine the extent to which company-relevant industry data is used to estimate the number, frequency, and loss value of reported and unreported incidents.
- Determine that a liability is recorded for any additional premium that may be owed for retrospectively rated policies.
- Review prior estimates and historical loss experience.
- Determine whether uncertainties related to self-insurance claims need to be disclosed in the auditor's report.
- Review the appropriateness of disclosures related to self-insurance.

17

Auditing Investments

* p. 517. *Replace entire chapter with:*

"Investments" is a broad term used to describe nonoperating, income-producing assets of a commercial or industrial enterprise that are held either as a means of using excess cash or to accomplish some special purpose. The term "securities" is commonly used interchangeably with investments, as it is in this chapter. Often, the description of investment assets in the financial statements gives further insight into the specific reasons they are held. Readers of financial statements should look at classifications, descriptions in captions, and descriptive notes to determine the nature and purpose of a company's investments in securities.

The term "security" is defined in Statement of Financial Accounting Standards (SFAS) No. 115, *Accounting for Certain Investments in Debt and Equity Securities* (Accounting Standards Section I80), as are the terms "equity security" and "debt security." A security represents either an ownership interest in property or in an enterprise or the right to acquire or dispose of an ownership interest in an enterprise, in which case it is an equity security, or it represents an obligation of the issuer, in which case it is a debt security. Debt securities exclude option contracts, financial futures contracts, forward contracts, lease contracts, and nonsecuritized trade accounts receivable and consumer, commercial, and real estate loans receivable. SFAS No. 115 does not apply to investments in equity securities accounted for under the equity method or to investments in consolidated subsidiaries.

At the date of acquisition, both debt securities and equity securities should be classified as indicated below. The appropriateness of the classification should be reassessed at each reporting date.

Debt securities should be classified into the following three categories:

- Held-to-maturity
- Trading
- Available-for-sale.

Equity securities should be classified into the following two categories:

- Trading
- Available-for-sale.

Investments in debt securities should be classified as held-to-maturity only if the entity has the positive intent and ability to hold the securities to maturity, which is distinct from a mere absence of an "intent to sell." The held-to-maturity category should not include debt securities that may be sold in response to changes in market interest rates, the security's prepayment risk, the enterprise's liquidity needs, foreign exchange risk, tax planning strategies, or other similar factors. An entity's held-to-maturity classification would not be considered inconsistent, however, if a security is sold or transferred, provided the action is due to certain changes in circumstances specified in SFAS No. 115. These changes in circumstances include a deterioration in the issuer's creditworthiness, a change in tax law, a major business combination, and changes in statutory or regulatory requirements regarding permissible investments, risk weights, and minimum capital.

In addition, other events that are isolated, nonrecurring, and unusual and that could not have been reasonably anticipated may cause the entity to sell or transfer a held-to-maturity security without necessarily calling into question its intent to hold other securities to maturity. Further, the held-to-maturity criterion would be deemed to be satisfied even though

- A security is sold within three months of its maturity date (or call date if exercise of the call is probable), or
- A security is sold after the entity has already collected 85 percent or more of the principal amount outstanding at acquisition due to either prepayments or scheduled payments.

Trading securities (both debt and equity) are bought principally for selling in the near term. They are generally held for a short period and are acquired with the objective of generating profits on short-term differences in price.

All investments within the scope of SFAS No. 115 that are neither held-to-maturity nor acquired for trading purposes are classified as available-for-sale.

SFAS No. 115, which superseded SFAS No. 12, is effective for fiscal years beginning after December 15, 1993. In general, initial application of the statement should be as of the beginning of a fiscal year. However, for fiscal years beginning prior to December 16, 1993, initial application of this statement is permitted as of the end of the fiscal year for which annual financial statements have not previously been issued. Interim financial statements for that year should *not* be restated. Prior years' financial statements should not be restated.

The effect on retained earnings of initially applying SFAS No. 115 should be reported similar to the cumulative effect of a change in accounting principle. For securities classified as available-for-sale, the net-of-tax unrealized holding gain or loss as of the date of initial application should be reported as an adjustment of the balance of the separate component of equity.

For entities presenting a classified balance sheet, all trading securities should be shown as current assets. All other securities should be shown as either current or noncurrent according to the provisions of Chapter 3A of Accounting Research Bulletin (ARB) No. 43 (Accounting Standards Section B05). (ARB No. 43 specifies that the term *current assets* designates assets that are reasonably expected to be realized in cash or sold or consumed in one year or during the normal operating cycle of the business, whichever is longer.) Balance sheets of banks, insurance companies, investment companies, and securities and commodities broker-dealers (which are discussed in Chapters 26, 32, 33, and 39, respectively) customarily do not classify assets as current or noncurrent.

Investments may also represent holdings of securities for purposes of control, affiliation, or financing of enterprises related to the investing company's operations. Those investments, which are classified as noncurrent assets, may require using the equity method of accounting. Sinking funds, building funds, and other funds accumulated for special purposes may consist of investments in securities and are also classified as noncurrent assets.

Income statement accounts related to investments are generally "interest income" (including amortization of premium and discount, as appropriate), "dividend income," "realized gain or loss on sale of securities," "unrealized holding gains and losses on trading securities," and "earnings or losses from investments accounted for by the equity method." Market value adjustments made for available-for-sale securities are reflected in the equity section of the balance sheet. Write-downs for other-than-temporary impairments of fair value of available-for-sale or held-to-maturity securities, however, are accounted for as realized losses in the income statement.

In the statement of cash flows, cash flows from trading securities should be presented as operating activities. Gross cash flows from held-to-maturity and available-for-sale securities should be presented separately under investing activities.

AUDIT OBJECTIVES

The auditor should design tests to provide reasonable assurance that

- Investments exist and the client has legal title to them at the balance sheet date. Establishing the existence (in either certificate form, electronic or "book entry" form, or a custodial account) and ownership of investments is paramount to the audit process, particularly because many securities are readily negotiable.
- All investments owned by the client at the balance sheet date are included in the investment accounts.
- The values at which investments are carried in the financial statements are appropriate and are adequately disclosed.

- The investments are properly classified between current and noncurrent components.
- Investments pledged as collateral or otherwise restricted are appropriately identified and disclosed.
- Income from investments, including realized and unrealized gains and losses, is appropriately reflected in the financial statements.

The nature, timing, and extent of substantive tests that the auditor applies to achieve those objectives, as well as tests of controls, are discussed later in this chapter. The auditor should be familiar with the key accounting measurement and disclosure concepts related to investments, as discussed in the following paragraphs.

Carrying Value

The value at which investments are carried in the financial statements varies with the type of investment and any specialized industry practices. The following is a synopsis of different bases for carrying values.

Amortized Cost.   Cost is the amount paid for an investment at the date of acquisition and includes such items as commissions and fees, but not accrued interest paid at acquisition. If securities are received as gifts (which occurs most commonly in not-for-profit institutions), cost is the fair value as of the date of the gift.[1]

Debt securities are normally acquired at a premium or discount, depending on the stated rate on the security compared with the market rate at the date of acquisition. For debt securities classified as held-to-maturity, the premium or discount should be amortized over the remaining life of the investment, using the effective interest method. Unless there is a decline in value that is other than temporary, the securities should be carried at amortized cost.

Debt securities carried at amortized cost should be written down to fair value if there is evidence that a decline in fair value below amortized cost is other than temporary. An auditing interpretation of Section 332, *Long-Term Investments*, of Statement on Auditing Standards (SAS) No. 1 (AU Section 9332.03) provides some guidance on evidential matter about the carrying amount of securities. As that interpretation indicates, the distinction between temporary and persistent (nontemporary) declines in value is largely undefined in the accounting and auditing literature.

The distinction was considered by the SEC staff in 1985, however, with respect to write-downs of noncurrent equity securities. Staff Accounting Bulletin (SAB) No. 59, which was subsequently reinforced by several accounting and auditing enforcement releases, cautioned that "other than temporary" should not be interpreted to mean "permanent" and stated that "unless evidence exists to support a realizable value equal to or greater than the carrying value of the investment, a write-down accounted for as a realized loss should be recorded." The SAB included examples of factors that should be considered in evaluating whether a

---

[1] SFAS No. 115 does not apply to not-for-profit organizations. The FASB has stated its intention to address accounting for investments by such organizations at a later date.

decline is other than temporary: the length of time and the extent to which fair value has been less than cost, the financial condition and near-term prospects of the issuer, and the intent and ability of the holder to retain its investment long enough for any anticipated recovery in fair value to occur. The conditions of paragraph 8 of SFAS No. 5, *Accounting for Contingencies* (Accounting Standards Section C59.105), also may be applicable, that is, a nontemporary impairment should be considered to have occurred when it is probable that the asset was impaired at the date of the financial statements and the loss can be reasonably estimated.

Equity.   The equity method is used for investments in a corporate joint venture and for other investments that confer the investor with "significant influence" over the investee. According to Accounting Principles Board (APB) Opinion No. 18, *Equity Method of Accounting for Investments in Common Stock* (Accounting Standards Section I82.104), an investment of 20 percent or more of the voting stock of an investee should lead to a presumption that, in the absence of evidence to the contrary, an investor has the ability to exercise significant influence over an investee. If it is clear that the investor exercises significant influence, the equity method is required even if less than 20 percent is owned.

Under the equity method, an investment is recorded at cost at the date of acquisition and is then adjusted each period for the investor's appropriate share of earnings, losses, and other changes in stockholders' equity of the investee corporation. The investor's share of earnings and losses should be adjusted for the accounting effects of the difference between cost and the investor's share of the underlying book value at the acquisition date. If the investor is not obligated to make further advances or investments, the carrying value of the investment ordinarily should not be reduced below zero as a result of investee losses. The equity method is appropriate for accounting for investments in (a) corporate joint ventures and (b) common stock of unconsolidated subsidiaries and other investments of 50 percent or less of the voting stock of the investee corporation if the investor has the ability to exercise significant influence over operating and financial policies of the investee.

Fair Value.   Under SFAS No. 115, investments in debt securities that are not classified as held-to-maturity (that is, those that are classified as trading securities and available-for-sale securities) should be measured at fair value. All investments in equity securities that have readily determinable fair values (as defined in the statement), except for investments accounted for under the equity method and investments in consolidated subsidiaries, also should be measured at fair value. Changes in fair value (that is, unrealized holding gains and losses) of trading securities are recognized in the income statement; changes in fair value of available-for-sale securities are reported as a separate component of shareholders' equity until realized, except for write-downs for other-than-temporary impairments, which are reported in the income statement. (Some industries with specialized accounting practices, such as brokers and dealers in securities, investment companies, and defined benefit pension plans, recognize all changes in fair value in income or its equivalent, but those industries are excluded from the scope of SFAS No. 115.)

SFAS No. 115 also provides guidance on accounting for transfers of securities between categories. It indicates that transfers into or from the trading category as well as transfers from the held-to-maturity category are expected to be rare. The statement specifies that all transfers between categories should be accounted for at fair value and provides detailed guidance on how unrealized holding gains and losses should be accounted for when transfers take place.

Income from Investments

The auditor is concerned primarily with the following accounts related to income from investments.

Interest and Dividend Income.   Interest income, including amortization of the premium or discount arising at acquisition, should be recorded as of the balance sheet date; dividends should be recorded on the "ex-dividend" date. Such amounts should be included in income.

Gains or Losses.   Realized gains or losses are recorded as part of earnings when securities classified as either available-for-sale or held-to-maturity are sold or, in certain cases, when they are exchanged for other securities. As noted earlier, declines in fair value of securities classified as available-for-sale or held-to-maturity that are determined to be other than temporary should be accounted for as realized losses and included in earnings.

A gain or loss from the sale of securities classified as available-for-sale or held-to-maturity is computed by deducting the carrying amount and costs of disposal from the proceeds, reduced by accrued interest or declared dividends, if any. (When available-for-sale securities are sold, the related unrealized holding gain or loss included in the separate component of shareholders' equity becomes part of the realized gain or loss on sale.) If only part of an investment in a security is sold, cost is usually apportioned on the basis of average cost, first-in, first-out, or identification of the cost of specific certificates. The method selected should be consistently followed.

The average cost method has the merit of recognizing the fungible character of different lots of the same security and is generally considered preferable to the other two methods. The identified cost method allows considerable choice in the amount of gain or loss to be recognized if different lots of a security were purchased at different prices.

The average cost method cannot be used for federal income tax purposes under current regulations. Either specific identification or the first-in, first-out method must be used. If the average cost method is used for financial statement reporting of sales of partial holdings, a difference arises between the book basis and tax basis of both the securities sold and the remaining holdings. Deferred tax accounting is necessary, and memorandum records of tax cost should be maintained.

As noted earlier, unrealized holding gains and losses on trading securities are included in earnings. Unrealized holding gains and losses on available-for-sale securities (including those classified as current assets) are excluded from earnings and reported net in a separate component of shareholders' equity until realized. SFAS No. 109, *Accounting for Income Taxes* (Accounting Standards Section I27), provides guidance on reporting the tax effects of unrealized gains and losses reported in the separate component of equity. SFAS No. 115 provides guidance on accounting for the unrealized gain or loss on a security that has been transferred between categories of investments.

Earnings or Losses from Investments Accounted for by the Equity Method. The mechanics of the equity method can be handled in either of two ways. The simpler way is to credit dividends received to the investment account and to adjust the investment periodically by the investor's appropriate share of the earnings or losses for the period, recording income or loss from the investment. However, since it is necessary to account for distributed earnings separately from equity in undistributed earnings for various reasons (e.g., SEC and federal income tax reporting), dividends received are commonly credited to an income account and the investment account is adjusted only for the net change in underlying equity (after adjustments equivalent to those made for consolidations).

Disclosures

SFAS No. 115 requires certain disclosures for all reporting enterprises and specifies additional disclosures for financial institutions, which include banks, savings and loan associations, savings banks, credit unions, finance companies, and insurance companies. The disclosure requirements discussed below are limited to those required of all enterprises.

Among the required disclosures are, for securities classified as available-for-sale and separately for securities classified as held-to-maturity, the aggregate fair value, gross unrealized holding gains, gross unrealized holding losses, and amortized cost basis by major security type, and information about the contractual maturities of debt securities as of the date of each balance sheet presented. Other required disclosures (for each period for which results of operations are presented) are detailed in SFAS No. 115, paragraphs 21 and 22, as follows:

a. The proceeds from sales of available-for-sale securities and the gross realized gains and gross realized losses on those sales

b. The basis on which cost was determined in computing realized gain or loss (that is, specific identification, average cost, or other method used)

c. The gross gains and gross losses included in earnings from transfers of securities from the available-for-sale category into the trading category

d. The change in net unrealized holding gain or loss on available-for-sale securities that has been included in the separate component of shareholders' equity during the period

e. The change in net unrealized holding gain or loss on trading securities that has been included in earnings during the period.

For any sales of or transfers from securities classified as held-to-maturity, the amortized cost amount of the sold or transferred security, the related realized or unrealized gain or loss, and the circumstances leading to the decision to sell or transfer the security shall be disclosed in the notes to the financial statements for each period for which the results of operations are presented.

INVESTMENT TRANSACTIONS AND INTERNAL CONTROL STRUCTURE POLICIES AND PROCEDURES

The steps involved in investment activity by industrial and commercial companies are more likely to be similar from one company to another than in many other areas of business operations. They are often rather formal and well organized, whether the purpose is short-term investment of temporary excess cash, long-term investment, or investment for purposes of affiliation or control. The activity begins with selection and authorization of an investment; subsequent steps are acquisition, safeguarding, accounting for income, appraisal, and disposition.

Management normally is aware of the amounts of funds available for investment as well as the future need for funds. In addition, many of the control procedures for investment activities are administered directly by management.

Selection and Authorization

If the investment activity is not significant, the selection and authorization of investments are generally specifically delegated to an executive officer, often the treasurer. If the activity is significant, it is usually overseen by top officers or by the board of directors itself, although investment transactions may be initiated automatically, for example, by overnight sweeps of cash balances into money market instruments, or by portfolio managers who operate discretionary accounts. Often an investment committee of officers or directors employs an investment advisor to whom it delegates the authority to make specific decisions about investment acquisitions and dispositions. Ultimately, however, the responsibility for investment decisions rests with management.

Control procedures for selecting investments include authorization by the board, either for specific investments or in the form of a general authorization to an officer or advisor to make investment decisions, and high-level management review and explicit approval of specific investment decisions before they are executed.

Acquisition

Control structure policies and procedures that are part of the acquisition process in general, for example, authorization for the disbursement of funds, are discussed in Chapter 13 of the main volume. The following discussion relates to additional policies and procedures that are specific to the acquisition of investments.

Investments are often acquired through financial institutions that deal in formal markets. Typically the control mechanism consists of some form of approved acquisition list, which may include maximum prices or minimum yields. In an effective control structure, the approved list would reflect the client's assessment of the risks inherent in various types of securities and the returns they generate. Acquisitions of investments that do not have readily determinable fair values are almost always unique events, even if a fairly large number of units is acquired at one time, such as acquisitions of nonmarketable equity securities or of real estate for an endowment fund or investment portfolio. Selecting investments and negotiating acquisition terms are likely to be delegated to an investment specialist;

high-level management review and approval are required before investment decisions are executed.

Safeguarding Investments

Physical protection of securities is vital because many such securities are readily negotiable; moreover, documents evidencing legal ownership have value even if securities are not readily negotiable. Therefore, restricted access and segregation of duties are particularly important aspects of the control structure for investments. Securities are generally kept in a vault or safe deposit box, or entrusted to a financial institution for safekeeping. The custodian and other personnel who have access to the securities should be independent of the functions of authorizing investment transactions, keeping investment records, handling cash, and maintaining the general ledger; preferably each of those employees should be independent of all the others.

If securities are kept in a safe deposit box, the number of people with authorized access is kept to a minimum, but it is preferable for two people to be present whenever the box is opened. A safe deposit box is an effective means of protection because a bank's provisions for physical security and procedures for restricting and controlling access to the vault are normally more extensive than most commercial and industrial organizations are able to maintain.

Other control procedures for investments generally include periodically inspecting and counting securities for which delivery has been taken, and reconciling and investigating differences. Those procedures are performed by people other than those responsible for authorizing and executing transactions and maintaining custody of the securities. Even if securities have been entrusted to a financial institution for safekeeping, or exist in electronic notation (book entry) form, the entity still needs to maintain records of transactions and balances and to periodically reconcile the records with those of the custodian.

Internal Control Structure Policies and Procedures for Complex Financial Instruments

Additional internal control structure policies and procedures for assessing and monitoring the risks associated with sophisticated and complex financial instruments are important. These policies and procedures are in addition to those that apply to investment transactions generally.

Selection and Authorization. Management should establish an overall corporate policy defining the objectives for entering into transactions involving financial instruments with off-balance-sheet credit or market risk or concentrations of credit risk. (See the discussions of these risks later in this chapter and in Chapter 21A of this Supplement.) The policy should cover selecting broker-dealers, portfolio managers, or investment advisors; limits on investments in financial instruments, counterparties, and traders; and procedures to ensure that the investor has possession of any collateral. This policy should be approved by the board of directors.

Monitoring and Evaluating Results. Transactions should be monitored on a regular basis and procedures should be in place to react to risks that have exceeded what the entity wishes to bear. Formal procedures should be established to monitor the economic health of counterparties (issuers). Appropriate levels of management reporting should exist.

Other. Procedures should exist to segregate duties effectively among individuals responsible for making investment and credit decisions, custody of securities, disbursing and receiving funds, record keeping, confirmation of positions, and performing reconciliations.

Internal auditors should periodically evaluate the effectiveness of the policies and procedures and recommend appropriate changes.

Valuation of Investments

Periodic valuation of investments is necessary for management decision-making purposes; it is also required so that fair value can be determined for financial statement purposes. If investments are few, have readily determinable fair values, and are not significant to a company's operations, the valuation process is sometimes performed informally by the officer responsible for investments. If investments are significant, the valuation should be formally executed and documented. The frequency of valuation depends on the amount of investment activity and how often financial statements are issued. (Some active investment portfolios are under virtually continual valuation.)

Disposition

Dispositions of investments are usually subject to the same procedures as acquisitions. Control procedures for the receipt and processing of proceeds from dispositions are discussed in Chapter 12 of the main volume.

Records of Investments

An investment ledger is desirable regardless of the size of a portfolio. The ledger generally contains an account for each investment, which is described completely: full title of the issue; number of shares or face value; certificate numbers (if the enterprise takes delivery of the securities); interest or dividend rate; maturities or other features such as call, conversion, or collateral; cost; and required amortization of premium or discount. If the tax basis is different from the book basis, the former may also be noted in the investment ledger account. The detail of the investment ledger is reconciled periodically to the general ledger control account.

Some investments, such as mortgages, are supported by a permanent file of documents controlled by a checklist: for example, note (bond) receivable, mortgage, record of registering the mortgage, insurance policies, and tax bills.

AUDIT TESTING PLAN

The investment portfolio of many industrial and commercial companies is not significant to the financial statements, and efficiency considerations often lead the auditor to adopt a testing plan that emphasizes substantive testing. In some situations, however, the auditor may choose to perform tests of controls as a basis for reducing the assurance needed from substantive tests. That strategy decision partly reflects the auditor's assessment of the inherent risk characteristics associated with the particular types of investments the client has.

Assessing those risks, which have both accounting and auditing implications, is especially important if the client's investment portfolio includes sophisticated, complex financial instruments whose terms and risks may not be widely understood. All investments contain elements of business risk, market risk, credit risk, and the risk of intentional or unintentional loss of securities (collateral risk).

- Business risk relates to the possibility that the investor will misunderstand the terms and the underlying economic substance of an investment, including the expected return. This can result in incorrect pricing of securities, inappropriate accounting for investment income, or unrealistic expectations about the marketability or liquidity of an investment.

- Market risk is the risk that changes in security prices may affect the investor's ability to continue to finance an investment made with borrowed funds, thus forcing the investment to be liquidated sooner than intended.

- Credit risk is the risk of default, either by the issuer of the securities or by the financial institution that holds securities as a custodian or has entered into a commitment to deliver securities some time in the future. Credit risk and market risk are interrelated; adverse price fluctuations may create losses that preclude a debtor or other obligor from honoring its commitments.

- Collateral risk is the risk that the custodian of securities in which the client has not perfected a security interest may not be able to deliver the securities.

The decision whether to perform tests of controls also reflects the auditor's understanding and assessment of control structure policies and procedures the client has created in response to those risks. Those policies and procedures should (1) ensure that the personnel authorized to enter into investment transactions are competent, (2) require that written contracts specify the rights and obligations inherent in the investment transaction, (3) establish trading limits, (4) require reviews of investment transactions by competent personnel, and (5) require periodic evaluation of credit, market, and collateral risk.

As mentioned earlier, many of the control procedures for investments are exercised directly by management. While management's close attention to investment transactions can be an effective factor in the control structure, the auditor must be alert for potential abuses and override of policies and procedures. Other key aspects of the control structure are asset protection policies and procedures and segregation of duties. These will usually be the focus of tests of controls, if the auditor does decide to perform them. In addition, the auditor may obtain evidence of the effectiveness of certain control procedures (such as those relating to depositing incoming receipts or disbursing funds) in connection with auditing the revenue and buying cycles, as discussed in Chapters 12 and 13 of the main volume.

Tests of controls of investment activity may also focus on the acquisition or disposal of investments. For example, the auditor may perform tests of controls of authorization of investment transactions and safeguarding of investments to obtain evidence that recorded investments exist and are owned at the balance sheet date. If those control procedures are found to be in place and operating effectively, the auditor may decide to reduce year-end confirmations (see below) or to perform them before year-end. Conversely, if those procedures are absent or ineffective, the auditor may need to revise the audit testing plan and perform 100 percent confirmation at year-end. The auditor may also test control procedures for recording investment income to obtain evidence of its accuracy.

SUBSTANTIVE TESTS

This section discusses tests of existence, ownership, accuracy, and completeness; carrying values; investment income; and classification and presentation. It concludes with tests related to investments in sophisticated financial instruments.

Existence, Ownership, Accuracy, and Completeness

Evidence of the existence and ownership of investments, as well as some assurance about the accuracy and completeness of the investment accounts, is normally obtained by confirmation or inspection. The auditor should agree the securities confirmed or inspected to the client's detailed records. Whether these procedures are performed at year-end or at an interim date will be based on the auditor's assessment of control risk and on efficiency considerations.

Counting Securities.   Most industrial and commercial companies do not own numerous securities, and physical inspection is not difficult. The auditor usually obtains a list of securities supporting the general ledger balance at the date of the count and arranges to visit the place where the securities are kept, accompanied by the custodian.

The list of securities owned (and those held as collateral or for safekeeping) at the date of the count is prepared from the security records and includes aggregate principal amount of bonds and notes; number of shares of stock; denomination of bonds or par value, if any, of stocks; maturity dates of bonds; and interest and preferred stock dividend rates. If available, information about the location of the securities is usually included on the list. The auditor examines the securities and compares them with the list. This process normally provides the auditor with evidence about the control structure; for example, an accurate security list, proper endorsement or evidence of ownership on the securities, proper division of duties between custodian and record keeper, adequate physical safeguards (such as use of a bank's safe deposit vault), and requirements that two people be present for access to the securities are all indications of an effective control structure.

Generally, the auditor should count the securities at the balance sheet date; if it is done at another date, the vault or safe deposit box should be sealed during the intervening period. Banks ordinarily seal a safe deposit box on a client's request and subsequently confirm to the auditor that no access to the box was granted during the specified period. Securities should be counted simultaneously with cash and other negotiable assets. A count is considered "simultaneous" if the securities are sealed or otherwise controlled until all negotiable assets have been examined.

The auditor should maintain control over the securities from the start of the count until it has been completed, the results have been compared with the list of securities, and all exceptions have been investigated to the extent possible at the time. Responsible officers and employees of the client should be present during the count to reduce the possibility of later questions about the handling of securities, and should acknowledge, in writing, the return of the securities intact upon conclusion of the count.

In the process of counting the securities, the auditor should also examine them. Although auditors are not qualified to assume responsibility for the genuineness or authenticity of certificates or instruments representing investments, they should be alert to the possibility of forged certificates. If any certificates appear to be unusual and if the auditor is unable to establish their authenticity by examining purchase documents, income records, or similar items, the security should be confirmed with the issuer or transfer agent.

Insurance companies and similar institutional investors often have in their portfolios registered instruments in large denominations that may have been reduced below face amount by partial payments. The auditor should confirm the amount of those instruments outstanding with the issuer, if it appears they do not have to be presented to the issuer or an agent for endorsement or reissue at the time a partial payment is received.

The auditor should note that stock certificates and registered bonds are in the name of the client or an accredited nominee or, if they are not, that certificates are appropriately endorsed or accompanied by powers of attorney. Bonds with interest coupons should be examined to determine that coupons not yet due have not been detached. If coupons presently coming due are not attached to the bonds, the auditor should ask where they are and either inspect them or confirm them with the holders. Likewise, explanations should be obtained and evaluated for any coupons past due that are attached and have not been presented for payment. Interest in default should be noted in the working papers for consideration in connection with the audit of accrued income and carrying amounts of investments.

The auditor should investigate reasons for differences between the count and the list of securities. Certain types of differences are normal and expected, for example, securities held by others and securities in transit. The holders of securities in other locations should be identified and requests for confirmation sent. In-transit items should be related to recent transactions; outgoing in-transit items should be confirmed with recipients. Securities received by the client through the mail for a few days following the date of the count should be examined to substantiate items in transit. Once the auditor is satisfied that all items on the security list have been counted or their location elsewhere has been confirmed and all differences have been reconciled, he or she may "release" control over securities.

The auditor should not overlook the possibility of substitutions. If, for example, examinations are being made of one or more trust accounts handled by the same trustee, securities in all accounts should be counted at the same time. Similarly, if different auditors are employed to examine several accounts, they should make their counts simultaneously. Otherwise, material shortages may be concealed by temporary transfers from accounts whose securities are not being counted. If a client is reluctant to permit an auditor to count securities of other accounts or is unwilling or unable to arrange for a simultaneous count by all auditors concerned, the auditor may identify securities owned by the client by accounting for certificate numbers of stocks and bonds; however, that procedure is difficult and time-consuming for a large portfolio with numerous purchases and sales. Securities owned or held as collateral or for safekeeping should also be counted simultaneously with cash funds and cash equivalents, undeposited receipts, notes receivable, and other negotiable assets if there is a possibility of substitution of one item for another.

Counts of Large Portfolios.   If an investment portfolio is relatively large and active (as in banks, insurance companies, investment companies, and stock brokerages), the count of securities may be a major undertaking requiring extensive planning, precise execution, and a large staff of auditors. The following matters should be considered in conjunction with those applicable to counts of small portfolios.

In counts of large portfolios, the auditor should make every effort to plan the count most expeditiously and also to institute the necessary controls with minimum inconvenience to the client. Especially if a "surprise" count is made without prior notice to the client, the auditor must ascertain the location of all securities, establish controls at various points necessary to record movements of securities, and plan the sequence of the count.

A properly controlled plan may consist of stationing an auditor—the "control" auditor—at each location to observe and record movements of securities, while other auditors perform the actual count. Bags, boxes, safes, or whole rooms may be sealed to be counted later. (The purpose of seals is to provide assurance to the auditor that no one has had access to the sealed items.)

If securities must be moved before the count is completed, the control auditor should observe the withdrawal or deposit, determine the reason for withdrawals, and record the transactions in the working papers. If securities that have already been counted must be removed to be mailed to correspondents, brokers, transfer agents, or others, they should be recorded and controlled until they are turned over to the postal authorities. Relatively inactive securities may be counted and placed under seal in advance of the main count or may be placed under seal and counted after the more active items have been examined.

The usual counting procedure is for the control auditor to release batches of securities to the counting auditors, keeping a record of batches released. The counting auditors count each issue of securities and call off the count to an auditor holding the security list. If the count and the list do not agree, the issue is recounted, sometimes by a different person, until the count agrees with the listed amount or it is determined that a difference exists.

Confirmation of Securities Not on Hand.   Items on the list of securities owned at the count date but not counted should be confirmed with the holders. If a client's entire portfolio is held by a custodian, confirmation procedures usually take the place of the security count.

Items not on hand ordinarily include securities held by banks as collateral for loans, securities left with broker-dealers as custodians for safekeeping, securities with transfer agents, securities that exist on computerized files in "book entry" form, and, if the client is a broker-dealer, items with other brokers on loan or awaiting delivery. The auditor should determine the location of those securities at the examination date, the appropriate responsible person acting as custodian, and the reasons they are held by the custodian. (If the securities are held by people or organizations unknown to the auditor, he or she may consider it necessary to inspect the securities physically rather than confirm them.) In examining the accounts of financial institutions, the auditor should also confirm contracts for the purchase or sale of securities on a "when issued" basis.

If the client's entire portfolio of securities is held in custody by a well-known, reliable financial institution independent of the client, the custodian should be requested to furnish directly to the auditor a list of securities held for the client at the examination date. The confirmation request should also ask whether the client has clear title to the securities. The auditor should compare the list with the client's security records and account for differences noted. It is sometimes desirable to corroborate the custodian's confirmation by counting the securities, for example, if the portfolio is large in relation to the custodian's assets or if the auditor seeks assurance about the adequacy of the custodian's procedures. A letter from the custodian's auditor addressing its internal control structure can also provide that assurance. Joint counts with other auditors having a similar interest are possible. (See the discussion in Chapter 6 of this Supplement of the auditor's responsibilities under SAS No. 70, *Reports on the Processing of Transactions by Service Organizations* [AU Section 324].)

If securities are in the custody of an affiliate or are under the control of a person or group of people who take an active part in the management of the client, the auditor is not justified in relying solely on written confirmation from the custodian. Instead, the auditing procedures outlined above for counting securities under the client's control should be followed.

Tests of Carrying Values

Cost of securities purchased and proceeds from securities sold are normally supported by brokers' advices. The auditor should examine these documents to substantiate the basis for initially recording those transactions. Additionally, the auditor should review the client's method of determining cost (first-in, first-out, average, or specific identification) of securities sold and ascertain that it is consistent during the year and with prior years.

The auditor should test the client's classification of securities and should determine that fair values have been appropriately determined. Normally, this is accomplished by comparing values with published sources. The client's support for fair values of investments that are determined on a basis other than published values should be tested for propriety and consistency. The auditor should be alert to any indication that declines in fair value may be other than temporary. Chapter 21A of this Supplement provides guidance on auditing required disclosures of fair value of financial instruments under SFAS No. 107. That guidance may be applicable in auditing fair values of securities recognized on the balance sheet.

The auditor should consider evidence related to the degree of influence or control the client can exercise over an investee, to evaluate whether the equity method of accounting or consolidation is appropriate in the circumstances. In addition, the auditor should exercise appropriate professional care to ensure that transactions involving investments are accounted for in accordance with their substance, regardless of their form.

If there are investments accounted for by the equity method and if the investee enterprise is audited by other auditors, the auditor will have to use the report of the investee's auditors to be able to report on the client investor's equity in the investee's underlying net assets and its share of the investee's earnings or losses and other transactions. This places the auditor in the position of a principal auditor who is using the work and reports of other auditors. The work and reports of other auditors may also serve as evidence with respect to investments carried at amortized cost or at fair value, which would similarly place the auditor in the position of a principal auditor. The procedures to be followed in those instances are discussed in Chapter 6 of the main volume; reporting aspects of using the work and reports of other auditors are discussed in Chapter 22 of the main volume.

For investments accounted for by the equity method, the investor's share of the investee's results of operations should be based on data from the investee's most recent reliable financial statements, which may be audited year-end statements or unaudited interim statements. If audited statements are used and there is a time lag, for example, three months, between the reporting dates of the investor and investee, the lag should be consistent from year to year. If the most recent reliable financial statements of the investee are unaudited interim statements as of the same date as the investor's year-end, the auditor should apply auditing procedures to those statements in light of the materiality of the investment in relation to the investor's financial statements. If audited financial statements of the investee cannot be obtained, which may happen particularly for foreign investees, a scope limitation is present that, depending on materiality, could result in a qualified opinion or a disclaimer. See the discussion and examples of scope limitations in Chapter 22 of the main volume.

The auditor should read available interim financial statements of the investee and inquire of the investor about events and transactions of the investee between the date of its financial statements and the date of the audit report on the investor's financial statements. Through such inquiries, the auditor should also ascertain that the investor is aware of any material events or transactions subsequent to the date of the investee's financial statements.

Tests of Investment Income

The auditor should determine that all income earned has been appropriately recorded and either collected or recognized as a receivable, and that all accrued income receivable has in fact been earned. The auditor usually obtains evidence about investment income and collection dates by referring to dates of purchase and disposal of investments, interest rates, and published dividend records. Interest should not be accrued on debt securities unless its collectibility is probable; previously accrued interest in arrears should be evaluated for collectibility and written off if it does not appear probable that it will be collected.

In testing income from investments, the auditor can often perform analytical procedures, for example, analyzing the rate of return or gross investment income on a month-to-month or quarter-to-quarter basis, or comparing income with budgeted or prior-year data. Fluctuations in investment income that do not conform to the auditor's expectations would indicate that recorded investments might not exist or that investments exist that have not been recorded. (Analytical procedures, however, are generally not relevant for achieving other audit objectives with respect to investments.)

Tests of Classification and Presentation

The auditor should determine that investments have been classified into the proper categories as held-to-maturity, trading, and available-for-sale. The auditor should also determine that the investments are properly classified between the current and noncurrent categories, if the balance sheet is so classified. The auditor should also ascertain that the financial statements contain all required disclosures regarding investment carrying values and realized and unrealized gains and losses. In addition, minutes, confirmation replies, loan agreements, bond indentures, and other appropriate documents should be reviewed to determine whether investments have been pledged as collateral or whether there is evidence of commitments to acquire or dispose of investments, both of which may require disclosures.

Financial statement classification of investments depends largely on management's objectives and intentions. The auditor can ascertain management's objectives through inquiry and by reviewing minutes of meetings of the board of directors and its investment committee. It may be desirable to include a statement of management's intent in the client representation letter (discussed in Chapter 21 of the main volume). To evaluate management's representations about its intentions, the auditor should consider whether they are reasonable in light of the enterprise's financial position, working capital requirements, debt agreements, other contractual obligations, past practices, and events that occur after the balance sheet date but before the auditor's report is issued. For example, the client's needs may indicate a reasonable presumption that securities will have to be sold to meet operating requirements and that therefore they should be classified as current assets that are available for sale.

Tests Related to Investments in Sophisticated Financial Instruments

More and more, enterprises are managing their available cash in ways that try to achieve the highest rates of return for a given level of acceptable risk. One result has been the increasing use of innovative, sophisticated, and often complex financial instruments to generate investment income. The proliferation and relatively short "shelf lives" of such investments make describing all of them and providing guidance for auditing them a most formidable task—far beyond the scope of this book.

The guidance that follows is, therefore, extremely "generic." It applies to all investments and should be considered in addition to the procedures discussed earlier in this chapter. The suggested guidance should, of course, be tailored to risks associated with the specific types of investments being audited. (Guidance on auditing some of these kinds of investments is also presented in Chapter 39 of the main volume, "Auditing Securities and Commodities Broker-Dealers.") The auditor should always consider the substance of the transaction, not its form, and should consult with experts, as appropriate in the circumstances.

1. Review the client's records for transactions involving purchases and sales of investments in financial instruments of all types.

2. Develop an understanding of the nature of each financial instrument the client has invested in.

3. Determine the appropriate accounting measurement and recognition principles for each type of instrument.

4. Assess the risks associated with each instrument and evaluate how those risks affect the realizability of the investment. Those risks include (a) the risk that the issuer of the instrument or the counterparty to the investment transaction will be unable to make payment or otherwise complete the transaction at its scheduled maturity, and (b) the risk that fluctuations in interest rates may reduce the underlying value of the investment.

5. Evaluate the appropriateness of the financial statement classification and disclosure of investment transactions and the degree of risk involved in them.

6. Count or confirm securities delivered to the client or its agent, as appropriate.

7. Determine where securities not transferred to the investor or its agent are being held and confirm their existence and the custodian's legal obligation to the investor.

8. Consider whether it is desirable to (a) obtain a report from the custodian's auditor on the custodian's internal control structure with respect to securities held in safekeeping, (b) request that specific tests be performed by that auditor, or (c) personally perform such tests.

19

Auditing Income Taxes

* **p. 564.** *Replace third through fifth paragraphs with:*

In 1992, the Financial Accounting Standards Board (FASB) issued Statement of Financial Accounting Standards (SFAS) No. 109, *Accounting for Income Taxes* (Accounting Standards Section I27). SFAS No. 109 supersedes what were the two primary standards on accounting for income taxes, APB Opinion No. 11 and SFAS No. 96. SFAS No. 109 is effective for fiscal years beginning after December 15, 1992.

The basic principles of SFAS No. 109 can be summarized as follows:

- A current tax liability or asset is recognized for estimated taxes payable or refundable on the current year's tax returns.
- A deferred tax liability or asset is recognized for the estimated future tax effects attributable to temporary differences and carryforwards.
- All measurements are based on regular tax rates and provisions of the enacted tax law; the effects of anticipated changes in tax laws or rates are not considered.
- The amount of deferred tax assets is reduced, if applicable, by any tax benefits that, based on available evidence, are not expected to be realized.

SFAS No. 109 requires that deferred tax assets be recognized for all temporary differences that will result in deductible amounts in future years and for carryforwards and then evaluated for realization based on available evidence. A valuation allowance is required if it is "more likely than not" (defined as a likelihood of greater than 50%) that some portion of or all deferred tax assets will not be realized. That determination is made based on evidence concerning the sources of taxable income that may be available to realize future tax benefits. SFAS No. 109 specifies the four sources that may be available for that purpose; they are discussed later in this chapter of the Supplement.

INCOME TAX TRANSACTIONS AND INTERNAL CONTROL STRUCTURE POLICIES AND PROCEDURES

Internal Control Structure

* **p. 567.** *Add after first full paragraph:*
The requirement in SFAS No. 109 for a valuation allowance for deferred tax assets that are not expected to be realized has increased the significance of tax planning. Tax planning strategies are one of the possible sources of taxable income specified in the statement as available to realize benefits for deductible temporary differences and carryforwards. SFAS No. 109 defines tax planning strategies as prudent and feasible actions that an enterprise might not ordinarily take but would take to prevent a carryforward from expiring unused and that would result in the realization of deferred tax assets.

AUDIT TESTING PLAN

Risk Characteristics

* **p. 568.** *Add after second paragraph in section:*
The requirement in SFAS No. 109 for a valuation allowance for deferred tax assets not expected to be realized increases the risk involved in auditing the deferred tax asset account. Management is required to consider both positive and negative evidence concerning the realizability of deferred tax assets; the more negative evidence that exists, the more positive evidence will be necessary to support a conclusion that a valuation allowance is not needed. SFAS No. 109 cites examples of negative evidence that must be overcome to justify not recording a valuation allowance. As the weight of negative evidence increases, the need for positive evidence increases, as do the amount of evidential matter and extent of audit testing required.

SUBSTANTIVE TESTS

* **p. 572.** *Add new subsection after fourth paragraph:*

Deferred Tax Assets (New)

Under SFAS No. 109, the auditor is required to evaluate the reasonableness of management's determination of the valuation allowance (if any) needed for deferred tax assets not expected to be realized. Future realization of deferred tax assets ultimately depends on sufficient taxable income of the appropriate type (e.g., ordinary income or capital gains) within the carryback or carryforward periods stipulated by the tax law. SFAS No. 109 specifies the four sources of taxable income that may be available to realize a future tax benefit for deductible temporary differences and carryforwards:

- Taxable income in prior carryback years.
- Taxable income from reversals of existing taxable temporary differences.
- Taxable income from tax planning strategies that would be implemented, if necessary, to avoid losing the benefit of a deferred tax asset.
- Expected future taxable income, exclusive of reversing temporary differences and carryforwards.

The auditor should follow the guidance in SAS No. 57, *Auditing Accounting Estimates*, in considering management's conclusion about the need for and amount of the valuation allowance.

The four sources of taxable income above are listed in order of the objectivity of the evidence they provide. SFAS No. 109 states that "the weight given to the potential effect of negative and positive evidence should be commensurate with the extent to which it can be objectively verified." The first two sources of taxable income are more objective and thus are more competent forms of evidential matter than the last two and should ordinarily be considered first in evaluating the realizability of deferred tax assets. If a deferred tax asset cannot be fully realized from carrybacks or reversals of temporary differences, tax planning strategies should be considered next. Finally, future taxable income, the least objective source, should be considered. If an analysis of future taxable income is the basis for a valuation allowance, management has primary responsibility for preparing the analysis, which should include all major underlying assumptions. The auditor should consider whether management has an objective basis for the analysis and should determine that the major assumptions are appropriately supported, especially those that are sensitive or susceptible to change, or inconsistent with historical trends. Concluding that a valuation allowance is not needed will be difficult, for example, when there is negative evidence such as cumulative losses in recent years.

Reaching a conclusion about the realizability of deferred tax assets and the valuation allowance may require the evaluation of large amounts of both positive and negative evidence that is of necessity surrounded by much uncertainty because it involves the occurrence or nonoccurrence of future events. Management must exercise judgment in weighing both types of evidence and their potential impact on the need for an allowance. If there is substantial negative evidence, the authors believe that a forecast of future taxable income by itself will not provide sufficient positive evidence to outweigh the negative evidence and support a conclusion that no valuation allowance is needed.

20

Auditing Debt and Equity

SUBSTANTIVE TESTS

Common Substantive Tests of Debt and Equity Accounts

p. 585. *Add after first full paragraph:*

Confirming Contingent Liabilities, Compensating Balances, Lines of Credit, and Other Arrangements. Auditors typically confirm clients' arrangements with financial institutions by requesting that the client send letters to specific officials of those institutions who are knowledgeable about the particular transactions or arrangements. The kinds of arrangements that auditors may confirm, usually at year-end, include compensating balances, lines of credit, and arrangements that may create contingent liabilities, such as oral and written guarantees, commitments to purchase foreign currencies, repurchase or reverse repurchase agreements, and letters of credit. In addition, the auditor may ask the client to request information about automatic investment services, bank acceptances, cash management services, futures and forward contracts, interest rate or loan swaps, loan agreements and related covenants, and other transactions or arrangements. The AICPA Auditing Standards Division has developed—and the American Bankers Association and Bank Administration Institute have approved—three illustrative letters for use in confirming transactions and arrangements with financial institutions involving contingent liabilities, compensating balances, and lines of credit. These letters are illustrated in Figures S20.1 through S20.3. Letters for use in confirming other transactions, arrangements, or information will have to be tailored to the specific item about which the auditor requests confirmation.

Figure S20.1   Illustrative Letter for Confirmation of Contingent Liabilities

(Date)

Financial Institution Official*
First United Bank
Anytown, USA 00000

Dear Financial Institution Official:

In connection with an audit of the financial statements of (name of customer) as of (balance-sheet date) and for the (period) then ended, we have advised our independent auditors of the information listed below, which we believe is a complete and accurate description of our contingent liabilities, including oral and written guarantees, with your financial institution. Although we do not request nor expect you to conduct a comprehensive, detailed search of your records, if during the process of completing this confirmation additional information about other contingent liabilities, including oral and written guarantees, between (name of customer) and your financial institution comes to your attention, please include such information below.

Name of Maker	Date of Note	Due Date	Current Balance

Interest Rate	Date Through Which Interest Is Paid	Description of Collateral	Description of Purpose of Note

Information related to oral and written guarantees is as follows:

_____
_____
_____
_____

*This letter should be addressed to a financial institution official who is responsible for the financial institution's relationship with the client or is knowledgeable about the transactions or arrangements. Some financial institutions centralize this function by assigning responsibility for responding to confirmation requests to a separate function. Independent auditors should ascertain the appropriate recipient.

Figure S20.1 *Continued*

Please confirm whether the information about contingent liabilities presented above is correct by signing below and returning this directly to our independent auditors (name and address of CPA firm).

Sincerely,

(Name of Customer)

_____

By: _____
        (Authorized Signature)

Dear CPA Firm:

The above information listing contingent liabilities, including oral and written guarantees, agrees with the records of this financial institution.* Although we have not conducted a comprehensive, detailed search of our records, no information about other contingent liabilities, including oral and written guarantees, came to our attention. [Note exceptions below or in an attached letter.]

_____

_____

_____

_____

_____

                                   _____
                                   (Name of Financial Institution)

                    By: _____ _____
                          (Officer and Title)   (Date)

*If applicable, comments similar to the following may be added to the confirmation reply by the financial institution: This confirmation does not relate to arrangements, if any, with other branches or affiliates of this financial institution. Information should be sought separately from such branches or affiliates with which any such arrangements might exist.

Figure S20.2   Illustrative Letter for Confirmation of Compensating Balances

(Date)

Financial Institution Official*
First United Bank
Anytown, USA 00000

Dear Financial Institution Official:

In connection with an audit of the financial statements of (name of customer) as of (balance-sheet date) and for the (period) then ended, we have advised our independent auditors that as of the close of business on (balance-sheet date) there (were) (were not) compensating balance arrangements as described in our agreement dated (date). Although we do not request nor expect you to conduct a comprehensive, detailed search of your records, if during the process of completing this confirmation additional information about other compensating balance arrangements between (name of customer) and your financial institution comes to your attention, please include such information below. Withdrawal by (name of customer) of the compensating balance (was) (was not) legally restricted at (date). The terms of the compensating balance arrangements at (date) were:

EXAMPLES:
1. The Company has been expected to maintain an average compensating balance of 20 percent of its average loan outstanding, as determined from the financial institution's ledger records adjusted for estimated average uncollected funds.
2. The Company has been expected to maintain an average compensating balance of $100,000 during the year, as determined from the financial institution's ledger records without adjustment for uncollected funds.
3. The Company has been expected to maintain a compensating balance, as determined from the financial institution's ledger records without adjustment for uncollected funds, of 15 percent of its outstanding loans plus 10 percent of its unused line of credit.
4. The Company has been expected to maintain as a compensating balance noninterest bearing time deposits of 10 percent of its outstanding loans.

In determining compliance with compensating balance arrangements, the Company uses a factor for uncollected funds of _____ (business) (calendar) days.[1]

There (were the following) (were no) changes in the compensating balance arrangements during the (period) and subsequently through the date of this letter.

* This letter should be addressed to a financial institution official who is responsible for the financial institution's relationship with the client or is knowledgeable about the compensating balance arrangements. Some financial institutions centralize this function by assigning responsibility for responding to confirmation requests to a separate function. Independent auditors should ascertain the appropriate recipient.

[1] Not applicable if compensating balances are based on the financial institution's ledger records without adjustment for uncollected funds. If some other method is used for determining collected funds for compensating balance purposes, the method used should be described.

Figure S20.2 *Continued*

The Company (was) (was not) in compliance with the compensating balance arrangements during the (period) and subsequently through the date of this letter.

There (were the following) (were no) sanctions (applied or imminent) by the financial institution because of noncompliance with compensating balance arrangements.[2]

During the (period), and subsequently through the date of this letter, (no) (the following) compensating balances were maintained by the Company at the financial institution on behalf of an affiliate, director, officer, or any other third party and (no) (the following) third party maintained compensating balances at the bank on behalf of the Company. (Withdrawal of such compensating balances (was) (was not) legally restricted.)

Please confirm whether the information about compensating balances presented above is correct by signing below, and returning this letter directly to our independent auditors (name and address of CPA Firm).

Sincerely,

(Name of Customer)

_____

By: _____
       (Authorized Signature)

Dear CPA Firm:

The above information regarding the compensating balance arrangements with this financial institution agrees with the records of this financial institution.* Although we have not conducted a comprehensive, detailed search of our records, no information about other compensating balance arrangements came to our attention. [Note exceptions below or in an attached letter.]

_____
_____
_____
_____

_____
(Name of Financial Institution)

By: _____ _____
       (Officer and Title)   (Date)

[2] Applicable only if the financial institution has applied sanctions during the (period) or notified the Company that sanctions may be applied. Indicate details.

* If applicable, comments similar to the following may be added to the confirmation reply by the financial institution: This confirmation does not relate to arrangements, if any, with other branches or affiliates of this financial institution. Information should be sought separately from such branches or affiliates with which any such arrangements might exist.

Figure S20.3   Illustrative Letter for Confirmation of Lines of Credit

---

(Date)

Financial Institution Official*
First United Bank
Anytown, USA 00000

Dear Financial Institution Official:

In connection with an audit of the financial statements of (name of customer) as of (balance-sheet date) and for the (period) then ended, we have advised our independent auditors of the information listed below, which we believe is a complete and accurate description of our line of credit from your financial institution as of the close of business on (balance-sheet date). Although we do not request nor expect you to conduct a comprehensive, detailed search of your records, if during the process of completing this confirmation additional information about other lines of credit from your financial institution comes to your attention, please include such information below.

The Company has available at the financial institution a line of credit totaling (amount). The current terms of the line of credit are contained in the letter dated (date). The related debt outstanding at the close of business on (date) was $(amount).

The amount of unused line of credit, subject to the terms of the related letter, at (date) was $(amount).

Interest rate at the close of business on (date) was _____%.

Compensating balance arrangements are_____
_____
_____
_____

This line of credit supports commercial paper (or other borrowing arrangements) as described below:
_____
_____
_____
_____

*This letter should be addressed to a financial institution official who is responsible for the financial institution's relationship with the client or is knowledgeable about the lines of credit. Some financial institutions centralize this function by assigning responsibility for responding to confirmation requests to a separate function. Independent auditors should ascertain the appropriate recipient.

Figure S20.3 *Continued*

Please confirm whether the information about lines of credit presented above is correct by signing below and returning this letter directly to our independent auditors (name and address of CPA Firm).

Sincerely,

(Name of Customer)

_____

By: _____
            (Authorized Signature)

_____

Dear CPA Firm:

The above information regarding the line of credit arrangements agrees with the records of this financial institution.* Although we have not conducted a comprehensive, detailed search of our records, no information about other lines of credit came to our attention. [Note exceptions below or in attached letter.]

_____

_____

_____

_____

_____
(Name of Financial Institution)

By: _____   _____
      (Officer and Title)   (Date)

*If applicable, comments similar to the following may be added to the confirmation reply by the financial institution: This confirmation does not relate to arrangements, if any, with other branches or affiliates of this financial institution. Information should be sought separately from such branches or affiliates with which any such arrangements might exist.

21

Completing the Audit

LAWYERS' LETTERS

Inquiry of a Client's Lawyer

p. 600. *Add before heading* **Evaluating Lawyers' Responses**:

Both audit inquiry letters and lawyers' responses may include explanatory language intended to emphasize that the letters do not constitute a waiver of the attorney–client privilege or the attorney work product privilege. An auditing interpretation of Section 337 of SAS No. 1 (AU Section 9337.28–.30) dated February 1990 clarifies that use of such language does not create an audit scope limitation.

21A

Auditing Financial Statement Disclosures (New)

Most of the auditor's work in obtaining and evaluating evidence about whether a set of financial statements is presented fairly in conformity with generally accepted accounting principles is done as part of the audit of specific transaction cycles and accounts. Some aspects of financial statement presentation, however, are more pervasive and cannot conveniently be associated with specific cycles or accounts. Chapter 21 of the main volume discusses various auditing procedures that are customarily applied at the conclusion of the audit. This chapter extends that discussion to include certain auditing considerations related to required financial statement disclosures that are not covered elsewhere in either the main volume or this Supplement because they are not related to specific transaction cycles and accounts.

As discussed in Chapter 5 of the main volume, management assertions that are embodied in financial statement components include those related to presentation and disclosure. SAS No. 31, *Evidential Matter* (AU Section 326), notes that "assertions about presentation and disclosure deal with whether particular components of the financial statements are properly classified, described, and disclosed." Those assertions are translated by auditors into audit objectives that they seek to achieve by performing auditing procedures.

The auditor's responsibility for the adequacy of disclosures derives from the third generally accepted auditing standard applicable to reporting, which states:

Informative disclosures in the financial statements are to be regarded as reasonably adequate unless otherwise stated in the report. (SAS No. 1 [AU Section 150.02])

That standard is discussed, in general terms, in SAS No. 32, *Adequacy of Disclosure in Financial Statements* (AU Section 431). SAS No. 32 requires material matters regarding the financial statements to be disclosed in the statements themselves or in notes to the statements; if they are not, the auditor should express a qualified or an adverse opinion and should, if practicable, provide the information in the auditor's report. The auditor's reporting responsibilities with regard to inadequate disclosures are discussed in Chapter 22 of the main volume.

The sections that follow discuss a number of disclosures required to be made in financial statements. As discussed in Chapter 21 of the main volume, auditors often use checklists to help ensure their compliance with the standard of informative disclosure.

INTERNAL CONTROL PROCEDURES RELATING TO FINANCIAL STATEMENT DISCLOSURES

The auditor's responsibilities with respect to auditing information contained in notes to financial statements are the same as those with respect to the basic financial statements (with the exception of unaudited information and supplementary disclosures). The information in many disclosures often is prepared by personnel not involved in or familiar with the client's accounting functions and is not subject to the same type or degree of control as the information used in preparing the basic financial statements.

The auditor, as a first step, should understand and evaluate the control procedures relating to the preparation of financial statement disclosures. Obviously, the procedures appropriate in each situation depend on the nature and complexity of the disclosures themselves, as well as the degree to which the information is derived from, and therefore subject to the control procedures relating to, the formal accounting records. The following are examples of control procedures that usually are appropriate:

1. Written procedures should be maintained with respect to the accumulation of data used in financial statement disclosures. These procedures should describe what information is needed, the sources from which it is to be obtained, and the functions or personnel who are responsible for its accumulation.

2. Control procedures should be developed to ensure the completeness and accuracy of data accumulated from sources not subject to procedures applied to the accounting records. For example, the amount of employee debt guaranteed by an employer is usually obtained by aggregating the amounts of individual loans from the loan documents. An appropriate way to control accuracy would be to maintain a list, by employee and by loan payment date, so the amount of debt outstanding can be tested readily for arithmetical accuracy. An appropriate completeness control procedure would be reconciling the total debt outstanding from this list to the amount of loans repaid during the year and amount of new loans guaranteed.

3. If information is supplied by outside specialists such as actuaries, attorneys, geologists, or engineers, formal procedures should be in place for requesting the information at the appropriate time and for providing the specialists with the information necessary for them to complete their work in a timely manner. Any data supplied to specialists should be subject to the completeness and accuracy control procedures discussed above.

4. Financial statement disclosures (usually, a complete set of statements, including notes) should be distributed to management of various functions within the company for their review to determine the adequacy of overall informative content with respect to any disclosures relating to their functions. For example, appropriate people in the employee benefits or human resources department should review the postretirement plan disclosures to determine the accuracy of the plan descriptions and reasonableness of the actuarial data contained therein.

The internal control structure over the preparation of financial statement disclosures affects the extent of the auditor's testing of the information. The amount of judgment required in determining what constitutes adequate informative disclosures means that no internal control structure, however effective, can ensure that all appropriate disclosures are made. Therefore, the auditor must make an evaluation of the disclosures contained in the statements for each period, using the knowledge of the client and its business and industry and all the specific information obtained during the audit, as well as technical knowledge of reporting and disclosure standards and the latest changes thereto.

DISCLOSURE OF ACCOUNTING POLICIES

To understand the financial statements, users must have information regarding the accounting policies followed by the reporting entity. APB Opinion No. 22, *Disclosure of Accounting Policies* (Accounting Standards Section A10), calls for disclosure of "all significant accounting policies," and specifically those policies that influence the accounting periods for which revenues and costs are included in the results of operations. In evaluating the client's accounting policy disclosures, the auditor should consider the following questions:

- Is there an alternative generally accepted accounting principle or method that would be suitable in lieu of the policy being followed?
- Is the accounting policy currently in use peculiar to the industry in which the entity operates?
- Is the current accounting policy or its application unusual or innovative?

If the answer to any of those questions is yes, and the accounting policy has a material effect on the entity's financial position, results of operations, or cash flows, the policy should be disclosed.

The evaluation of materiality should be based on the effect of the accounting policy in use on financial position, results of operations, or cash flows, and not on whether the application of an alternative policy would produce a materially different result. In many cases, a comparison with the effects of an acceptable alternative policy would be impracticable. The existence of an alternative policy is not a pertinent consideration unless it would be acceptable for the specific application. The existence of an alternative policy that might be considered preferable to the policy in use, however, is a strong argument for disclosure. If disclosure of a particular policy is considered necessary, there is no requirement to refer to alternative accounting principles or to make comparisons with alternatives. The information called for is limited to a description of the policy in use.

The term "peculiar to an industry," used in Opinion No. 22 in defining criteria for disclosures, should be interpreted broadly to include transactions with characteristics that have led to the development of special accounting policies. Leasing, for example, cuts across many industry lines. Special accounting policies have been developed to consider the economic characteristics of these transactions, and such policies should be disclosed.

Evaluating the need to disclose policies with respect to transactions that are nonrecurring or that recur infrequently requires judgment. Generally, accounting policies covering nonrecurring or infrequently recurring transactions need be disclosed only for those years in which amounts relating to such transactions are included in the financial statements presented, unless disclosure of information is necessary to ensure that the financial statements are not misleading.

In considering the materiality of accounting policies relating to recurring transactions, recognition should be given to the possible effects under various operating conditions that might be anticipated. Consideration should not be limited to whether or not the transactions have a material effect on the current year.

Opinion No. 22 expresses a preference for a separate summary of accounting policies, either apart from the notes to financial statements or as the first note. In some cases, it is acceptable to combine the description of an accounting policy with other data related to the policy. For example, disclosure of the accounting and funding policies with respect to pension costs may be combined with the other pension-related disclosures required by SFAS No. 87.

DISCLOSURE OF RELATED PARTY TRANSACTIONS

SFAS No. 57, *Related Party Disclosures* (Accounting Standards Section R36), requires disclosure in financial statements of material related party transactions (related parties are explicitly defined in Appendix B of SFAS No. 57 and in Chapter 8 of the main volume). That statement also requires disclosure of the nature of control relationships (with other enterprises) that could affect the operating results or financial position of the reporting enterprise, even though there were no transactions between the enterprises. AU Section 334, *Related Parties,* outlines specific audit procedures that the auditor may consider in determining the existence of related parties, procedures intended to provide guidance for identifying material transactions with related parties, and procedures that should be considered in examining identified related party transactions. Audit procedures regarding related party transactions are described in Chapter 8 of the main volume.

EARNINGS PER SHARE

APB Opinion No. 15, *Earnings Per Share* (Accounting Standards Section E09), requires that EPS information be presented by all enterprises whose capital structures contain common stock or securities that should be considered the equivalent of common stock. Therefore, the opinion does not apply to mutual enterprises, registered investment enterprises, government-owned enterprises, or not-for-profit enterprises. In addition, the opinion does not apply to parent company financial statements accompanied by consolidated financial statements or to financial statements of wholly owned subsidiaries. SFAS No. 21 (Accounting Standards Section E09), issued in 1978, suspended the requirements of Opinion No. 15 for nonpublic enterprises. If a nonpublic enterprise presents EPS information in its financial statements, however, such information must be presented in accordance with the requirements of Opinion No. 15.

Auditing EPS information usually involves more than a simple recalculation of the arithmetic involved. The process may be viewed as consisting of the following three general steps:

1. Obtaining an understanding of the client's capital structure.
2. Determining that the client's securities have been properly classified under the provisions of APB Opinion No. 15 and that the required EPS amounts have been correctly calculated.
3. Determining that the financial statements comply with the presentation and disclosure requirements of Opinion No. 15.

Much of the understanding of the client's capital structure is obtained in the course of auditing the debt and equity accounts. The auditor should review and document the conversion rights and terms of convertible securities and the exercise conditions of options or warrants when auditing the related debt or equity accounts. The terms of plans, contracts, and agreements for the issuance of stock to employees often contain provisions for contingent shares, restrictions on stock issued, and options, all of which may affect the EPS computations. Other agreements, such as the sale or purchase of an affiliate, may also contain provisions that affect EPS. For purposes of computing EPS, a company's capital structure often comprises more than the amounts presented in the equity section of the balance sheet. Consequently, the evidence needed to support the audit of the EPS computation and related disclosures may be gathered most efficiently at various stages of the audit and should be planned accordingly.

Opinion No. 15 was issued in recognition of the importance that users of financial statements attach to earnings per share. Because the computation of EPS under the opinion includes the effect on EPS of securities that enable the holders to obtain common stock, assumptions must be made regarding the exercise, conversion, and issuance of securities, and prices to be used. To promote comparability in the computation of EPS, the opinion specifies how those assumptions are to be made, and also requires the use of specified methods to reflect the effect of certain securities. For example, the opinion specifies the "if-converted" method for convertible securities and the "treasury stock" method for options and warrants. The AICPA has issued over 100 unofficial accounting interpretations of Opinion No. 15, which are intended to explain its provisions. In the majority of situations, questions regarding the computation of EPS may be answered by reference to the opinion, the interpretations, or the FASB statements and interpretations relating to EPS (all included in Accounting Standards Section E09). Even though EPS has been the subject of exhaustive explanation, auditors may encounter transactions or events that have not been specifically addressed in the literature. In those cases, the auditor should ascertain that the provisions of the opinion have been applied to the substance of the transactions.

SEGMENT INFORMATION

When a public enterprise issues a complete set of financial statements in conformity with GAAP, SFAS No. 14 (as amended by Statement Nos. 18, 21, 24, and 30) requires that those statements include information regarding the enterprise's operations in different industries, its foreign operations and export sales, and its major customers. The following statement of the auditor's objective with respect to segment information is included in SAS No. 21 (AU Section 435.03):

> The objective of auditing procedures applied to segment information is to provide the auditor with a reasonable basis for concluding whether the information is presented in conformity with FASB Statement No. 14 in relation to the financial statements taken as a whole. The auditor performing an audit of financial statements in accordance with generally accepted auditing standards considers segment information, as other informative disclosures, in relation to the financial statements taken as a whole, and is not required to apply auditing procedures that would be necessary to express a separate opinion on the segment information.

The preparation of segment information involves disaggregation of the financial statements and consequently may require the accumulation of information that would not otherwise be available from the accounting system. The auditor should consider the effect of segment information on the audit during the planning stage. This is necessary for both promoting audit efficiency and determining that the procedures used by the client to develop the segment information are sufficient to enable the auditor to form a conclusion regarding the information. SAS No. 21 discusses the types of auditing procedures that the auditor should consider when financial statements include segment information. The nature and extent of the specific procedures depend on the number of industry and geographic segments in which the client operates, the procedures used by the client to accumulate the information, and the client's operating structure. For example, a company with several relatively autonomous divisions or subsidiaries, each operating in a different industry segment, may be able to accumulate most of the required information directly from the financial statements of the divisions or subsidiaries. Another company that operates in the same industry segments but whose operations are more integrated may need to employ a number of additional procedures to disaggregate its financial statements. In the first instance, the auditor may be able to test the segment information by a few additional audit procedures, while in the second instance, many additional audit tests may be required.

SFAS No. 21 suspended the segment reporting requirements of SFAS No. 14 (as well as the requirements of APB Opinion No. 15) for nonpublic enterprises. Consequently, most financial statements that include segment information are those of SEC registrants. The disclosure requirements of Regulation S-K covering the annual report to shareholders and Form 10-K are similar to those of SFAS No. 14, but include certain additional information. This additional information is not required to be audited, but companies often include parts of it in the notes to financial statements along with the information required by SFAS No. 14. In addition, companies often include segment information in a section of the report to shareholders that is outside of the basic financial statements and notes thereto. In these situations, the notes to financial statements should contain a cross-reference to the segment data. During the planning stage, the auditor should discuss with the client the anticipated form and location of all segment information.

The auditor should read a draft of the annual report to determine whether all of the segment information included has been audited and covered by the audit report on the financial statements. If the annual report contains other segment data that is not required by SFAS No. 14 and has not been audited, such information should be presented in a manner that clearly distinguishes it from the information covered by the auditor's report. The auditor's report should not refer to segment information unless such information is materially misstated or omitted, there has been an accounting change with respect to the segment information that is material in relation to the financial statements taken as a whole, or a scope limitation has been placed on the auditor with respect to such information. A separate auditor's report should not be issued on the segment information unless the auditor has been engaged to report separately on such information and has issued the type of special report covered in SAS No. 62 (AU Sections 623.11–623.17) and SAS No. 21 (AU Section 435.18), as discussed in Chapter 23 of the main volume.

DISCLOSURE OF INFORMATION ABOUT FINANCIAL INSTRUMENTS

Off-Balance-Sheet Risk and Concentrations of Credit Risk

In 1990, the FASB issued SFAS No. 105, *Disclosure of Information about Financial Instruments with Off-Balance-Sheet Risk and Financial Instruments with Concentrations of Credit Risk* (Accounting Standards Section F25), which establishes requirements for disclosure of information about financial instruments by all entities—both financial and nonfinancial. (The statement does not change any requirements for recognition, measurement, or classification of financial instruments in financial statements. These requirements are being addressed in separate phases of the FASB's financial instruments project.)

SFAS No. 105 requires disclosures about financial instruments that have off-balance-sheet credit or market risk. Off-balance-sheet risk is the risk that an entity may incur an accounting loss that exceeds the amount recognized in its financial statements. (The SFAS defines credit risk as "the possibility that a loss may occur from the failure of another party to perform according to the terms of a contract" and market risk as "the possibility that future changes in market prices may make a financial instrument less valuable or more onerous.") Examples of financial instruments with off-balance-sheet risk are commitments to lend, financial guarantees, options, recourse obligations on receivables sold, obligations to repurchase securities sold, commitments to purchase or sell other financial instruments at predetermined prices, futures contracts, interest rate and foreign currency swaps, and obligations arising from financial instruments sold short.

SFAS No. 105 also requires disclosures about concentrations of credit risk for all financial instruments—both on and off balance sheet. Concentration of credit risk can be viewed in several ways, for example, by region, by industry, or by type of issuer. A company can have different types of concentrations for different classes of financial instruments. For example, a company can have industry and type of issuer concentration in its common stock investments and region and industry concentration in its convertible bond investments.

The disclosures should be made by class of financial instruments (typically represented by a line item on the balance sheet) either in the body of the financial statements or in the accompanying notes. For each class of financial instruments with off-balance-sheet credit or market risk, the entity should disclose

- The face or contract amount of the class of financial instruments (or, if none, the notional principal amount).
- The nature and terms, including at a minimum
  - •• The credit and market risk of those instruments.
  - •• The cash requirements of those instruments.
  - •• The accounting policy relating to recognition of revenue and allocation of asset costs to current and future periods.

Additional required disclosures relate to both off-balance-sheet credit risk and concentrations of credit risk.

- Information regarding the entity's policy of
  - •• Requiring collateral or other security to support financial instruments subject to credit risk.
  - •• The entity's access to that collateral or other security.
  - •• The nature and a brief description of the collateral or other security supporting the financial instruments.
- The amount of accounting loss the entity would incur if any party to the financial instrument failed to perform completely according to the terms of the contract and the collateral or other security, if any, proved to be of no value to the entity.

For concentrations of credit risk, the entity should also disclose information about the activity, region, or economic characteristic that identifies the concentrations.

Auditing procedures specifically designed to identify financial instruments with off-balance-sheet credit or market risk or concentrations of credit risk include

- Reviewing the minutes of meetings of the board of directors and its executive or operating committees for information about material transactions authorized or discussed and for approval of overall corporate policy as to the company's investment, financing, and hedge philosophy and guidelines.
- Inquiring of management as to whether such transactions are occurring and, if so, how they are being recognized.
- Reviewing, to the extent practicable, accounting records for large, unusual, or nonrecurring transactions that may expose the company to significant credit or market risk.

- Obtaining a representation from management that financial instruments with off-balance-sheet risk and financial instruments with concentrations of credit risk have been properly recorded or disclosed in the financial statements.

Fair Value

In 1991, the FASB issued SFAS No. 107, *Disclosures about Fair Value of Financial Instruments* (Accounting Standards Section F25). Like SFAS No. 105, No. 107 applies to all types of entities, not just those in the financial services industry. It is effective for fiscal years ended after December 15, 1992, except for entities with less than $150 million in total assets; for those entities, the effective date is three years later.

Financial instruments for which fair value disclosures are required under SFAS No. 107 include financial assets and liabilities both on and off the balance sheet. Examples include investments, loans receivable, current and long-term debt, repurchase agreements, interest rate and currency swap contracts, option contracts, foreign exchange contracts, letters of credit, and commitments to lend.

If available, quoted market prices are to be used to determine fair values. Sources for quoted prices include the public exchange markets, dealer markets, and quotation services. If quoted prices are not available, fair values should be estimated using quoted prices of similar instruments or techniques such as present value of expected cash flows or option pricing models. The statement also requires disclosure of the methods and significant assumptions used to estimate fair values.

The fair value disclosures under SFAS No. 107, however, are required only if it is practicable to estimate those values. Practicable means that an estimate of fair value can be made without incurring excessive costs. Deciding whether costs are considered excessive will require exercise of judgment.

If it is not practicable to estimate fair value of a financial instrument or a class of financial instruments, the entity must disclose:

- Information pertinent to estimating the fair value (for example, the carrying amount, effective interest rate, and maturity).
- The reasons why it is not practicable to estimate fair value (that is, why estimation of values would require excessive costs).

Auditing procedures specifically designed to audit disclosures required by SFAS No. 107 include

- Determine how the client identifies financial instruments whose fair value needs to be disclosed under SFAS No. 107.
- Obtain a listing of financial instruments held or issued at year-end, both on and off the balance sheet; reconcile the on-balance-sheet instruments to the balance sheet; determine whether financial instruments identified through other auditing procedures have been included in the listing.

- Identify the method(s) the client uses to estimate fair value; evaluate the reasonableness of any client determinations that it is not practicable to estimate fair value because of excessive costs.
- For fair values obtained from external sources (as appropriate)
  - • Compare market prices with an independent published source.
  - • Confirm quotations from dealers and quotation services.
  - • Follow procedures appropriate for using the work of a specialist for financial instruments valued using outside pricing services or other valuation specialists.
- For estimates developed internally
  - • Review the supporting documentation describing the methodology, underlying assumptions, factors, and input used and supporting calculations.
  - • Determine whether the valuation principles are acceptable and whether the assumptions are reasonable and reflect adjustments for differences in security characteristics such as credit risk and maturities.
- Determine whether the disclosures are in accordance with SFAS No. 107.
- Determine whether there have been any significant events subsequent to the balance sheet date that would materially affect fair values and would require disclosure.
- Determine whether all appropriate items related to fair value disclosures have been included in the client representation letter, including support for management's decision not to disclose fair values when it was determined not to be practicable to estimate them.

In addition to disclosing the fair value of financial instruments as required by SFAS No. 107, an entity may disclose voluntarily the fair value of other assets and liabilities not encompassed by that statement. An auditing interpretation of SAS No. 57, *Auditing Accounting Estimates,* issued in February 1993 (AU Section 9342), indicates that the voluntary information may be audited only if the measurement and disclosure criteria used to prepare the fair value information are reasonable and competent persons using those criteria would ordinarily obtain materially similar measurements and disclosures. The interpretation provides reporting guidance when the audited disclosures constitute a complete balance sheet presentation and also when they do not. For voluntary disclosures that are not audited, the interpretation also provides reporting guidance when the disclosures are included in an auditor-submitted document and when they are included in a client-prepared document.

DISCLOSURE OF RISKS AND UNCERTAINTIES

In March 1993, the American Institute of Certified Public Accountants issued an exposure draft of a proposed Statement of Position, *Disclosure of Certain Significant Risks and Uncertainties and Financial Flexibility.* The proposed SOP is intended to be responsive to user demands that financial statements include more information to help in assessing the risks and uncertainties about future cash flows and results of operations. It would require the financial statements of all entities to include disclosures about the nature of the entity's operations, the use of estimates in the preparation of the financial statements, certain significant estimates, current vulnerability due to concentrations, and financial flexibility. The first two proposed disclosures are already found in some financial statements, and the concepts associated with them are not believed to be controversial. The last three, however, have created significant debate. If approved for issuance as an SOP, the effective date (as specified in the exposure draft) would be for financial statements issued for fiscal years ending after December 15, 1994, with earlier application encouraged.

22

The Auditor's Report

STANDARD REPORTS

The Meaning of Fair Presentation in Conformity with GAAP

* **p. 639.** *Add after carryover paragraph:*

Revisions to the GAAP Hierarchy. In early 1992, the Auditing Standards Board issued SAS No. 69, *The Meaning of* Present Fairly in Conformity With Generally Accepted Accounting Principles *in the Independent Auditor's Report* (AU Section 411), which superseded SAS No. 5. SAS No. 69, which became effective for audits of financial statements for periods ended after March 15, 1992, recognizes explicitly, for the first time, that a consensus of the FASB's Emerging Issues Task Force is also a source of established accounting principles; that for SEC registrants, SEC rules and interpretive releases should be viewed as having the same level of authority as pronouncements covered by Rule 203 of the AICPA Code of Professional Conduct; and that the relative standing of FASB and GASB pronouncements depends on the type of entity under consideration. The SAS contains a chart, reproduced as Figure S22.1, that summarizes the new GAAP hierarchy. (The summary excludes SEC rules and interpretive releases.)

The SAS notes that in addition to SEC rules and interpretive releases, the staff of the SEC's Division of Corporation Finance and the Office of the Chief Accountant issue Staff Accounting Bulletins (SABs) that "represent practices followed by the staff in administering SEC disclosure requirements." Of note is the emergence in the last few years of a new source of established accounting principles, namely, observations of "the SEC observer" (in reality, the Chief Accountant of the SEC) at meetings of the Emerging Issues Task Force—observations that also represent practices followed by the SEC staff in administering SEC accounting

Figure S22.1   GAAP Hierarchy Summary

	Nongovernmental Entities	*State and Local Governments*
Established Accounting Principles	FASB Statements and Interpretations, APB Opinions, and AICPA Accounting Research Bulletins	GASB Statements and Interpretations, plus AICPA and FASB pronouncements if made applicable to state and local governments by a GASB Statement or Interpretation
	FASB Technical Bulletins, AICPA Industry Audit and Accounting Guides, and AICPA Statements of Position	GASB Technical Bulletins, and the following pronouncements if specifically made applicable to state and local governments by the AICPA: AICPA Industry Audit and Accounting Guides and AICPA Statements of Position
	Consensus positions of the FASB Emerging Issues Task Force and AICPA Practice Bulletins	Consensus positions of the GASB Emerging Issues Task Force‡ and AICPA Practice Bulletins if specifically made applicable to state and local governments by the AICPA
	AICPA accounting interpretations, "Qs and As" published by the FASB staff, as well as industry practices widely recognized and prevalent	"Qs and As" published by the GASB staff, as well as industry practices widely recognized and prevalent
Other Accounting Literature†	Other accounting literature, including FASB Concepts Statements; APB Statements; AICPA Issues Papers; International Accounting Standards Committee Statements; GASB Statements, Interpretations, and Technical Bulletins; pronouncements of other professional associations or regulatory agencies; AICPA *Technical Practice Aids;* and accounting textbooks, handbooks, and articles	Other accounting literature, including GASB Concepts Statements; pronouncements in categories (*a*) through (*d*) of the hierarchy for nongovernmental entities when not specifically made applicable to state and local governments; APB Statements; FASB Concepts Statements; AICPA Issues Papers; International Accounting Standards Committee Statements; pronouncements of other professional associations or regulatory agencies; AICPA *Technical Practice Aids;* and accounting textbooks, handbooks, and articles

† In the absence of established accounting principles, the auditor may consider other accounting literature, depending on its relevance in the circumstances.

‡ As of the date of this Statement, the GASB had not organized such a group.

Source: Statement on Auditing Standards No. 69, *The Meaning of* Present Fairly in Conformity With Generally Accepted Accounting Principles *in the Independent Auditor's Report.*

and financial reporting requirements. These observations have come to be known colloquially as "turbo-SABs," since they have much the same effect as SABs.

EXPLANATORY LANGUAGE ADDED
TO THE STANDARD REPORT

Uncertainties

p. 648.   *Add after third full paragraph:*
Certain investment securities may not have readily ascertainable values and therefore may be included in financial statements at valuations determined by management. Those valuations may be subjective and highly judgmental; moreover, the range of possible values may be quite broad. In these circumstances, the auditor usually does not have a basis for either agreeing or disagreeing with management's conclusion. An uncertainty, therefore, exists that requires an explanatory paragraph in the auditor's report, assuming that management's valuation principles and procedures are reasonable and supported by underlying documentation. Statement of Position 89-1, *Reports on Audited Financial Statements of Brokers and Dealers in Securities,* illustrates an explanatory paragraph related to an uncertainty about the valuation of investment securities that are not readily marketable.

[*Separate paragraph following the opinion paragraph*]

As discussed in Note 1 to the financial statements, investment securities not readily marketable amounting to $10,730,685 (27 percent of stockholders' equity) as of December 31, 19X1, have been valued at fair value as determined by the Board of Directors. We have reviewed the procedures applied by the directors in valuing such securities and investments and have inspected underlying documentation, and in the circumstances, we believe the procedures are reasonable and the documentation appropriate. However, because of the inherent uncertainty of valuation, the Board of Directors' estimate of fair values may differ significantly from the values that would have been used had a ready market existed for the securities, and the differences could be material.

p. 651.   *Add at bottom of page:*
SAS No. 64, *Omnibus Statement on Auditing Standards—1990,* amended SAS No. 59 (AU Section 341.12 and .13) to clarify that the auditor's conclusion about the entity's ability to continue as a going concern should be expressed using the phrase "substantial doubt about its ability to continue as a going concern" or similar wording that includes both of the terms, "substantial doubt" and "going concern."

p. 652.   *Add at bottom of page:*
In November 1990, the AICPA issued Statement of Position (SOP) 90-7, *Financial Reporting by Entities in Reorganization Under the Bankruptcy Code,* which provides detailed guidance on the accounting treatment of entities that enter into and emerge from bankruptcy. The SOP recommends that when an entity emerges from bankruptcy and meets specified criteria, it should adopt fresh-start reporting; in that

situation, it should not present comparative financial statements in the first year after emerging from bankruptcy.

Lack of Consistency

p. 654. *Add after last paragraph:*

Correction of Errors.   There are two types of corrections of errors. Both are accounted for as prior-period adjustments, and previous periods' statements are retroactively restated. The first type, which requires an explanatory paragraph following the auditor's opinion, involves a change from an accounting principle that is not generally accepted to one that is, including the correction of a mistake in applying a principle.

The second type of error correction involves errors in previously issued financial statements resulting from mathematical mistakes, oversight, or misuse of facts that existed at the time the financial statements were originally prepared, and does not involve the consistency standard. A correction of an error of this type should be reported in a note to the financial statements but need not be recognized in the auditor's report. The auditor may, however, include an explanatory paragraph to emphasize the revision. An example of such a paragraph when there has been a correction of an error resulting from an oversight is

> As more fully described in note A of notes to statements of consolidated earnings (loss), certain errors resulting in overstatements of previously reported year-end inventories as of April 28, 1993, April 29, 1992 and April 30, 1991 were discovered by management of the Company during the course of determining year-end inventory as of May 3, 1994. Accordingly, the consolidated balance sheet as of April 28, 1993 and the statements of consolidated earnings (loss), consolidated stockholders' equity, and consolidated cash flows for each of the three years then ended have been restated to reflect corrections to previously reported year-end inventories and the related tax effect.

If the auditor had previously reported on the financial statements containing the error, he or she should refer to the section of Chapter 22 of the main volume entitled "Discovery of Information After the Report Date."

DEPARTURES FROM UNQUALIFIED OPINIONS

Distinguishing Among Situations Involving Scope Limitations, Uncertainties, and Departures from GAAP

p. 666. *Add after third full paragraph:*
Concern has been expressed that auditors have sometimes issued unqualified opinions, with an explanatory paragraph describing the existence of an uncertainty, in situations that require a qualified or an adverse opinion because of a departure from GAAP. Those situations usually involve uncertainties facing management about market or other business conditions that are inappropriately

treated in auditors' reports as uncertainties about the likelihood of occurrence of future events. The presence of uncertainties in the economic environment in which an entity typically conducts business does not negate management's responsibility to make accounting estimates as a basis for the application of accounting principles. Management's unwillingness to make reasonable estimates in those situations indicates a possible departure from GAAP, which would require either a qualified or an adverse opinion. The auditor's inability to reach a conclusion about an accounting measurement or estimate made by management may indicate a scope limitation, which would require either a qualified opinion or a disclaimer.

23

Special Reporting Situations

NONAUDITS, COMPILATIONS, AND REVIEWS

Indirect Association with Financial Data

* **p. 677.** *Replace first full paragraph with:*
A client may ask the accountant merely to type or reproduce financial statements that the accountant has not otherwise prepared or assisted in preparing. Previously, an accountant was prohibited from rendering such a service for a non-public entity, but Statement on Standards for Accounting and Review Services (SSARS) No. 7 (AR Section 100.07) eliminates the prohibition.

Personal Financial Statements in a Financial Plan

p. 678. *Add after carryover paragraph:*
In May 1991, an interpretation of SSARS No. 6, *Reporting on Personal Financial Statements Included in Written Personal Financial Plans* (AR Section 9600.01-.03), was issued to clarify what activities are encompassed by the term "developing the client's financial goals and objectives." The interpretation states that developing personal financial goals and objectives encompasses implementation of a personal financial plan submitted by an accountant and that therefore the exemptive provisions of SSARS No. 6 extend to written personal financial plans containing unaudited personal financial statements to be used in implementing, as well as developing, the plan. The interpretation also lists examples of client advisors who may use the plan as part of the implementation process, namely, an insurance broker who might identify specific insurance products, an investment advisor who might recommend specific investments, and an attorney who might draft a will or trust documents. Such uses would not void the exemption from complying with SSARS No. 1.

Reviews of Financial Statements

* p. 680. *Replace last sentence of carryover paragraph with:*

Reviews (as discussed in AR Section 100) may be performed only for nonpublic entities[4.1] and for those public companies that do not have their annual financial statements audited. Some states have established securities laws that permit public companies to raise a limited amount of capital with financial statements that have been reviewed, rather than audited. At the federal level, entities with "small offerings" may also be exempt from the requirement to have their financial statements audited.

* p. 681. *Replace from top of page to the major heading on page 686 with:*

If other accountants have been engaged to audit or review the financial statements of significant components of the reporting entity, its subsidiaries, or other investees, the principal accountant should obtain reports from the other accountants as a basis, in part, for his or her report on the review of the reporting entity's financial statements. SSARS No. 7 also requires the accountant to obtain a representation letter from the client to confirm the oral representations made in the course of the review. That letter also serves as a means of reducing the possibility of misunderstanding and of documenting some of the more important inquiries.

Based on the results of the review, the accountant should consider whether the financial statements appear to conform with GAAP. Material departures from GAAP should cause the accountant to modify the standard review report, unless the financial statements are revised. If modifying the report is not adequate to indicate the deficiencies in the financial statements taken as a whole, the accountant may have to withdraw from the engagement.

Form of Reporting. The accountant's report on reviewed financial statements expresses limited assurance. The opinion is in the form of "negative assurance" that the accountant is not aware of any material modifications that should be made to the financial statements in order for them to be in conformity with GAAP. The standard form of review report to be issued, as specified in SSARS No. 1 (AR Section 100.35), follows:

> I (we) have reviewed the accompanying balance sheet of XYZ Company as of December 31, 19XX, and the related statements of income, retained earnings, and cash flows for the year then ended, in accordance with Statements on Standards for Accounting and Review Services issued by the American Institute of Certified Public Accountants. All information included in these financial statements is the representation of the management (owners) of XYZ Company.

> A review consists principally of inquiries of company personnel and analytical procedures applied to financial data. It is substantially less in scope than an audit in

---

[4.1] SSARS No. 1 defines "nonpublic entity" in paragraph 4 (AR Section 100.04) as follows: "A nonpublic entity is any entity other than (a) one whose securities trade in a public market either on a stock exchange (domestic or foreign) or in the over-the-counter market, including securities quoted only locally or regionally, (b) one that makes a filing with a regulatory agency in preparation for the sale of any class of its securities in a public market, or (c) a subsidiary, corporate joint venture, or other entity controlled by an entity covered by (a) or (b)."

accordance with generally accepted auditing standards, the objective of which is the expression of an opinion regarding the financial statements taken as a whole. Accordingly, I (we) do not express such an opinion.

Based on my (our) review, I am (we are) not aware of any material modifications that should be made to the accompanying financial statements in order for them to be in conformity with generally accepted accounting principles.

The accountant's report should be dated as of the date the review was completed. Each page of the financial statements should include a reference such as "See Accountant's Review Report."[5]

Interpretations of SSARS No. 1 (New)

A number of interpretations of SSARS No. 1 have been issued. Interpretation No. 15 (AR Section 9100.54–.57), issued in September 1990, discusses attributes that help distinguish between a financial statement presentation, which is covered by the SSARSs, and other presentations such as a trial balance, which are not. Accountants should consider those attributes in determining whether accounting services performed fall under the provisions of the SSARSs. Interpretation No. 16 (AR Section 9100.58–.60), also issued in September 1990, defines "submission" of financial statements and contrasts services that fit the definition with those that do not and therefore do not require the accountant to comply with the provisions of the SSARSs.

Three other interpretations (Nos. 17 and 18, issued in September 1990, and 19, issued in February 1991; AR Section 9100.61–.75) address submitting draft financial statements, the application of the SSARSs to special-purpose financial statements prepared to comply with contractual agreements or regulatory provisions that specify a special basis of presentation, and reporting on a compilation or review engagement when financial statements contain a departure from promulgated accounting principles that prevents the statements from being misleading.

Finally, in May 1991, Interpretation No. 20 (AR Section 9100.76–.79) was issued, dealing with the applicability of SSARSs to litigation services. The interpretation clarifies that the SSARSs apply to only those litigation services engagements in which the accountant

- Submits unaudited financial statements of a nonpublic entity that are the representation of management to other parties who, under the rules of the proceeding, will not be able to analyze and challenge the accountant's work, or
- Is specifically engaged to submit, in accordance with the SSARSs, financial statements that are the representation of management.

---

[5] SSARS No. 2, *Reporting on Comparative Financial Statements* (AR Section 200), provides guidance for reporting on comparative financial statements of a nonpublic entity when financial statements of one or more periods presented have been compiled or reviewed.

In establishing which services are and are not covered by the SSARSs, this interpretation follows closely an interpretation of the attestation standards (AT Section 9100.47–.55) issued in July 1990 to clarify the applicability of those standards to litigation services engagements. The attestation interpretation is discussed in Chapter 24 of this Supplement.

Reporting When the Accountant Is Not Independent

Lack of independence precludes an accountant from issuing a review report. The accountant may, however, issue a report on a compilation engagement for a nonpublic company with respect to which the accountant is not independent, provided the report includes language specifically stating the lack of independence. The reason for lack of independence should not be described.

The staff of the AICPA issued *Compilation and Review Alert—1992,* which provides accountants with an overview of recent practice, regulatory, and professional developments that may affect the performance of compilations and reviews. In addition to summarizing new pronouncements, the Alert is intended to clarify existing standards and to suggest ways of avoiding pitfalls that frequently occur in such engagements. Some of the subjects discussed are

- *Going Concern.* The Alert provides an example of an emphasis of a matter paragraph related to a going concern issue. When financial statements include appropriate disclosure about a going concern matter, the accountant may, but is not required to, add an explanatory paragraph to the compilation or review report. Such paragraph does not use the term "substantial doubt," because compilation or review procedures do not yield evidence for determining substantial doubt.
- *Reporting on Supplementary Information.* Examples are presented of reports on supplementary information that has been either compiled or reviewed.
- *Internal Control Weaknesses.* The Alert states that, although it might be beneficial to a client to be made aware of internal control weaknesses, it is unrealistic to expect an accountant to provide this service as part of a compilation or review engagement and it is not required by professional standards.
- *Computer-Generated Financial Statements.* A caution is provided to the accountant to ensure that suitable financial statement titles and wording are used when the basis of accounting is other than GAAP.

INTERIM REVIEWS

A public accountant may be requested to perform a preissuance review of interim financial information for a client for a number of reasons. The client may wish to include a representation that the information has been reviewed in a document issued to stockholders or third parties or in Form 10-Q, a quarterly report required to be submitted to the SEC pursuant to Section 13 or 15(d) of the Securities Exchange Act of 1934. Such representation may also be included or incorporated by reference in a registration statement.

Larger, more widely traded companies meeting specified criteria are also required by Item 302(a) of SEC Regulation S-K to include selected quarterly financial data in their annual reports or other documents filed with the SEC that contain audited financial statements. The selected quarterly financial data is required to be reviewed, on either a preissuance or retrospective basis. Other entities may voluntarily include similar information in documents containing audited financial statements. In the latter instance, the interim financial information may or may not have been reviewed. It is unlikely that an entity not required to include that information would do so without having it reviewed, since that would give rise to an expansion of the auditor's report. (See the discussion later in this chapter of the Supplement under "Interim Financial Information Presented in Annual Reports to Shareholders.")

Companies that include quarterly financial information with their audited annual financial statements may want their accountants to review the information periodically throughout the year, rather than retrospectively at year-end. There are a number of tangible benefits to this approach. First, a preissuance review helps bring accounting problems to light early enough to avoid year-end "surprises." Second, there may be some offsetting reductions in the audit fee for the year because, even though the review does not entail actual audit tests, it involves procedures that, if the work is coordinated, the auditor can utilize in performing the audit. Finally, it may prevent the need to publish at year-end quarterly financial information that differs from amounts previously reported during the year.

The National Commission on Fraudulent Financial Reporting (Treadway Commission) recommended that "the SEC should require independent public accountants to review quarterly financial data of all public companies before release to the public" (p. 53). The SEC staff subsequently issued, and later withdrew, a concepts release on timely reviews of interim financial information. This release asked for comments on whether the SEC should propose a requirement that (1) interim financial data of registrants be reviewed by independent accountants before it is filed with the SEC, and (2) a report issued by the independent accountants be included in the registrant's Form 10-Q and any registration statements that include the interim financial information.

Objective of Reviews of Interim Financial Information

A review of interim financial information is intended to provide the accountant with a basis for reporting whether he or she is aware of material modifications that should be made to such information in order for it to conform with GAAP. The accountant does this by applying a knowledge of financial reporting practices to significant accounting matters that come to his or her attention through inquiries and analytical procedures.

Nature of Reviews

SAS No. 71, *Interim Financial Information* (AU Section 722), which supersedes SAS Nos. 36 and 66, sets forth the procedures established by the profession for a review of interim financial information. Those procedures are similar to the procedures discussed in Chapter 23 of the main volume relating to review engagements conducted under Statements on Standards for Accounting and Review Services (SSARSs). In order to select the inquiries and analytical procedures to be performed and to assess the nature and likelihood of material misstatements, the accountant needs sufficient knowledge of a client's internal control structure policies and procedures as they relate to both annual and interim information. An accountant who has not previously audited the client's annual financial statements and does not have the requisite knowledge of the control structure should perform procedures to acquire that knowledge. The SAS also establishes requirements for communicating errors, irregularities, and illegal acts that the accountant becomes aware of in performing an interim review.

SAS No. 71 also requires an accountant who, as a result of assisting the entity in preparing its interim financial information or performing any review procedures (other than merely reading it), becomes aware of a probable material misstatement in interim financial information filed or to be filed with a regulatory agency to discuss the matter with the appropriate level of management as soon as practicable. If management does not respond appropriately, the accountant should inform the audit committee or others with equivalent authority. If there is still no appropriate response, the accountant should consider whether to resign from the interim engagement and whether to remain as the entity's auditor or stand for re-election to audit the entity's financial statements.

Timing of Reviews

The timing of procedures to be performed depends largely on whether the accountant has been engaged to perform a preissuance (or "timely") review of the interim financial information or a retrospective review.

While adequate planning by the accountant is essential to the timely completion of a preissuance review, the most critical element is the client's interim reporting system. It must permit the preparation of reliable interim financial information; otherwise, the scope of the accountant's engagement may be restricted. In addition, the client's interim financial control procedures should be adequate so that a preissuance review is not unduly expensive or time-consuming.

On the other hand, if a review is done retrospectively, there must be sufficient documentation, including the rationale for conclusions reached during the year, available for the accountant's purpose. For example, the accountant may review the client's documentation in deciding whether an adjustment arising in a later quarter of the year is a change in estimate or correction of an error.

Extent of Reviews

The extent to which the accountant makes inquiries and performs analytical procedures on the financial information to be reported on depends on a number of considerations. First, the accountant needs a knowledge of the client's accounting and reporting practices, as well as its control structure policies and procedures as a practical basis for the inquiry and other procedures. The accountant ordinarily acquires this knowledge as a result of having audited the client's previous annual financial statements. Knowledge of deficiencies in control structure policies and procedures, accounting changes, and changes in the nature or volume of the client's business activities; the issuance of new accounting pronouncements; and questions raised during the review all may prompt the accountant to make more extensive inquiries or to employ other procedures to assess interim financial information.

If there appear to be deficiencies in the client's control structure policies and procedures that prevent the preparation of interim financial information in conformity with GAAP, and, as a result, the accountant cannot effectively apply his or her knowledge of financial reporting practices to the interim financial information, the accountant should consider whether there is a restriction on the scope of the engagement sufficient to preclude completing the review. Furthermore, the accountant should inform senior management and the board of directors (or its audit committee) of these circumstances.

There are also a number of practical considerations that affect the extent of review procedures. Examples are selecting locations to be visited if the accounting records are maintained at multiple client locations, and acquiring the appropriate level of knowledge when there has been a change in auditors and the current accountant does not have an audit base to work from. These are special matters that the accountant should consider in determining the review strategy.

Reporting Standards

An accountant may address a report on interim financial information to the company, its board of directors, or its stockholders. The report should be dated as of the date the review was completed and is similar to a review report conducted under the SSARSs, as discussed in Chapter 23 of the main volume. The standard form of interim review report presented in AU Section 722.28 follows:

Independent Accountant's Report

We have reviewed the accompanying [*describe the statements or information reviewed*] of ABC Company and consolidated subsidiaries as of September 30, 19X1, and for the three-month and nine-month periods then ended. These financial statements (information) are (is) the responsibility of the company's management.

We conducted our review in accordance with standards established by the American Institute of Certified Public Accountants. A review of interim financial information consists principally of applying analytical procedures to financial data and making inquiries of persons responsible for financial and accounting matters. It is substantially less in scope than an audit conducted in accordance with generally accepted auditing standards, the objective of which is the expression of an opinion regarding the financial statements taken as a whole. Accordingly, we do not express such an opinion.

Based on our review, we are not aware of any material modifications that should be made to the accompanying financial statements (information) for them (it) to be in conformity with generally accepted accounting principles.

[*Signature*]

[*Date*]

Each page of the interim financial information should be marked as "unaudited."

When an accountant requires reports from other accountants as a basis, in part, for a report on a review of consolidated interim financial information, the accountant may refer in the report to the reports of the other accountants to indicate a division of responsibility for performance of the review.

Modifications to the Standard Review Report.   Since an accountant reporting on a review of interim financial information is not expressing an opinion on audited financial statements, the circumstances that require modifying the standard review report are somewhat different than for an audit report. The accountant should modify the standard review report only if the interim financial information departs from GAAP. Such departures include inadequate disclosure, as well as changes in accounting principles that are not in conformity with GAAP. The existence of an uncertainty, substantial doubt about the entity's ability to continue as a going concern, or a lack of consistency in the application of GAAP, however, would not cause the accountant to modify the standard review report as long as such matters were adequately disclosed in the interim financial information. The accountant may wish, however, to emphasize such matters in a separate paragraph of the report.

Interim Financial Information Presented in Annual Reports to Shareholders.   Selected quarterly financial data may be presented in a note to the audited financial statements or as supplementary information outside the audited financial statements. If such information is presented in a note to the audited financial statements, the information should be marked as "unaudited." If it is included in an annual report to shareholders, either voluntarily or as required by Item 302(a) of SEC Regulation S-K, there is a presumption in the absence of an indication to the contrary that the data has been reviewed in accordance with the established professional standards previously discussed. Because of this presumption, if an accountant has reviewed the data, the audit report on the annual financial statements ordinarily need not be modified, nor does the accountant have to report separately on the review.

The auditor's report on the annual financial statements should be expanded if the selected quarterly financial data required by Item 302(a) of Regulation S-K is omitted or if interim financial data presented (a) is not appropriately marked as "unaudited," (b) has not been reviewed, (c) does not appear to be presented in conformity with GAAP, or (d) includes an indication that a review was made but fails to state that "the review is substantially less in scope than an audit conducted in accordance with generally accepted auditing standards, the objective of which is an expression of opinion regarding the financial statements taken as a whole, and accordingly, no such opinion is expressed" (AU Section 722.42).[6]

---

[6] Under its present rules, it is unlikely the SEC would accept any expansion of the auditor's report in this regard. A possible exception might be if the auditor could not review the selected quarterly financial data in the annual report because the company's system for preparing interim financial information did not provide an adequate basis for conducting such a review. In that case, however, there is a possibility that the client might be in violation of the "accounting standards" provisions of the Foreign Corrupt Practices Act, as discussed in Chapter 7 of the main volume.

SEC Filings.　If the client includes a representation in a Form 10-Q that an accountant has reviewed interim financial information set forth in that document, the accountant should request that the review report be included.

An accountant's report based on a review of interim financial information also may be presented or incorporated by reference in a registration statement. In that event, the prospectus should discuss the independent accountant's involvement and the legal status of the review report. The discussion should make it clear that, under SEC rules, the accountant's statutory responsibility as to liability for the report does not extend to the effective date of the registration statement. Suitable wording for this purpose is included in SAS No. 37, *Filings Under Federal Securities Statutes,* paragraph 9 (AU Section 711.09).

SPECIAL REPORTS

Non-GAAP Financial Statements

p. 688.　*Add at the end of the extract:*
An auditing interpretation of SAS No. 62 (AU Section 9623) addresses reporting on current-value financial statements that supplement historical-cost financial statements in a general-use presentation of a real estate entity. The interpretation states that if the measurement and disclosure criteria used in preparing the current-value statements are reasonable and if competent persons using the criteria would ordinarily arrive at similar conclusions, an auditor may report on the statements in accordance with the provisions in SAS No. 62 for non-GAAP and non-OCBOA presentations. An example of a report that an auditor might issue in these circumstances is presented in the interpretation (AU Section 9623.58).

REPORTS ON INTERNAL CONTROL

Management Reporting on the Internal Control Structure

* **p. 699.**　*Replace from second paragraph in this subsection to the major heading on page 702 with:*
In its 1987 report, the Treadway Commission recommended that the auditor's standard report should be revised to describe the independent public accountant's work with respect to understanding and evaluating the control structure. The Treadway Commission also recommended that companies be required to issue management reports on the effectiveness of their internal controls. In developing SAS No. 58, the Auditing Standards Board (ASB) considered implementing the former recommendation, but decided instead to develop a standard under which the auditor could attest to management's assertion about an entity's internal control structure. Statement on Standards for Attestation Engagements (SSAE) No. 2, *Reporting on an Entity's Internal Control Structure Over Financial Reporting,* was issued in early 1993 to provide guidance for examining and reporting on such an assertion. SSAE No. 2, which is discussed further in Chapter 24 of this Supplement, superseded SAS No. 30, *Reporting on Internal Accounting Control.* In

addition, in September 1992, the Committee of Sponsoring Organizations of the Treadway Commission issued its report, *Internal Control—Integrated Framework.* The report, authored by Coopers & Lybrand, provides integrated guidance on internal control, including a definition, description of its components, and criteria as to what constitutes an effective system. It also includes implementation guidelines for designing, evaluating, and monitoring internal control systems. The guidance is intended to provide "reasonable criteria" against which management's assertions about an entity's internal control structure can be evaluated.

Over the years, legislators and regulators have initiated several proposals involving internal control. Proposed legislation has included requirements that management assess and report on the effectiveness of its internal controls and that an independent accountant attest to the management reports. One such bill, relating to banks, has become law, in the form of the Federal Deposit Insurance Corporation Improvement Act of 1991.

Reports on the Processing of Transactions by a Service Organization

Service organizations may record transactions, process related data, or even execute and account for transactions on behalf of others. Companies that provide such services include, for example, trust departments of banks (which invest and hold securities for others), computer service centers (which process data for others), and securities depositories (which hold and account for securities for others). A service organization may seek a special-purpose report from an auditor on the policies and procedures placed in operation surrounding the processing of those transactions or on both the policies and procedures placed in operation and tests of their operating effectiveness. SAS No. 70, *Reports on the Processing of Transactions by Service Organizations* (AU Section 324), which superseded SAS No. 44, provides guidance on the responsibilities of an auditor who issues these types of special reports. These reports are frequently used by auditors of the enterprises whose transactions are executed or processed by the service organization (see the discussion in Chapter 6 of this Supplement).

OPINIONS ON ACCOUNTING PRINCIPLES

Pooling Letters

* **p. 705.** *Add at end of section:*
The NYSE deleted the requirements for pooling-of interests letters from companies and auditors in 1992. The proposed rule changes were contained in SEC Release No. 34-30167; the rule changes were approved in SEC Release No. 34-30662.

MATTERS RELATING TO SOLVENCY

p. 707. *Add at bottom of page:*
In July 1990, an interpretation (AT Section 9100.47-.55) of the attestation standards was issued that, among other things, clarified a previous interpretation

(*Responding to Requests for Reports on Matters Relating to Solvency*) to specify that a practitioner may, when involved in formal legal or regulatory proceedings in which the parties to the dispute have the opportunity to analyze and challenge the matters relating to solvency and the criteria used by the practitioner in evaluating those matters, provide an expert opinion or consulting advice about matters relating to solvency. The 1990 interpretation is discussed in more detail in Chapter 24 of this Supplement.

AUDITORS' CONSENTS (NEW)

Section 11(a) of the Securities Act of 1933 imposes civil liability on a registrant's management personnel, underwriters, legal counsel, independent auditors, and all other parties involved if a 1933 Act registration statement is found to contain untrue statements or material omissions. Damages are generally limited to the excess of the purchase price (not exceeding the public offering price) over the later value of the security. Under Section 11(b), however, officers, directors, and underwriters may not be liable with respect to information included in any part of the registration statement that is purported to be included "on the authority of an expert." Because of the protection afforded to officers, directors, and underwriters by this provision, lawyers for the registrant and the underwriters usually request the insertion of language in the registration statement to specify that the audited financial statements and supporting schedules are included in reliance on the report of the independent auditors as "experts." There is no regulatory requirement for the inclusion of an experts section; however, if the independent auditors are referred to as experts, Section 7 of the Act requires their written consent to such reference.

The auditor should read the wording in the registration statement referring to the independent auditors as experts to ensure that it does not impute responsibility for financial data the auditor does not intend to, or should not, assume. The expertising declaration should be limited to financial statements and supporting schedules covered by the auditor's report. (If the auditor's report is qualified or modified to explain the existence of an uncertainty, including an uncertainty related to the entity's ability to continue as a going concern, or of a change in accounting principles, the declaration should be modified or qualified to disclose that fact.) The expertising language is usually similar to the following:

Experts

The consolidated balance sheets as of December 31, 19X4 and 19X3 and the consolidated statements of income, retained earnings, and cash flows for each of the three years in the period ended December 31, 19X4, included [or incorporated by reference] in this prospectus, have been included [or incorporated] herein in reliance on the report of ABC, independent auditors, given on the authority of that firm as experts in accounting and auditing.

Consents in 1933 Act filings are typically worded as follows:

Consent of Independent Accountants

We consent to the inclusion in this registration statement on Form S-1 (File No. 2-0000) of our report dated February 7, 19X5, on our audits of the financial statements and financial statement schedules of XYZ Company. We also consent to the reference to our firm under the caption "Experts."

The auditor's consent must be dated, signed manually, and included in Part II of the 1933 Act registration statement. The consent is usually dated as of, or a few days prior to, the filing date of the registration statement. Any changes in the financial data covered by the auditor's report that occur between the initial 1933 Act filing and the filing of an amendment necessitate the inclusion in the amendment of a new manually signed consent as of a more current date. While technically not required, it is not uncommon for a registrant's counsel to request that the auditor manually sign a new consent every time an amendment is filed regardless of whether the financial information has changed.

A manually signed auditor's consent is required to be included in a document filed under the Securities Exchange Act of 1934 in certain situations, including when

- The auditor's report in the document is being incorporated by reference into a currently effective 1933 Act registration statement.
- The auditor's report included in a document filed under another of the Acts administered by the SEC is being incorporated by reference.
- Audited financial information previously included in a 1934 Act filing is being amended on Form 8.

A consent is not required in a document filed under the 1934 Act when financial information is being incorporated by reference from another 1934 Act filing or when financial statements are incorporated by reference in Form 10-K from the annual report to shareholders. In all such instances, however, the auditor must manually sign at least one copy of his or her report when it is filed with the SEC.

In certain circumstances, a client may propose to refer to the independent auditors as experts in a document that is not filed with the SEC—such as a bond offering document filed with a state agency—and may request the auditors to consent to that reference. An auditing interpretation of AU Section 711, published in August 1992, states that an auditor should not consent to be named, or referred to, as an expert in an offering document in connection with securities offerings other than those registered under the 1933 Act. This is because the term "expert" is typically undefined outside the context of the 1933 Act, and the auditor's responsibility, as a result of the use of that term, would also be undefined.

When a client wishes to refer to the auditors' role in a non-1933 Act offering document, the caption "Independent Accountants" should be used in the title of that section of the document instead of the caption "Experts," and the auditors should not be referred to as experts anywhere in the document. The following language should be used to describe the auditors' role:

Independent Accountants

The financial statements as of December 31, 19XX and for the year then ended, included in this offering circular, have been audited by ABC, independent auditors, as stated in their report(s) appearing herein.

A second auditing interpretation of AU Section 711, also published in August 1992, states that it is usually not necessary for the auditor to provide a consent when his or her report is included in a non-1933 Act offering document. A consent may be provided, however, if requested, and the following illustrative language is presented in the interpretation:

Consent of Independent Accountants

We agree to the inclusion in this offering circular of our report, dated February 5, 19XX, on our audit of the financial statements of XYZ Company.

LETTERS FOR UNDERWRITERS

* **p. 708.** *Replace entire section with:*

The SEC's requirements for disclosures to be made in prospectuses and registration statements are complicated and periodically undergo significant changes. Accordingly, all parties to an SEC filing go to great lengths to ensure that the contents of those filings comply with the applicable requirements. In particular, as part of their "due diligence" duties, underwriters have had a long-standing practice of seeking specific assurance from lawyers and accountants that the SEC rules and regulations have been complied with. A common practice for underwriters is to seek "comfort" from an auditor on financial information in registration statements that is not covered by the auditor's report and on events subsequent to the report date.

As public expectations have grown and been reflected in legal and other attacks on those associated with disclosures, underwriters and their counsel have sought to obtain more and more "comfort" from accountants, which is formally expressed in a letter called a comfort letter. (Some lawyers still use the phrase common in earlier, more austere times: "cold comfort" letter.) While the comfort letter may originally have been an informal or semiformal helpful gesture on the part of an accountant, it is now a significant formal communication. In drafting comfort letters, formally called "letters for underwriters," accountants must therefore be especially careful not to assume unwarranted responsibility, either explicitly or implicitly.

SAS No. 72, *Letters for Underwriters and Certain Other Requesting Parties*[15] (AU Section 634), provides guidelines intended to minimize misunderstandings in connection with comfort letters. The importance attached to comfort letters is reflected in the length and details of the numerous paragraphs in the statement. It covers the kinds of matters that may properly be commented on by accountants in comfort letters and how the matters should be phrased, suggests forms of letters and how to prepare them, and recommends ways of reducing or avoiding

---

[15] SAS No. 72 was issued in February 1993 and is effective for letters issued on or after June 30, 1993. It supersedes SAS No. 49. SAS No. 72 amends SAS No. 35, *Special Reports—Applying Agreed-Upon Procedures to Specified Elements, Accounts, or Items of a Financial Statement;* Section 100, "Attestation Standards," and Section 200, "Financial Forecasts and Projections," of SSAE No. 1; and SAS No. 26, *Association With Financial Statements,* to preclude their use to circumvent its provisions.

misunderstandings about responsibility. Accountants who are asked to prepare letters for underwriters should become thoroughly familiar with SAS No. 72. While the following paragraphs summarize and paraphrase the SAS, the treatment in this book is not intended to serve as a substitute for a thorough understanding of the statement.

Comfort letters are required not by the SEC but by the underwriters as part of meeting their due diligence responsibilities; the letters are not "filed" with the SEC. Underwriting agreements usually set forth the requirement for and scope of a comfort letter. As soon as an underwriting is planned, the accountant, underwriter, and client meet to discuss the comfort letter. All parties usually recognize their respective objectives and welcome such a conference. The underwriter wants to have as much comfort as possible, the client is concerned with avoiding unnecessary problems and delays in the underwriting, and the accountant must determine whether he or she can provide the comfort called for by the underwriting agreement. Furthermore, an accountant who understands the client in the breadth and depth presumed throughout this book can usually benefit both the underwriter and the client by clarifying what is possible and what is not possible. An early conference often results in timely recognition of desirable clarifying changes both in the registration statement itself and in the underwriting agreement.

The accountant should obtain a copy of the underwriting agreement as soon as it is in draft form. After reading the draft agreement, the accountant may wish to prepare a draft of the comfort letter. The purpose of the draft letter is to inform all parties what they may expect, provide an opportunity to discuss and change contemplated procedures, and enhance a smooth execution of the subsequent steps in the underwriting.

Preparing and reviewing the comfort letter also gives the accountant the opportunity to emphasize that responsibility for the sufficiency of procedures carried out in the comfort review is the underwriter's, not the accountant's. The accountant's purpose is to preclude allegations in support of a claim against the accountant that the underwriter relied on the accountant for the sufficiency of the procedures if they subsequently appear to have been insufficient. An accountant must take great care to make clear to all parties that a CPA may advise on procedures but may not assume responsibility for adequacy or sufficiency.

The assistance accountants can provide through comfort letters is subject to limitations. Among them is that independent accountants can properly comment in their professional capacity only on matters to which their professional expertise is substantially relevant. Another limitation is that procedures short of an audit, such as those contemplated in a comfort letter, provide accountants with a basis for expressing, at the most, negative assurance (see below).

Applicability

Accountants may provide a comfort letter to underwriters or to other parties with a statutory due diligence defense under Section 11 of the Securities Act of 1933 (the Act) in connection with financial statements and financial statement schedules included in registration statements filed with the SEC under the Act. A comfort letter may be addressed to parties with a statutory due diligence defense under Section 11 of the Act other than underwriters only when an attorney for the requesting party issues a written opinion to the accountant stating that such party has a due diligence defense. If the requesting party cannot provide such a letter, it must provide a representation letter stating that the review process is substantially consistent with a due diligence review that would be performed if securities were being registered pursuant to the Act.

Accountants may also issue a comfort letter to a broker-dealer or other financial intermediary in connection with foreign offerings, transactions that are exempt from the registration requirements of Section 5 of the Act, and offerings of securities issued or backed by governmental, municipal, banking, tax-exempt, or other entities that are exempt from registration under the Act. The representation letter just described must be provided in these situations.

In addition, a comfort letter may be issued in connection with acquisitions in which there is an exchange of stock, provided that the comfort letter is requested by the buyer or seller, or both, and the representation letter described above is provided.

There may be situations in which more than one accountant is involved in the audit of the financial statements and in which the reports of more than one accountant appear in the registration statement. The letters of the other accountants reporting on significant units should contain statements similar to those contained in the comfort letter prepared by the principal accountant, including statements about their independence (see below). The principal accountant should state in the comfort letter that reading the letters of the other accountants was one of the procedures performed and that the other procedures performed by the principal accountant relate solely to the companies audited by the principal accountant and the consolidated financial statements.

Dating and Addressing the Letter

A comfort letter usually is requested at or shortly before the "effective date" of the registration statement. Underwriting agreements generally specify the date, often referred to as the "cutoff date," through which procedures specified in the letter are to be performed (perhaps five business days before the effective date). The letter should make clear that the period between the cutoff date and the date of the letter is not covered by the procedures and disclosures set forth in the letter. The comfort letter usually is updated to a new cutoff date at or shortly before the "closing date" (the date the securities are to be delivered to the underwriter in exchange for the proceeds of the offering) or to several closing dates, as might happen when securities are issued under a shelf registration.[16]

The letter should not be addressed or given to any parties other than the client and the named underwriters, broker-dealer, financial intermediary, or buyer or seller. The appropriate addressee is the intermediary who negotiated the agreement with the client, and with whom the accountants will deal in discussions regarding the scope and sufficiency of the letter.

---

[16] Rule 415 of the 1933 Act permits, in certain circumstances, the registration of securities to be offered on a delayed or continuous basis over an extended period of time—known as a shelf registration.

Contents of the Letter

The following subjects may be covered in a comfort letter: the independence of the accountants; whether the audited financial statements and financial statement schedules in the registration statement conform in all material respects with the applicable accounting requirements of the Act and the related published rules and regulations; unaudited financial statements, condensed interim financial information, capsule financial information, pro forma financial information, financial forecasts, and changes in selected financial statement items during a period after the latest financial statements in the filing; tables, statistics, and other financial information in the registration statement; and negative assurance as to whether certain nonfinancial statement information conforms in all material respects with Regulation S-K. Since there is no way of anticipating other matters that would be of interest to an underwriter, accountants should not make a general statement in the letter that, as a result of carrying out the specified procedures, nothing else has come to their attention that would be of interest to the underwriter. The following paragraphs illustrate a typical comfort letter. They need not be presented in the same order in an actual letter.

Introductory Paragraph.   A typical introductory paragraph is as follows:

June 30, 19X6

(Addressee)

Gentlemen:

We have audited the consolidated balance sheets of X Company (the company) and subsidiaries as of December 31, 19X5 and 19X4, and the consolidated statements of income, retained earnings, and cash flows for each of the three years in the period ended December 31, 19X5, and the related financial statement schedules included in the registration statement (No. _____) on Form _____ filed by the company under the Securities Act of 1933 (the Act); our reports with respect thereto are also included in that registration statement. The registration statement, as amended on [date], is herein referred to as the registration statement.

The underwriter may request the accountants to repeat in the comfort letter their report on the audited financial statements included in the registration statement. Because of the special significance of the date of the accountants' report, the accountants should not repeat their opinion.

The underwriter may also request the accountants to give negative assurance on the accountants' report or on the financial statements and financial statement schedules that have been audited and are reported on in the registration statement by other accountants. Because accountants have a statutory responsibility with respect to their opinion as of the effective date of a registration statement, and because the additional significance, if any, of negative assurance is unclear and such assurance may be misunderstood, accountants should not give such negative assurance.

Accountants may refer in the introductory paragraph to the fact that they have issued reports on other financial information: condensed financial statements that are derived from audited financial statements, selected financial data, interim financial information, pro forma financial information, or a financial forecast.

For example, if the auditor refers to the fact that a review of interim financial information was performed, an additional paragraph, such as the following, may be added:

> Also, we have reviewed the unaudited condensed consolidated financial statements as of March 31, 19X6 and 19X5 and for the three-month periods then ended, as indicated in our report dated May 15, 19X6, which is included in the registration statement.

Independence.   It is customary in conjunction with SEC filings to make an assertion about independence, substantially as follows:

> We are independent certified public accountants with respect to X Company, within the meaning of the Act and the applicable published rules and regulations thereunder.

In a non-SEC filing, the assertion about independence would be substantially as follows:

> We are independent certified public accountants with respect to X Company, under Rule 101 of the AICPA's *Code of Professional Conduct* and its interpretations and rulings.

When the accountant reports on a predecessor company rather than the registrant named in the registration statement and is no longer associated and therefore does not need to be independent currently, the assertion begins along the following lines:

> As of [date of the predecessor accountant's report] and during the period covered by the financial statements on which we reported, we were independent . . .

Compliance with SEC Requirements.   It is also customary to require comfort on compliance with SEC requirements as to form, which may be expressed as follows:

> In our opinion, the consolidated financial statements and schedules audited by us and included or incorporated by reference in the registration statement comply as to form in all material respects with the applicable accounting requirements of the Act and the related published rules and regulations.

In the rare case of a material departure from the published requirements, either the paragraph would include the phrase "except as disclosed in the registration statement" or the departure would be disclosed in the letter. Normally, a departure would not be considered unless representatives of the SEC had agreed to it in advance; in that event, the agreement should be mentioned in the comfort letter.

Comfort on conformity with SEC requirements is limited to negative assurance when the financial statements or financial statement schedules have not been audited.

Commenting on Unaudited Information.   Comments in a comfort letter on information other than audited financial statements often concern: unaudited condensed interim financial information; capsule financial information; pro forma financial information; financial forecasts; or changes in capital stock, increases in long-term debt, and decreases in other specified financial statement items. In all instances, terms of uncertain meaning, such as "general review," "limited review," "check," or "test," should not be used to describe the work unless they are defined in the letter. Guidance for commenting on these matters and illustrative comments follow.

Internal Control Structure.   Accountants should not comment in a comfort letter on unaudited condensed interim financial information, capsule information, a forecast (when historical financial statements provide a basis for one or more significant assumptions for the forecast), or changes in capital stock, increases in long-term debt, and decreases in selected financial statement items, unless they have obtained knowledge of a client's internal control structure policies and procedures as they relate to the preparation both annual and interim financial information. Sufficient knowledge would ordinarily have been acquired by accountants who audited a client's financial statements for one or more periods. If the accountants have not acquired sufficient knowledge of the entity's internal control structure policies and procedures, they should perform procedures to obtain that knowledge.

Identifying Unaudited Information.   In commenting on unaudited condensed interim financial information, capsule financial information, or pro forma financial information, accountants should specifically and explicitly identify the financial information and should clearly state the responsibility taken with respect to each item. The following is an example of how this might be done in a letter on unaudited condensed interim financial statements:

> We have not audited any financial statements of the company as of any date or for any period subsequent to December 31, 19X5; although we have conducted an audit for the year ended December 31, 19X5, the purpose (and therefore the scope) of the audit was to enable us to express our opinion on the consolidated financial statements as of December 31, 19X5, and for the year ended, but not on the financial statements for any interim period within that year. Therefore, we are unable to and do not express any opinion on the unaudited condensed consolidated balance sheet as of March 31, 19X6, and unaudited condensed consolidated statements of income, retained earnings, and cash flows for the three-month periods ended March 31, 19X6 and 19X5, included in the registration statement, or on the financial position, results of operations, or cash flows as of any date or for any period subsequent to December 31, 19X5.

Enumerating Procedures.   The limited procedures carried out by the accountants, which should have been agreed on in advance, as described above, should be set forth in the letter. To avoid any misunderstanding about the responsibility for the sufficiency of the agreed-upon procedures for the underwriter's purposes, the accountants should not state, or imply, that they have applied procedures that they determined to be necessary or sufficient for the underwriter's purposes. The following is an example of a description of agreed-upon procedures performed on unaudited financial statements:

> For purposes of this letter, we have read the 19X6 minutes of the meetings of the stockholders, the board of directors, and [include other appropriate committees, if any] of the company and its subsidiaries as set forth in the minute books at June 25, 19X6, officials of the company having advised us that the minutes of all such meetings through that date were set forth therein; and we have carried out other procedures to June 25, 19X6 (our work did not extend to the period from June 26, 19X6, to June 30, 19X6, inclusive), as follows:
>
> a. With respect to the three-month periods ended March 31, 19X6 and 19X5, we have
>
> (i) Performed the procedures specified by the American Institute of Certified Public Accountants for a review of interim financial information as described in SAS No. 71, *Interim Financial Information,* on the unaudited condensed consolidated balance sheet as of March 31, 19X6, and unaudited condensed consolidated statements of income, retained earnings, and cash flows for the three-month periods ended March 31, 19X6 and 19X5, included in the registration statement.
>
> (ii) Inquired of certain officials of the company who have responsibility for financial and accounting matters whether the unaudited consolidated condensed financial statements referred to in a(i) comply as to form in all material respects with the applicable accounting requirements of the Act and the related published rules and regulations.
>
> b. With respect to the period from April 1, 19X6, to May 31, 19X6, we have
>
> (i) Read the unaudited consolidated financial statements of the company and subsidiaries for April and May of both 19X5 and 19X6 furnished us by the company, officials of the company having advised us that no such financial statements as of any date or for any period subsequent to May 31, 19X6 were available.
>
> (ii) Inquired of certain officials of the company who have responsibility for financial and accounting matters whether the unaudited consolidated financial statements referred to in b(i) are stated on a basis substantially consistent with that of the audited financial statements included in the registration statement.
>
> The foregoing procedures do not constitute an audit conducted in accordance with generally accepted auditing standards. Also, they would not necessarily reveal matters of significance with respect to the comments in the following paragraph. [See the paragraph illustrated below under "Negative Assurance" for the "following paragraph" referred to.] Accordingly, we make no representations regarding the sufficiency of the foregoing procedures for your purposes.

Negative Assurance.   Procedures short of an audit provide accountants with a basis for expressing, at the most, negative assurance. Accountants may give negative assurance on unaudited condensed interim financial information, capsule financial information, or pro forma financial information only when they have, among other requirements, conducted a review in accordance with SAS No. 71, *Interim Financial Information.* Otherwise, accountants are limited to reporting on procedures performed and findings obtained.

Accountants may not provide negative assurance on the results of procedures performed or with respect to compliance of a financial forecast with Rule 11-03 of Regulation S-X unless they have performed an examination of the forecast in accordance with Statement on Standards for Accountants' Services on Prospective Financial Information, *Financial Forecasts and Projections.*

The following is an example of how negative assurance on unaudited condensed interim financial statements may be expressed:

> Nothing came to our attention as a result of the foregoing procedures, however, that caused us to believe that:
>
> a. (i) Any material modifications should be made to the unaudited condensed consolidated financial statements described in [cite paragraph number] for them to be in conformity with generally accepted accounting principles.
>
> (ii) The unaudited condensed consolidated financial statements described in [cite paragraph number] do not comply as to form in all material respects with the applicable accounting requirements of the Act and related published rules and regulations.
>
> b. (i) At May 31, 19X6, there was any change in capital stock, increase in long-term debt, or decrease in consolidated net current assets or stockholders' equity of the consolidated companies as compared with amounts shown in the March 31, 19X6 unaudited condensed consolidated balance sheet included in the registration statement, or (ii) for the period from April 1, 19X6, to May 31, 19X6, there were any decreases, as compared with the corresponding period in the preceding year, in consolidated net sales or in the total or per-share amounts of income before extraordinary items or of net income, except in all instances for changes, increases, or decreases that the registration statement discloses have occurred or may occur.

Subsequent Changes.   Comments regarding subsequent changes typically relate to whether there has been any change in capital stock, increase in long-term debt, or decreases in other specified financial statement items during the "change period" (period between the date of the latest financial statements and the cutoff date). Comments on the occurrence of these changes should be limited to changes not disclosed in the registration statement. Comments on subsequent changes should not relate to "adverse changes" since that term is not clearly understood. The procedures followed for interim periods may not disclose changes in capital stock, increases in long-term debt, or decreases in specified financial statement items, inconsistencies in the application of GAAP, instances of noncompliance as to form with accounting requirements of the SEC, or other matters about which negative assurance is requested. An appropriate way of making this clear is shown in the caveat included in the illustrative paragraphs under "Enumerating Procedures."

Negative assurance may be given as to subsequent changes in specified financial statement items as of a date less than 135 days from the end of the most recent period for which the audit or review was performed. Otherwise, accountants may not provide negative assurance and are limited to reporting on procedures performed and findings obtained. Wording describing procedures performed and expressing negative assurance with respect to subsequent changes might be as follows:

As mentioned in [cite paragraph number], company officials have advised us that no consolidated financial statements as of any date or for any period subsequent to May 31, 19X6, are available; accordingly, the procedures carried out by us with respect to changes in financial statement items after May 31, 19X6, have, of necessity, been even more limited than those with respect to the periods referred to in [cite paragraph number]. We have inquired of certain company officials who have responsibility for financial and accounting matters regarding whether (a) at June 25, 19X6, there was any change in the capital stock, any increase in long-term debt, or any decreases in consolidated net current assets or stockholders' equity of the consolidated companies as compared with amounts shown on the March 31, 19X6, unaudited condensed consolidated balance sheet included in the registration statement or (b) for the period from April 1, 19X6, to June 25, 19X6, there were any decreases, as compared with the corresponding period in the preceding year, in consolidated net sales or in the total or per share amounts of income before extraordinary items or of net income. On the basis of these inquiries and our reading of the minutes as described in [cite paragraph number], nothing came to our attention that caused us to believe that there was any such change, increase, or decrease, except in all instances for changes, increases, or decreases that the registration statement discloses have occurred or may occur.

Tables, Statistics, and Other Financial Information.   The underwriting agreement may call for a comfort letter that includes comments on tables, statistics, and other financial information appearing in the registration statement. Accountants should refrain from commenting on matters to which their competence as independent accountants has little relevance. It is appropriate for an accountant to comment on information expressed in dollars or in percentages derived from dollar amounts and on other quantitative information obtained from accounting records by analysis or computation. Accountants should not comment on matters involving the exercise of management judgment, like explanations of the reasons for changes in income or operating ratios. Nor should they comment on matters that are not subject to internal control structure policies and procedures, like square footage of facilities and backlog information. As with all other comments, the procedures followed by accountants in support of comments on tables, statistics, and other financial information should be set out clearly in the letter and agreed on in advance. They should also be accompanied by a disclaimer of responsibility for their sufficiency.

The expression "present fairly" should not be used in comments concerning tables, statistics, and other financial information. As discussed more fully in Chapter 22 of the main volume, "present fairly" is meaningful only in relation to a specific frame of reference which, for an accountant, usually is conformity with generally accepted accounting principles. Without that qualifying phrase, "present fairly" is too broad and imprecise and is likely to give rise to misunderstandings.

The comfort letter should state that the accountants make no representations regarding any matter of legal interpretation. Since accountants are not in a position to make any representations about the completeness or adequacy of disclosure or about the adequacy of procedures followed, the letter should so state.

Accountants may comment as to whether certain financial information is in conformity with the disclosure requirements of Regulation S-K if certain conditions are met. They are limited, however, to giving negative assurance or reporting procedures and findings, since this information is not given in the form of financial statements and generally has not been audited.

Concluding Paragraph.   To avoid the possibility of misunderstanding about the purpose and intended use of the comfort letter, it is customary to conclude the letter with a paragraph along the following lines:

> This letter is solely for the information of the addressees and to assist the underwriters in conducting and documenting their investigation of the affairs of the company in connection with the offering of the securities covered by the registration statement, and it is not to be used, circulated, quoted, or otherwise referred to within or without the underwriting group for any other purpose, including, but not limited to, the registration, purchase, or sale of securities, nor is it to be filed with or referred to in whole or in part in the registration statement or any other document, except that reference may be made to it in the underwriting agreement or in any list of closing documents pertaining to the offering of the securities covered by the registration statement.

Subsequently Discovered Matters

When matters that may require mention in the final comfort letter were not mentioned in the draft letter furnished to the underwriter, the accountants should discuss them with the client to consider whether disclosure should be made in the registration statement. If disclosure is not made, the accountants should inform the client that the matters will be mentioned in the comfort letter and should suggest that the underwriter be informed promptly. It is recommended that the accountants be present when the client and the underwriter discuss such matters.

24

Attestation Engagements

ATTESTATION STANDARDS

Interpretations of Attestation Standards

* **p. 728.** *Replace first sentence with:*
Three interpretations of the attestation standards have been issued that indicate how the standards may be used, and a fourth is under development.

p. 728. *Add after second bulleted paragraph:*

- *Applicability of Attestation Standards to Litigation Services* (AT Section 9100.47-.55), issued in July 1990, clarifies that the attestation standards apply to only those litigation services in which the practitioner (1) expresses a written conclusion about the reliability of a written assertion that is the responsibility of another party and the conclusion and assertion are for the use of others who, under the rules of the proceeding, will not be able to analyze and challenge the practitioner's work, or (2) is specifically engaged, in connection with litigation services, to perform work in accordance with the attestation standards.

Paragraph 2.f of Section 100 of Statement on Standards for Attestation Engagements (SSAE) No. 1 (AT Section 100.02f) provides the following examples of litigation services that are not attest engagements: "engagements in which a practitioner is engaged to testify as an expert witness in accounting, auditing, taxation, or other matters, given certain stipulated facts." The July 1990 interpretation clarifies the meaning of the term "stipulated facts" to mean facts or assumptions specified by one or more parties to a dispute as forming the basis for the development of an expert opinion.

In addition, the interpretation clarifies a previous interpretation (*Responding to Requests for Reports on Matters Relating to Solvency;* AT Section 9100.28-.41) that prohibits accountants, when reporting on an examination, review, or agreed-upon procedures engagement, from providing assurance on matters relating to solvency. The July 1990 interpretation specifies that a practitioner may provide an expert opinion or consulting advice about matters relating to solvency, in connection with formal legal or regulatory proceedings. The rationale given in the interpretation for allowing expert testimony concerning solvency is that "as a part of the legal or regulatory proceedings, each party to the dispute has the opportunity to analyze and challenge the legal definition and interpretation of the matters relating to solvency and the criteria the practitioner uses to evaluate matters related to solvency." This is the same reason stated in Section 200 of SSAE No. 1 (AT Section 200) for excluding from its provisions engagements involving prospective financial statements used solely in connection with litigation support services.

* An interpretation of the attestation standards relating to management's discussion and analysis of financial condition and results of operations (MD&A) is being developed at the time of this writing. In February 1987, an exposure draft of an attestation standard on MD&A was issued, containing guidance for examining and reporting on MD&A, including descriptions and examples of procedures to be followed. Because of time constraints and other commitments, the Auditing Standards Board (ASB) decided to defer discussions. The staff of the AICPA's Auditing Standards Division has now proposed that the exposure draft be incorporated, with some modifications, into an interpretation of the attestation standards.

* ## REPORTING ON AN ENTITY'S INTERNAL CONTROL STRUCTURE OVER FINANCIAL REPORTING (NEW)

In June 1993, the ASB issued SSAE No. 2, *Reporting on an Entity's Internal Control Structure Over Financial Reporting* (AT Section 400). It provides guidance to a practitioner in examining and reporting on management's written assertion about the effectiveness of an entity's internal control structure over financial reporting. The SSAE also permits a practitioner to perform agreed-upon procedures relating to that assertion, but it does not permit accepting an engagement to review and report on that assertion. SSAE No. 2 supersedes SAS No. 30, *Reporting on Internal Accounting Control.*

Attestation Procedures in Examination Engagements

To express an opinion on management's assertion, the practitioner should obtain an understanding of the internal control structure and accumulate sufficient evidence about its design and operating effectiveness. When evaluating the design effectiveness of specific control structure policies and procedures, the practitioner should consider whether a policy or procedure is suitably designed to prevent or detect material misstatements on a timely basis. When evaluating operating effectiveness, the practitioner should consider how the policy or procedure was applied, the consistency with which it was applied, and by whom it was applied.

The nature and extent of the attestation procedures will vary from entity to entity and be influenced by factors such as the extent of monitoring performed by the entity's internal auditors and the appropriateness of the available documentation of the internal control structure policies and procedures.

Management may perform tests of the operating effectiveness of certain internal control structure policies and procedures and provide the results to the practitioner. Although the practitioner should consider the results of such tests, evidence obtained through personal knowledge, observation, reperformance, and inspection is more persuasive than information obtained indirectly, such as from management.

For a practitioner to examine and report on management's assertion for general distribution, the assertion must be based on reasonable criteria against which it can be evaluated. (SSAE No. 2 notes that the COSO Report, discussed in Chapter 7 of this Supplement, provides reasonable criteria.) If the assertion is based on criteria established by a regulatory agency that has not followed due process procedures, a general distribution report cannot be issued.

Reporting on Examination Engagements

The practitioner is not permitted to report directly on the entity's internal control structure; the report is on management's assertion about the internal control structure. The assertion may be in either a separate report that will accompany the practitioner's report or a representation letter to the practitioner. The practitioner's report must be restricted to management and other specified parties if the assertion is presented only in a representation letter. Management's assertion may be as of a point in time or apply to a period of time, although the guidance in the SSAE is geared to point-in-time reporting.

An example of a report by management that contains an assertion about an enterprise's internal control structure at a point in time, based on the COSO Report, *Internal Control—Integrated Framework,* follows:

Report on Internal Control System

XYZ Company maintains a system of internal control over financial reporting, which is designed to provide reasonable assurance to the Company's management and board of directors regarding the preparation of reliable published financial statements. The system contains self-monitoring mechanisms, and actions are taken to correct deficiencies as they are identified. Even an effective internal control system, no matter how well designed, has inherent limitations—including the possibility of the circumvention or overriding of controls—and therefore can provide only reasonable assurance with respect to financial statement preparation. Further, because of changes in conditions, internal control system effectiveness may vary over time.

The Company assessed its internal control system as of December 31, 19XX in relation to criteria for effective internal control over financial reporting described in *Internal Control—Integrated Framework* issued by the Committee of Sponsoring Organizations of the Treadway Commission. Based on this assessment, the Company believes that, as of December 31, 19XX, its system of internal control over financial reporting met those criteria.

A practitioner's attestation report on the assertion in the above management report might read as follows:

Independent Accountant's Report

We have examined management's assertion that XYZ Company's system of internal control over financial reporting as of December 31, 19XX included in the accompanying Report on Internal Control System met the criteria for effectiveness described in *Internal Control—Integrated Framework* issued by the Committee of Sponsoring Organizations of the Treadway Commission.

Our examination was made in accordance with standards established by the American Institute of Certified Public Accountants and, accordingly, included obtaining an understanding of the system of internal control over financial reporting, testing, and evaluating the design and operating effectiveness of the internal control system, and such other procedures as we considered necessary in the circumstances. We believe that our examination provides a reasonable basis for our opinion.

Because of inherent limitations in any system of internal control, errors or irregularities may occur and not be detected. Also, projections of any evaluation of the internal control system over financial reporting to future periods are subject to the risk that the internal control system may become inadequate because of changes in conditions, or that the degree of compliance with the policies or procedures may deteriorate.

In our opinion, management's assertion that XYZ Company's system of internal control over financial reporting as of December 31, 19XX met the criteria for effectiveness described in *Internal Control—Integrated Framework* issued by the Committee of Sponsoring Organizations of the Treadway Commission is fairly stated, in all material respects.

Another way that management might express its assertion about the enterprise's internal control structure is implicit in SSAE No. 2. Under this alternative, the last sentence of management's report might state, "The Company believes that, based on those criteria, it maintained an effective system of internal control over financial reporting as of December 31, 19XX."

The practitioner's report on this alternative might read as follows:

Independent Accountant's Report

We have examined management's assertion that XYZ Company maintained an effective system of internal control over financial reporting as of December 31, 19XX included in the accompanying Report on Internal Control System.

[*Standard scope and inherent limitations paragraphs*]

In our opinion, management's assertion that XYZ Company maintained an effective system of internal control over financial reporting as of December 31, 19XX is fairly stated, in all material respects, based upon criteria for effective internal control over financial reporting described in *Internal Control—Integrated Framework* issued by the Committee of Sponsoring Organizations of the Treadway Commission.

Agreed-Upon Procedures Engagements

A practitioner may be engaged, under SSAE No. 2, to perform agreed-upon procedures on (a) management's assertion about the effectiveness of an entity's internal control structure or (b) *part* of an entity's existing or proposed control structure. (The latter situation is the only one in which an assertion from management is not required by this SSAE.) For example, the practitioner may provide management with a report on procedures and findings regarding the internal control procedures over the design of a new accounts receivable system. The practitioner's report must be restricted to management and other specified parties. SSAE No. 2 states that a practitioner performing agreed-upon procedures on an entity's internal control structure should not express negative assurance either on management's assertion about the effectiveness of the control structure or on the effectiveness of the control structure or any part of it. (This is in contrast to Section 100 of SSAE No. 1, which permits negative assurance to be expressed based on agreed-upon procedures, as discussed on page 727 of the main volume.)

Material Weakness

The existence of a material weakness would preclude an assertion that the internal control structure is effective. ("Material weakness" is defined by SAS No. 60, *Communication of Internal Control Structure Related Matters Noted in an Audit* (AU Section 325), as "a condition in which the design or operation of one or more of the internal control structure elements does not reduce to a relatively low level the risk that errors or irregularities in amounts that would be material in relation to the financial statements may occur and not be detected within a timely period by employees in the normal course of performing their assigned functions."

If a material weakness in the internal control structure exists, and management appropriately modifies its assertion in light of that weakness, the opinion paragraph of the attestation report should include a reference to the material weakness mentioned in the assertion and an explanatory paragraph should be added following the opinion paragraph describing the weakness. If management disagrees with the practitioner about the existence of a material weakness, and does not include a discussion of the material weakness in its assertion and appropriately modify the assertion as to effectiveness, the practitioner must issue an adverse opinion on management's assertion.

* COMPLIANCE ATTESTATION (NEW)

In early 1993, the ASB exposed a proposed SSAE, *Compliance Attestation*, for comment. The ASB developed the proposed SSAE because it recognized a growing need for broadly applicable guidance on attesting to assertions about entities' compliance with specified requirements of laws and regulations. The ASB's objective in promulgating a "generic" attestation statement on compliance was to preclude the need for separate statements covering individual laws and regulatory requirements. The proposed SSAE provides guidance to a practitioner who is engaged to report on management's assertion about either an entity's compliance with specified requirements or the effectiveness of an entity's internal control structure over compliance with specified requirements. The specified requirements may be either financial or operational in nature.

Specifically, the proposed SSAE provides guidance to assist the practitioner in

- Accepting either an agreed-upon procedures or an examination engagement;
- Planning the engagement;
- Obtaining an understanding of the internal control structure relating to compliance with specified requirements in an examination engagement;
- Testing the entity's compliance with specified requirements; and
- Reporting on management's assertion.

The proposed SSAE would provide immediate guidance to auditors of insured depository institutions who perform agreed-upon procedures to test compliance with specified safety and soundness laws, as required by the FDIC Improvement Act of 1991 (FDICIA). (The FDICIA regulations were finalized in May 1993 and are discussed in Chapter 26 of this Supplement.)

Agreed-Upon Procedures Engagements

Under the proposed SSAE, although the practitioner would be required to perform only those procedures that had been agreed to by the users of the report, the practitioner should obtain an understanding of the specified compliance requirements and should plan the engagement in accordance with Section 100 of SSAE No. 1, prior to performing those procedures.

The practitioner's report should enumerate procedures and findings and should not provide negative assurance about whether management's assertion is fairly stated. The report must be restricted to only management and other specified parties.

Use of Internal Audit.   The issue of whether the practitioner may use the work of internal auditors in an agreed-upon procedures engagement is currently under consideration by a task force established by the ASB. An agreement has been reached between the ASB and the FDIC regarding agreed-upon procedures engagements in connection with FDICIA. According to the agreement, internal auditors of financial institutions meeting specified size criteria may perform the agreed-upon procedures; the practitioner is then required to perform four specified procedures on the internal auditors' working papers and to perform the agreed-upon procedures on a smaller sample of items than would otherwise be tested for compliance with the relevant laws.

Examination Engagements

Under the proposed SSAE, management could present its assertion in a separate report to accompany the practitioner's report or only in a representation letter to the practitioner. If management presented its assertion only in a representation letter, the practitioner should modify the report to include management's assertion and add a paragraph that limits the distribution of the report to specified parties.

If the examination disclosed material noncompliance with the specified requirements and management disclosed the noncompliance and appropriately modified its assertion, the practitioner should refer to the noncompliance in the opinion paragraph and add an explanatory paragraph after the opinion paragraph. If management did not disclose the material noncompliance and modify its assertion, the practitioner should express either a qualified or an adverse opinion on management's assertion, depending on the materiality of the noncompliance.

PROSPECTIVE FINANCIAL INFORMATION

* **p. 734.** *Add after third bullet:*

- SOP 92-2, *Questions and Answers on the Term* Reasonably Objective Basis *and Other Issues Affecting Prospective Financial Statements.* The SOP was issued to clarify and expand on areas where guidance in the AICPA guide is limited. The SOP discusses how the responsible party evaluates whether a reasonably objective basis exists for presenting a financial forecast and provides guidance regarding the practitioner's consideration of whether the responsible party has such a basis. The SOP also discusses the need for certain disclosures about the effects of anticipated events and circumstances beyond the forecast period and the practitioner's consideration of the length of the forecast period. (On the latter issue, the SOP indicates that it would ordinarily be difficult to establish a reasonably objective basis for financial forecasts extending beyond three to five years.)

pp. 742–744. *Replace section* **Prospective Financial Statements for Internal Use Only and Partial Presentations** *with:*

Prospective Financial Statements for Internal Use Only and Partial Presentations

In 1990, the AICPA issued SOP 90-1, *Accountants' Services on Prospective Financial Statements for Internal Use Only and Partial Presentations.* Guidance included in Part I of the SOP, entitled "Guidance on the Accountant's Services and Reports on Prospective Financial Statements for Internal Use Only," replaces section 900 of the AICPA *Guide for Prospective Financial Statements;* Part II, entitled "Partial Presentations of Prospective Financial Information," replaces guide section 1000.[4.1]

Internal Use Only. A practitioner may be engaged to provide services on prospective financial statements that are restricted to internal use only. Examples are giving advice and assistance to a client on the tax consequences of future

---

[4.1] Guide sections 900 and 1000 were rendered obsolete by the adoption of the AICPA Code of Professional Conduct in 1988.

actions or on deciding whether to buy or lease an asset. In obtaining satisfaction that the prospective financial statements will be restricted to internal use, absent contrary information, the practitioner may rely on either the written or oral representation of the responsible party.

The SOP provides the following guidance for determining whether prospective financial statements are considered internal use only:

> In deciding whether a potential use is *internal use,* the accountant should consider the degree of consistency of interest between the responsible party and the user regarding the forecast [or projection]. If their interests are substantially consistent (for example, both the responsible party and the user are employees of the entity about which the forecast [or projection] is made), the use would be deemed internal use. On the other hand, where the interest[s] of the responsible party and the user are potentially inconsistent (for example, the responsible party is a nonowner manager and the user is an absentee owner), the use would not be deemed internal use. In some cases, this determination will require the exercise of considerable professional judgment. (ftn. 1 to para. 1)

The practitioner may perform services or procedures other than a compilation, examination, or agreed-upon procedures, such as merely assembling the statements, tailored to the particular engagement circumstances. The SOP does not require the practitioner to report on such "other" services performed on prospective financial statements for internal use only. For example, a practitioner may submit computer-generated prospective financial statements without reporting on them, provided the statements are restricted to internal use only.

A practitioner may, however, elect to issue a report on other services performed on prospective financial statements for internal use only, provided the statements include a summary of significant assumptions. Such a report typically would

- Be addressed to the responsible party.
- Identify the statements being reported on.
- Describe the work performed and the degree of responsibility taken with respect to the prospective financial statements.
- Include a caveat that the prospective results may not be achieved.
- Indicate the restrictions as to the distribution of the prospective financial statements and report.
- Be dated as of the date of the completion of the procedures.

In addition, the practitioner's report on a financial projection for internal use only preferably would describe the limitations on the usefulness of the presentation.

An illustrative report follows that is appropriate for use when a practitioner has assembled a financial projection for internal use only:

> We have assembled, from information provided by management, the accompanying projected balance sheet and the related projected statements of income, retained earnings, and cash flows of XYZ Company as of December 31, 19XX, and for the year then ending. (This financial projection omits the summary of significant accounting

policies.)ᵃ The accompanying projection and this report were prepared for [state special purpose, for example, "presentation to the Board of Directors of XYZ Company for its consideration as to whether to add a third operating shift"] and should not be used for any other purpose. We have not compiled or examined the financial projection and express no assurance of any kind on it. Further, even if [state hypothetical assumption, for example, "the third operating shift is added"] there will usually be differences between the projected and actual results, because events and circumstances frequently do not occur as expected, and those differences may be material. In accordance with the terms of our engagement, this report and the accompanying projection are restricted to internal use and may not be shown to any third party for any purpose.

ᵃThis sentence would be included, if applicable.

When prospective financial statements intended for internal use only are accompanied by a practitioner's written communication (for example, a transmittal letter), the communication should state that the prospective results may not be achieved and that the statements are for internal use only.

Partial Presentations. A partial presentation is a presentation of prospective financial information that excludes one or more of the items required to be included in prospective financial statements, as described on page 736 in the main volume. A partial presentation may include either forecasted or projected information and may be either extracted from a presentation of prospective financial statements or prepared specifically as a partial presentation. The following are examples of partial presentations:

- Sales forecasts.
- Presentations of forecasted or projected capital expenditure programs.
- Other presentations of specified elements, accounts, or items of prospective financial statements (for example, projected production costs) that might be part of the development of a full presentation of prospective financial statements.
- Forecasts that present operating income, but not net income.
- Projections of taxable income or forecasted tax returns that do not show significant changes in financial position.
- Presentations that provide enough information to be translated into elements, accounts, or items of a financial forecast or projection. Examples include a forecast of sales units and unit selling prices, or a forecast of occupancy percentage, number of rooms, and average rates.

Uses of Partial Presentations.   Partial presentations may be appropriate in many "limited use" circumstances. For example, in analyzing whether to lease or buy a piece of equipment, or in evaluating the income tax implications of a given election, it may be necessary to assess the impact of a decision on one aspect of financial results rather than on the financial statements taken as a whole. Partial presentations are not ordinarily appropriate for general use. That is, a partial presentation ordinarily should not be distributed to third parties who will not be negotiating directly with the responsible party.

Preparation and Presentation.   Much of the discussion of the preparation and presentation of prospective financial statements generally, as contained in Chapter 24 of the main volume, is also applicable to partial presentations. The SOP provides guidance on certain matters relating specifically to partial presentations, as follows:

a. If a partial presentation is prepared but full prospective financial statements are not, the responsible party should consider key factors affecting elements, accounts, or items of prospective financial statements that are interrelated with those presented.

b. Titles of partial presentations should be descriptive of the presentation, state whether the presentation is of forecasted or projected information, and disclose the limited nature of the presentation.

c. Relevant accounting principles and policies should be disclosed.

d. The concept of materiality should be related to the partial presentation taken as a whole.

e. Significant assumptions, such as those having a reasonable possibility of a variation that may significantly affect the prospective results, should be disclosed.

f. The introduction preceding the summary of assumptions should include a description of the purpose of the presentation and any limitations on the usefulness of the presentation.

Services Relating to Partial Presentations.   A practitioner may compile, examine, or apply agreed-upon procedures to a partial presentation.

The nature and scope of procedures for examinations and compilations of prospective financial statements, described in Chapter 24 of the main volume, generally are also applicable to partial presentations. Because of the limited nature of partial presentations, however, the practitioner may need to tailor the procedures. For instance, he or she may need to consider the impact that key factors affecting elements, accounts, or items that are not included in the presentation may have on elements, accounts, or items that are included, such as considering productive capacity in a sales forecast.

Applying agreed-upon procedures to partial presentations is similar to performing that service for full prospective financial statements (see Chapter 24 of the main volume).

The discussion of prospective financial statements for internal use only earlier in this chapter of the Supplement applies also to partial presentations that are restricted to internal use only.

Reporting.   Reporting on partial presentations (both standard and modified reports) generally follows the same form as for full prospective financial statements. SOP 90-1 presents illustrative standard reports for an examination of forecasted data, a compilation of forecasted data, and an engagement to apply agreed-upon procedures to forecasted data. Those reports are reproduced next.

Examination Report on a Partial Presentation
of Forecasted Information

We have examined the accompanying forecasted statement of net operating income before debt service, depreciation, and income taxes of the AAA Hotel for the year ending December 31, 19X1 (the forecasted statement). Our examination was made in accordance with standards established by the American Institute of Certified Public Accountants and, accordingly, included such procedures as we considered necessary to evaluate both the assumptions used by management and the preparation and presentation of the forecasted statement.

The accompanying forecasted statement presents, to the best of management's knowledge and belief, the expected net operating income before debt service, depreciation, and income taxes of AAA Hotel for the forecast period. It is not intended to be a forecast of financial position, results of operations, or cash flows. The accompanying forecasted statement and this report were prepared for ABC Bank for the purpose of negotiating a proposed construction loan to be used to finance expansion of the hotel and should not be used for any other purpose.

In our opinion, the forecasted statement referred to above is presented in conformity with the guidelines for presentation of forecasted information established by the American Institute of Certified Public Accountants, and the underlying assumptions provide a reasonable basis for management's forecasted statement. However, there will usually be differences between forecasted and actual results because events and circumstances frequently do not occur as expected, and those differences may be material. We have no responsibility to update this report for events and circumstances occurring after the date of this report.

Compilation Report on a Partial
Presentation of Forecasted Information

We have compiled the accompanying forecasted statement of net operating income before debt service, depreciation, and income taxes of AAA Hotel for the year ending December 31, 19X1 (the forecasted statement) in accordance with guidelines established by the American Institute of Certified Public Accountants.

The accompanying forecasted statement presents, to the best of management's knowledge and belief, the net operating income before debt service, depreciation, and income taxes of AAA Hotel for the forecast period. It is not intended to be a forecast of financial position, results of operations, or cash flows. The accompanying forecasted statement and this report were prepared for the ABC Bank for the purpose of negotiating a proposed construction loan to be used to finance expansion of the hotel and should not be used for any other purpose.

A compilation is limited to presenting forecasted information that is the representation of management and does not include evaluation of the support for the assumptions underlying such information. We have not examined the forecasted statement and, accordingly, do not express an opinion or any other form of assurance on the accompanying statement of assumptions. Furthermore, there will usually be differences between forecasted and actual results because events and circumstances frequently do not occur as expected, and those differences may be material. We have no responsibility to update this report for events and circumstances occurring after the date of this report.

Agreed-Upon Procedures Report on a
Partial Presentation of Forecasted Information

At your request, we have performed certain agreed-upon procedures, as enumerated below, with respect to the sales forecast of XYZ Company for the year ending December 31, 19X1. These procedures, which were specified by the Boards of Directors of XYZ Company and ABC Corporation, were performed solely to assist you, and this report is solely for your information and should not be used by those who did not participate in determining the procedures.

a. We assisted the management of XYZ Company in assembling the sales forecast.
b. We read the sales forecast for compliance in regard to format with the AICPA presentation guidelines for a partial presentation of forecasted information.
c. We tested the sales forecast for mathematical accuracy.

Because the procedures described above do not constitute an examination of a presentation of forecasted information in accordance with standards established by the American Institute of Certified Public Accountants, we do not express an opinion on whether the sales forecast is presented in conformity with AICPA presentation guidelines or on whether the underlying assumptions provide a reasonable basis for the presentation.

In connection with the procedures referred to above, no matters came to our attention that caused us to believe that the format of the sales forecast should be modified or that the presentation is mathematically inaccurate. Had we performed additional procedures or had we made an examination of the sales forecast in accordance with standards established by the American Institute of Certified Public Accountants, matters might have come to our attention that would have been reported to you. Furthermore, there will usually be differences between forecasted and actual results because events and circumstances frequently do not occur as expected, and those differences may be material. We have no responsibility to update this report for events and circumstances occurring after the date of this report.

25

Compliance Auditing

* **p. 746.** *Add at top of page:*

Note: A number of pronouncements affecting the topics covered in Chapter 25 have been revised or issued, by both government agencies and the profession, since the main volume of this book was written. Among them are

- Office of Management and Budget (OMB) Circular A-133, "Audits of Higher Education and Other Nonprofit Agencies," and draft of a related *Compliance Supplement.*
- Revisions to the *Compliance Supplement* to OMB Circular A-128, "Audits of State and Local Governments."
- SAS No. 68, *Compliance Auditing Applicable to Governmental Entities and Other Recipients of Governmental Financial Assistance,* which supersedes SAS No. 63.
- SOP 92-7, *Audits of State and Local Governmental Entities Receiving Federal Financial Assistance.*
- SOP 92-9, *Audits of Not-for-Profit Organizations Receiving Federal Awards.*
- Exposure draft of a proposed SOP, *Compliance and Internal Control Auditing for Student Financial Assistance Programs Using Service Organizations.*
- Notice to Practitioners—Audits Conducted in Accordance with HUD Audit Guide.

The following material incorporates significant aspects of those pronouncements.

SPECIAL CONSIDERATIONS IN PLANNING
A GOVERNMENTAL AUDIT

* **p. 749.** *Add after first full paragraph:*

In December 1991, the Auditing Standards Board issued SAS No. 68, *Compliance Auditing Applicable to Governmental Entities and Other Recipients of Governmental Financial Assistance* (AU Section 801), which superseded SAS No. 63. SAS No. 68 incorporates the requirements of both professional standards and regulations issued subsequent to SAS No. 63 relating to audits of certain nonprofit organizations receiving federal grants. It also clarifies certain issues related to auditing under the Single Audit Act, most notably, that a report on the "general requirements" is required even if there are no "major programs." Those changes are discussed in more detail later in this chapter of the Supplement.

In addition, SAS No. 68 requires the auditor to communicate to management or the audit committee if the auditor became aware during an audit that the entity was subject to a legal, regulatory, or contractual audit requirement that was not covered by the terms of the engagement. For example, if the auditor was engaged only to conduct an audit in accordance with generally accepted auditing standards and became aware that the entity was also subject to the provisions of government auditing standards, that fact should be communicated to the entity.

GOVERNMENT AUDITING STANDARDS

* **p. 749.** *Add after first paragraph in section:*

In July 1993, the GAO exposed for comment a draft of a major revision of *Government Auditing Standards*. The GAO expects the revision to become effective for audits under GAGAS for periods ending on or after December 31, 1994.

* **p. 755.** *Replace from last paragraph through end of chapter with:*

SAS No. 60 (AU Section 325.17) specifically prohibits the auditor from issuing a written report representing that no reportable conditions were noted during an audit. Therefore, if no reportable conditions were noted, the paragraphs of the report on the internal control structure illustrated on page 755 of the main volume that describe reportable conditions and material weaknesses would be replaced by the following paragraph (SAS No. 68, para. 42):

> Our consideration of the internal control structure would not necessarily disclose all matters in the internal control structure that might be material weaknesses under standards established by the American Institute of Certified Public Accountants. A material weakness is a condition in which the design or operation of one or more of the specific internal control structure elements does not reduce to a relatively low level the risk that errors or irregularities in amounts that would be material in relation to the financial statements being audited may occur and not be detected within a timely period by employees in the normal course of performing their assigned functions. We noted no matters involving the internal control structure and its operation that we consider to be material weaknesses as defined above.

However, we noted certain matters involving the internal control structure and its operation that we have reported to the management of [name of entity] in a separate letter dated August 15, 19X1.

No mention is made of reportable conditions. The report refers only to the fact that no matters involving the internal control structure and its operation were noted that the auditor considered to be material weaknesses. This language both satisfies GAGAS and is permissible under SAS No. 60.

Reporting on Audits of HUD Programs (New).   At the time of this writing, the U.S. Department of Housing and Urban Development's Office of Inspector General is in the process of revising its October 1991 *Consolidated Audit Guide for Audits of HUD Programs* to give effect to changes in program regulations and experience in implementing the guide. In the meantime, the AICPA Auditing Standards Division has provided guidance on reporting on audits conducted in accordance with the present guide for entities not subject to the requirements of OMB Circulars A-128 or A-133. This guidance was published in the form of a Notice to Practitioners. (The notice also withdrew SOP 90-4, *Auditors' Reports Under U.S. Department of Housing and Urban Development's Audit Guide for Mortgagors Having HUD Insured or Secretary Held Multifamily Mortgages.*)

The Notice to Practitioners indicates that a separate report on the procedures performed to test compliance with the "common" requirements (i.e., cash management and federal financial reports, which are two of the general requirements applicable to federal financial assistance programs discussed later in this chapter) and with the "specific" requirements related to civil rights (i.e., marketing and nondiscrimination) should be issued, providing positive assurance on matters tested and negative assurance with respect to items not tested. Reporting on compliance with "specific" requirements, other than those related to civil rights, should be in a manner similar to reporting for major programs and nonmajor programs; illustrative audit reports in SOP 92-7 (discussed later) may be adapted for this purpose.

SINGLE AUDIT ACT

Background

Before the enactment of the Single Audit Act of 1984 (the Act), a federal agency that issued a grant to a state or local government had the authority to establish its own audit guidelines. There was no oversight body or any other means of controlling the scope or number of audits required for a particular agency or other entity receiving federal financial assistance. Often the federal assistance came from several different federal agencies. As a result, the same internal control procedures and transactions often were tested more than once, frequently by different independent auditors, and sometimes even simultaneously. These duplicative audits caused organizational inefficiencies and led to increased audit costs.

The Single Audit Act created a single, coordinated audit (often called a "single audit," "organization-wide audit," or "entity-wide audit") of all federal financial assistance provided to a recipient agency during a fiscal year. The Act emphasizes audits of those federal financial assistance programs that the federal government has defined as major, as discussed later. The objectives of the Act are to

- Promote the efficient and effective use of audit resources.
- Improve state and local governments' financial management of federal financial assistance programs through more effective auditing.
- Establish uniform requirements for audits of federal financial assistance provided to state and local governments.
- Ensure that federal departments and agencies, to the greatest extent practicable, are audited in accordance with the requirements of the Single Audit Act.

The Office of Management and Budget is responsible for setting policies regarding the frequency and scope of audits required for federal agencies to meet government auditing standards. In 1985, the OMB issued Circular A-128, "Audits of State and Local Governments," to facilitate the implementation of the Single Audit Act. Together, Circular A-128 and the Act require (1) an audit of the entity's general-purpose or basic financial statements, (2) the performance of additional audit tests for compliance with applicable laws and regulations related to grants received, and (3) tests of control structure policies and procedures designed to ensure compliance with laws and regulations of applicable federal financial assistance programs. In addition, Circular A-128 prescribes the responsibilities for monitoring those requirements.

In 1976, the Office of Management and Budget (OMB) issued Circular A-110, which set forth audit requirements for institutions of higher education, hospitals, and other nonprofit organizations receiving federal grants. However, the audit requirements were not clear and were often misunderstood. In 1990, the OMB issued Circular A-133, "Audits of Higher Education and Other Nonprofit Agencies," which extends to colleges and universities (discussed in Chapter 27) and to nonprofit agencies receiving federal financial assistance, requirements similar to those in Circular A-128. Clarification and guidance on audits of not-for-profit organizations performed under A-133 are provided in *Q and A on OMB Circular A-133*, published by the Government Printing Office. Hospitals, other than those associated with a university, are specifically excluded from Circular A-133.

While the provisions of Circular A-133 are similar to those of A-128, there are some significant differences.

- The definition of a "major" program (discussed below) is different under A-133 than under A-128 (the larger of 3% of total federal expenditures or $100,000 under A-133 vs. the larger of 3% of total federal expenditures or $300,000 under A-128).
- Unlike A-128, A-133 does not require the auditor to describe instances of immaterial noncompliance in the audit reports; such instances are required to be communicated separately to the institution in writing.
- A-133 permits a "coordinated audit approach," which is described as one in which the different auditors performing auditing procedures at an institution

consider each others' work in determining the scope of their work. Although the coordinated audit approach contemplates different auditors providing the various reports required under A-133, it is not intended to preclude a single independent auditor from meeting the objectives and reporting requirements of A-133.

Applicability of the Single Audit Act

The requirements of the Act apply to each state and local government that receives a total amount of federal financial assistance of $100,000 or more in a fiscal year. A government that receives $25,000 or more, but less than $100,000 in any fiscal year, may elect to implement the Single Audit Act requirements in lieu of the separate financial and compliance audit requirements of the various applicable federal financial assistance programs. Governments receiving less than $25,000 in any fiscal year are exempt from the requirements of the Act, as well as all other federal audit requirements.

Certain not-for-profit organizations that are primary recipients of assistance from federal agencies may be required by a state or local government to be audited in accordance with the Act. These single audits are performed by state or local governmental auditors or public accountants who meet the Yellow Book's independence and qualification standards.

Auditing Compliance with Specific Requirements of Major Federal Financial Assistance Programs

Under the Single Audit Act, the auditor must report on whether the entity has complied with laws and regulations that have a material effect on each *major* federal financial assistance program. The Act defines a major federal financial assistance program based on the total expenditures of federal financial assistance during a program year. These major programs are listed in the *Catalog of Federal Domestic Assistance;* examples include the National School Lunch program and Headstart programs.

Management is responsible for identifying those federal financial assistance programs from which it receives funding. OMB Circular A-128 states

> In order to determine which major programs are to be tested for compliance, state and local governments shall identify in their accounts all federal funds received and expended and the programs under which they were received. This shall include funds received directly from federal agencies and through other state and local governments.

Circular A-133 contains a similar requirement.

On a single audit, it is the auditor's responsibility to test for compliance with the specific requirements of every applicable major federal financial assistance program. This is in addition to the GAGAS requirement to design tests to assess the risk that noncompliance with laws and regulations could have a direct and material effect on the financial statements. The Single Audit Act requirement is much more stringent; thus, after testing compliance with the requirements of the

Single Audit Act, the auditor may often consider that no further testing of compliance with laws and regulations is necessary to fulfill the GAGAS requirement.

The single audit must include the selection and testing of a representative number of charges from each major federal financial assistance program identified. The extent and selection of items to be tested depends on the auditor's professional judgment. For *all* major programs, Circulars A-128 and A-133 require the auditor to specifically consider

- *Types of Services Allowed*—Is the entity using financial assistance to purchase goods and services allowed by the program?
- *Eligibility*—Were the recipients of the goods and services eligible to receive them?
- *Matching Requirement*—Did the entity contribute the necessary amount from its own resources toward projects paid for with financial assistance?
- *Reporting*—Did the entity file all the reports required by the federal financial assistance program?
- *Special Tests and Provisions*—Could the federal financial assistance programs be materially affected by noncompliance with other federal provisions?

The details of these items vary with each federal financial assistance program. To help the auditor determine which federal compliance requirements should be tested, the OMB publishes the *Compliance Supplement for Single Audits of State and Local Governments* (the *Compliance Supplement*), which specifies program compliance requirements and suggests auditing procedures for the larger federal financial assistance programs. The *Compliance Supplement* also includes references to the *Code of Federal Regulations* and other applicable statutes. The auditor should consult this supplement when considering the nature, timing, and extent of procedures to perform as a basis for expressing an opinion on compliance.

In 1991, the OMB exposed for comment a draft of a *Compliance Supplement for Single Audits of Nonprofit Organizations*. This *Compliance Supplement* is intended to assist auditors in performing organization-wide audits of entities covered by the requirements of Circular A-133.

In addition to the specific requirements that recipient agencies must comply with and that the auditor must test, Circulars A-128 and A-133 require that independent auditors determine whether

- Financial reports and claims for advances and reimbursements contain information that is supported by the books and records used to prepare the basic financial statements.
- Amounts claimed or used for matching were determined in accordance with the particular grant requirements.

The Circulars require that the auditor's report on compliance (illustrated later in this chapter) specifically address the above requirements. In determining whether these requirements have been met, the auditor should consider the following, as appropriate, when testing charges to federal financial assistance programs:

- Are the charges necessary and reasonable for the proper administration of the program?
- Do the charges conform to any limitations or exclusions in the federal assistance agreement?
- Were the charges given consistent accounting treatment and applied uniformly to both federally assisted and other activities of the recipient?
- Were the charges net of applicable credits?
- Were only costs applicable to federal financial assistance programs charged to those programs?
- Were the charges properly recorded (that is, correct purpose, amount, date) and supported by source documentation?
- Were the charges approved in advance, if required?
- Were the charges incurred in accordance with competitive purchasing procedures, if required by the particular financial assistance program?
- Were the charges allocated equitably to the activities that benefited, including nonfederal activities?

Materiality Under the Single Audit Act

The concept of materiality for financial statements covered by the Act differs somewhat from that prescribed by GAAS. Under the Act, materiality is considered in relation to each major federal financial assistance program. Also, a material amount pertaining to one major program may not be considered material to another major program of a different size or nature.

Risk Assessment Under the Single Audit Act

Risk assessment in an audit performed under GAGAS is identical to that under GAAS. Under the Single Audit Act, however, the auditor has responsibilities over and above those of GAAS and GAGAS, namely, testing and reporting on the entity's compliance with the specific requirements of a particular program and the general requirements (discussed later) that apply to all programs. Thus, in assessing risk in a compliance audit of a major federal program, the auditor must also consider the risk that he or she may fail to appropriately modify his or her opinion on compliance with such a program. This risk has three aspects.

- Inherent risk—the risk that material noncompliance with requirements applicable to a major federal financial assistance program could occur assuming there were no related control structure policies or procedures.
- Control risk—the risk that material noncompliance that could occur in a major federal financial assistance program will not be prevented or detected on a timely basis by the entity's internal control structure policies and procedures.
- Detection risk—the risk that the auditor's procedures will lead him or her to conclude that noncompliance that could be material to a major federal

financial assistance program does not exist when in fact such noncompliance does exist.

The following paragraphs summarize the requirements of the Single Audit Act that pertain to each of the risk components, and explain how the requirements, taken together, provide a basis for the auditor's report on compliance.

Inherent Risk.   The auditor's assessment of inherent risk conditions is pervasive to the entire entity. In other words, the inherent risk conditions that exist would most likely affect both the entity's ability to record financial transactions and its compliance with laws and regulations. Therefore, a separate assessment for financial and compliance purposes may be unnecessary.

Control Risk.   Under the Single Audit Act the auditor is required to determine and report whether the government has internal control structure policies and procedures to provide reasonable assurance that it is managing federal financial assistance programs in compliance with applicable laws and regulations. SOP 92-7 elaborates on the tests that should be performed to make that determination. Paragraph 4.4 of the SOP states that the auditor should

a. Perform tests of controls to evaluate the effectiveness of the design and operation of the policies and procedures in preventing or detecting material noncompliance.
b. Examine the organization's control system for monitoring its subrecipients and obtaining and acting on subrecipients' audit reports.

The auditor should obtain a sufficient understanding of each of the three elements of the entity's control structure relating to major federal financial assistance programs to plan the audit of the entity's compliance with the requirements applicable to those programs. Control structure policies and procedures relating to those programs may be separate from policies and procedures applied to other transactions the entity enters into. For example, the policies and procedures in place to ensure eligibility might be totally separate from those relating to the processing of financial transactions. The auditor's understanding should include knowledge about relevant control environment factors and the design of policies, procedures, and records used in administering federal financial assistance programs and whether they have been placed in operation. The understanding should include knowledge about the design and extent of the supervisory control procedures in place to ensure that laws and regulations are being complied with. This understanding may be documented separately from the auditor's understanding of the overall control environment, the accounting system used to process financial transactions, and related control procedures.

The total amount of major federal financial assistance program expenditures may be less than 50 percent of the recipient organization's total federal financial assistance expenditures. In such circumstances, the auditor should extend the understanding to include the largest nonmajor programs so that at least 50 percent of federal financial assistance program expenditures are documented.

The auditor's understanding should be sufficient to enable him or her to

- Identify the types of potential material noncompliance.
- Consider matters that affect the risk of material noncompliance.
- Design effective tests of the entity's compliance with applicable requirements of major federal financial assistance programs.

Once the auditor has obtained the understanding of control structure policies and procedures relating to compliance, he or she should perform tests of controls, or consider tests of controls performed concurrently with obtaining the understanding, to determine whether the design and operation of relevant policies and procedures are effective for preventing or detecting material noncompliance. This assessment of control risk helps the auditor evaluate the risk that material noncompliance exists in a major federal financial assistance program.

Detection Risk.   OMB Circulars A-128 and A-133 require that in an audit of an entity that has major federal financial programs, a representative number of charges from each major program be selected for testing. The objective of these tests of compliance with requirements is to restrict detection risk. Just as in a financial statement audit, in a single audit the auditor determines how much substantive testing is necessary to reduce detection risk to an appropriately low level on the basis of the risk assessment activities. As the assessed level of control risk decreases, the acceptable level of detection risk increases.

General Requirements Applicable to Federal Financial Assistance Programs

The OMB *Compliance Supplement* identifies six general requirements that are applicable to all or most federal financial assistance programs. These requirements involve significant national policy, and failure to comply could have a material effect (though not necessarily a *direct* effect) on an organization's financial statements. The *Compliance Supplement* requires, as part of all audits of state and local governments that receive federal financial assistance, that compliance with applicable general requirements be tested, if failure to comply could materially affect the entity's financial statements. Therefore, where applicable, the auditor is required to perform tests that address compliance with these requirements.

- *Political Activity* (Hatch Act and Intergovernmental Personnel Act of 1970, as amended)—Federal funds cannot be used for political activity of any kind.
- *Construction Contracts* (Davis–Bacon Act)—Laborers and mechanics employed by contractors of federally funded projects must be paid wages not less than those established by the Secretary of Labor as the prevailing local wage rate.
- *Civil Rights*—No person shall be excluded from participation in, or be subjected to discrimination in connection with, a federally funded program because of race, color, national origin, sex, or physical impairment.

- *Cash Management*—Cash should be withdrawn only in amounts necessary to meet immediate needs or cover program disbursements.
- *Relocation Assistance and Real Property Acquisition*—Federally funded programs involving the acquisition of property must provide certain services for the households and businesses they displace.
- *Federal Financial Reports*—Specified financial reports must be periodically submitted.

Three additional general requirements have been added to the *Compliance Supplement* to A-128 and the draft *Compliance Supplement* to A-133, as follows:

- *Allowable Costs/Cost Principles*—A portion of operating costs may be charged to federal programs as indirect costs. To be eligible for reimbursement under those programs, indirect costs must be allocated in conformity with an indirect cost allocation plan prepared in accordance with OMB Circular A-87, "Cost Principles for State and Local Governments," OMB Circular A-21, "Cost Principles for Educational Institutions," or OMB Circular A-122, "Cost Principles for Nonprofit Organizations."
- *Drug-Free Workplace Act of 1988*—Regulations requiring grant recipients to certify that they have a drug-free workplace were issued by 35 federal agencies. The regulations apply to grants approved or awarded on or after March 18, 1989, and require that grantees
  - •• Publish a statement notifying employees that the illegal manufacturing, distribution, dispensation, possession, or use of a controlled substance is prohibited in the workplace.
  - •• Implement a drug-free awareness program to provide information on the availability of drug counseling and rehabilitation.
  - •• Notify the granting agency within ten days after receiving notice of an employee's conviction under any criminal anti-drug statute and impose a sanction on any employee convicted of such a crime.
- *Administrative Requirements*—Federal assistance programs, with certain exceptions, are subject to the provisions of "Uniform Administrative Requirements for Grants and Cooperative Agreements to State and Local Governments." The auditor should consider the administrative requirements related to the following:
  - •• Interest earned on advances
  - •• Period of availability of funds
  - •• Program income
  - •• Real property
  - •• Equipment
  - •• Supplies
  - •• Subawards to debarred and suspended parties
  - •• Procurement
  - •• Subgrants
  - •• Revolving fund payments.

Nonmajor Programs

The discussion of the Single Audit Act thus far has related to those programs defined as major federal financial assistance programs. Many state and local governments, however, receive some or all of their federal financial assistance from programs that do not meet the federal definition of major programs. These programs are referred to as nonmajor programs. The procedures required to be performed on nonmajor programs are substantially more limited in scope than those for major programs. As part of the audit of the financial statements or of considering the internal control structure, the auditor may have selected for testing some transactions from nonmajor programs; if so, he or she should test those transactions for compliance with the applicable requirements. The auditor is not required to address compliance with the specific requirements of other transactions from nonmajor programs.

SAS No. 68 cites, in paragraph 88, an example of the extent of testing necessary for a nonmajor program.

> If in the audit of the general-purpose or basic financial statements an auditor examined a payroll transaction that was charged to a nonmajor program, the auditor should determine that the position could reasonably be charged to that program and that the individual's salary was correctly charged to that program.

Reporting Under the Single Audit Act

The reporting requirements of the Single Audit Act are more extensive than those under GAAS and GAGAS. In addition to the report required by GAAS on the financial statements and the reports required by GAGAS on the internal control structure and on compliance with laws and regulations, the auditor performing a single audit must issue reports on

- The supplementary schedule of federal financial assistance (discussed below).
- Compliance with specific requirements applicable to major federal financial assistance programs.
- Compliance with requirements applicable to nonmajor federal financial assistance programs tested.
- Compliance with the general requirements applicable to federal financial assistance programs.
- The internal control structure used in administering federal financial assistance programs.

Report on Supplementary Schedule of Federal Financial Assistance.   OMB Circulars A-128 and A-133 require an auditor's report on the schedule of federal financial assistance program expenditures. This schedule must show the total expenditures for each federal financial assistance program as identified in the *Catalog of Federal Domestic Assistance.* The schedule of federal financial assistance is a type of additional information in an auditor-submitted document, as discussed in Chapter 23 of the main volume. The auditor's report on the schedule falls under the reporting guidelines of SAS No. 29, *Reporting on Information Accompanying the Basic Financial Statements in Auditor-Submitted Documents* (AU Section 551), and might read as follows:

> We have audited the general-purpose financial statements of the City of _____ for the year ended June 30, 19XX, and have issued our report thereon dated September 8, 19XX. These general-purpose financial statements are the responsibility of the City's management. Our responsibility is to express an opinion on these general-purpose financial statements based on our audit.
>
> We conducted our audit in accordance with generally accepted auditing standards and *Government Auditing Standards,* issued by the Comptroller General of the United States. Those standards require that we plan and perform the audit to obtain reasonable assurance about whether the general-purpose financial statements are free of material misstatements. An audit includes examining, on a test basis, evidence supporting the amounts and disclosures in the general-purpose financial statements. An audit also includes assessing the accounting principles used and significant estimates made by management, as well as evaluating the overall financial statement presentation. We believe that our audit provides a reasonable basis for our opinion.
>
> Our audit was made for the purpose of forming an opinion on the general-purpose financial statements of the City of _____ taken as a whole. The accompanying schedule of federal financial assistance is presented for purposes of additional analysis and is not a required part of the general-purpose financial statements. The information in that schedule has been subjected to the auditing procedures applied in the audit of the general-purpose financial statements and, in our opinion, is fairly presented in all material respects in relation to the general-purpose financial statements taken as a whole.

SOPs 92-7 and 92-9 provide additional guidance to the auditor when conducting an audit in accordance with OMB Circulars A-128 and A-133. Numerous report illustrations, not previously available, are included. (SOP 92-7 incorporated and superseded SOP 90-9, *The Auditor's Consideration of the Internal Control Structure Used in Administering Federal Financial Assistance Programs Under the Single Audit Act.*)

Reporting on Compliance with Specific Requirements of Major Federal Financial Assistance Programs.   The auditor is required to report on the governmental entity's compliance with the specific requirements applicable to major federal financial assistance programs. As illustrated in the report that follows (SAS No. 68, para. 81), an unqualified report expresses positive assurance on such compliance.

> We have audited the financial statements of [*name of entity*] as of and for the year ended June 30, 19X1, and have issued our report thereon dated August 15, 19X1.
>
> We have also audited the [*name of entity*]'s compliance with the requirements governing [*list specific requirements tested*] that are applicable to each of its major federal financial assistance programs, which are identified in the accompanying schedule of federal financial assistance, for the year ended June 30, 19X1. The management of [*name of entity*] is responsible for [*name of entity*]'s compliance

with those requirements. Our responsibility is to express an opinion on compliance with those requirements based on our audit.

We conducted our audit of compliance with those requirements in accordance with generally accepted auditing standards; *Government Auditing Standards,* issued by the Comptroller General of the United States; and OMB Circular A-128, "Audits of State and Local Governments." Those standards and OMB Circular A-128 require that we plan and perform the audit to obtain reasonable assurance about whether material noncompliance with the requirements referred to above occurred. An audit includes examining, on a test basis, evidence about [*name of entity*]'s compliance with those requirements. We believe that our audit provides a reasonable basis for our opinion.

[*Following paragraph is omitted if there are no instances of noncompliance.*]

The results of our audit procedures disclosed immaterial instances of noncompliance with the requirements referred to above, which are described in the accompanying schedule of findings and questioned costs. We considered these instances of noncompliance in forming our opinion on compliance, which is expressed in the following paragraph.

In our opinion, [*name of entity*] complied, in all material respects, with the requirements governing [*list of requirements tested*] that are applicable to each of its major federal financial assistance programs for the year ended June 30, 19X1.

[*Following paragraph is omitted if report is not part of the public record.*]

This report is intended for the information of the audit committee, management, and [*specify legislative or regulatory body*]. However, this report is a matter of public record and its distribution is not limited.

Scope Limitations. Any restrictions on the scope of the audit, that is, on the auditor's ability to perform all the procedures considered necessary in the circumstances, may require the auditor to qualify the opinion or disclaim an opinion. This decision depends on the auditor's judgment about the nature and magnitude of the potential effects of the scope limitation and their significance to each applicable major federal financial assistance program. Paragraphs 83 and 84 of SAS No. 68 illustrate the appropriate wording when a qualification or disclaimer of opinion is necessary.

Material Noncompliance. The auditor is also precluded from issuing an unqualified opinion on compliance when the auditing procedures performed reveal instances of noncompliance that the auditor believes could have a material effect on a program. In these circumstances, the auditor must use his or her professional judgment to determine if a qualified or an adverse opinion is required. Report language for both a qualified and an adverse opinion is illustrated in SAS No. 68, paragraphs 85 and 86.

Regardless of the auditor's opinion on compliance, Circular A-128 requires him or her to report *any* instance of noncompliance found and any resulting questioned costs. Circular A-133, on the other hand, does not require instances of immaterial noncompliance to be reported, but does require such instances to be separately communicated to management or the audit committee. The auditor is not required to report likely questioned costs; that is, the auditor does not project known questioned costs to the population to arrive at likely questioned costs. The auditor reports only those questioned costs that are known to have been incurred.

If an auditor reports material findings of noncompliance relating to major programs on the part of an entity subject to the provisions of Circular A-133, the auditor is required to disclose the following details, either in the report or in an attachment to it:

- The population size of transactions,
- The sample size of transactions tested, and
- The instances of noncompliance.

For each of the items, both the number and dollar amount should be disclosed.

Reporting on Compliance with Requirements of Nonmajor Programs.   The auditor's report on compliance with requirements applicable to nonmajor programs contains a disclaimer of opinion on compliance with the requirements, a statement of positive assurance with respect to the items tested, and a statement of negative assurance with respect to items not tested.

Reporting on Compliance with the General Requirements of Federal Financial Assistance Programs.   As previously noted, the auditor is required to test compliance with the general requirements applicable to federal financial assistance programs. The auditor's report on compliance with the general requirements contains a disclaimer of opinion on compliance with the general requirements, and expresses positive assurance that the results of procedures performed on the items tested disclosed no material instances of noncompliance (if that is the case) and negative assurance with respect to items not tested. In addition, the report states that the auditor's procedures were limited to the applicable procedures described in the appropriate *Compliance Supplement,* or describes alternative procedures.

Reporting on Internal Control Structure Policies and Procedures Used in Administering Federal Assistance Programs.   The Single Audit Act requires the auditor to issue a report on the internal control structure policies and procedures used in administering federal financial assistance programs. SOP 92-7 contains an example of such a report, as follows:

> We have audited the general-purpose financial statements of City of Example, Any State, as of and for the year ended June 30, 19X1, and have issued our report thereon dated September 8, 19X1. We have also audited the compliance of City of Example, Any State, with requirements applicable to major federal financial assistance programs and have issued our report thereon dated September 8, 19X1.

> We conducted our audits in accordance with generally accepted auditing standards; *Government Auditing Standards,* issued by the Comptroller General of the United States; and Office of Management and Budget (OMB) Circular A-128, *Audits of State and Local Governments.* Those standards and OMB Circular A-128 require that we plan and

perform the audit to obtain reasonable assurance about whether the general-purpose financial statements are free of material misstatement and about whether City of Example, Any State, complied with laws and regulations, noncompliance with which would be material to a major federal financial assistance program.

In planning and performing our audits for the year ended June 30, 19X1, we considered the internal control structure of City of Example, Any State, in order to determine our auditing procedures for the purpose of expressing our opinions on the general-purpose financial statements of City of Example, Any State, and on the compliance of City of Example, Any State, with requirements applicable to major programs and to report on the internal control structure in accordance with OMB Circular A-128. This report addresses our consideration of internal control structure policies and procedures relevant to compliance with requirements applicable to federal financial assistance programs. We have addressed internal control structure policies and procedures relevant to our audit of the general-purpose financial statements in a separate report dated September 8, 19X1.

The management of City of Example, Any State, is responsible for establishing and maintaining an internal control structure. In fulfilling this responsibility, estimates and judgments by management are required to assess the expected benefits and related costs of internal control structure policies and procedures. The objectives of an internal control structure are to provide management with reasonable, but not absolute, assurance that assets are safeguarded against loss from unauthorized use or disposition, that transactions are executed in accordance with management's authorization and recorded properly to permit the preparation of general-purpose financial statements in accordance with generally accepted accounting principles, and that federal financial assistance programs are managed in compliance with applicable laws and regulations. Because of inherent limitations in any internal control structure, errors, irregularities, or instances of noncompliance may nevertheless occur and not be detected. Also, projection of any evaluation of the structure to future periods is subject to the risk that procedures may become inadequate because of changes in conditions or that the effectiveness of the design and operation of policies and procedures may deteriorate.

For the purpose of this report, we have classified the significant internal control structure policies and procedures used in administering federal financial assistance programs in the following categories [*identify internal control structure categories*].

For all of the internal control structure categories listed above, we obtained an understanding of the design of relevant policies and procedures and determined whether they have been placed in operation, and we assessed control risk.

During the year ended June 30, 19X1, City of Example, Any State, expended X percent of its total federal financial assistance under major federal financial assistance programs.

We performed tests of controls, as required by OMB Circular A-128, to evaluate the effectiveness of the design and operation of internal control structure policies and procedures that we considered relevant to preventing or detecting material noncompliance with specific requirements, general requirements, and requirements governing claims for advances and reimbursements and amounts claimed or used for matching that are applicable to each of City of Example, Any State's major federal financial assistance programs, which are identified in the accompanying Schedule of Federal Financial Assistance. Our procedures were less in scope than would be necessary to render an opinion on these internal control structure policies and procedures. Accordingly, we do not express such an opinion.

We noted certain matters involving the internal control structure and its operation that we consider to be reportable conditions under standards established by the American Institute of Certified Public Accountants. Reportable conditions involve matters coming to our attention relating to significant deficiencies in the design or operation of the internal control structure that, in our judgment, could adversely affect the City of Example, Any State's ability to administer federal financial assistance programs in accordance with applicable laws and regulations.

[*Include paragraphs to describe the reportable conditions noted.*]

A material weakness is a reportable condition in which the design or operation of one or more of the internal control structure elements does not reduce to a relatively low level the risk that noncompliance with laws and regulations that would be material to a federal financial assistance program may occur and not be detected within a timely period by employees in the normal course of performing their assigned functions.

Our consideration of the internal control structure policies and procedures used in administering federal financial assistance would not necessarily disclose all matters in the internal control structure that might be reportable conditions and, accordingly, would not necessarily disclose all reportable conditions that are also considered to be material weaknesses as defined above. However, we believe none of the reportable conditions described above is a material weakness.

We also noted other matters involving the internal control structure and its operation that we have reported to the management of City of Example, Any State, in a separate letter dated September 8, 19X1.

This report is intended for the information of the audit committee, management, and [*specify legislative or regulatory body*]. However, this report is a matter of public record and its distribution is not limited.

With appropriate changes to refer to Circular A-133 instead of A-128, the above report can be used for entities subject to the requirements of Circular A-133.

26

Auditing Banks

* **p. 809.** *Add after third paragraph:*

RECENT DEVELOPMENTS

Industry and Economic

During the early 1990s, the banking industry has begun to recover from the banking and thrift crisis that began in the 1980s. This recovery resulted largely from a favorable interest rate environment in which net interest rate margins enabled depository institutions to replenish capital, while affording borrowers relief in the form of lower interest payments. At the same time, depository institutions have been subjected to numerous new laws, regulations, and accounting and auditing developments with special implications for auditors.

The industry experienced record earnings as a byproduct of successive Federal Reserve Board (FRB) cuts in interest rates to stimulate economic growth. These cuts resulted in enhanced interest spreads and gains on sales of debt securities. Yet, economic weakness continues to threaten individual institutions. Performance is hampered by asset quality problems arising from persistent weakness in commercial real estate markets in the Northeast and West. Despite improved earnings and increased capital ratios, the capital and credit crunch continues as loan volumes fall and institutions continue to redeploy funds into security holdings.

Competitive forces have brought about several megamergers that will increase the number of U.S. $100 billion-plus banks. Continued industry consolidation is expected as institutions deal with overcapacity, reduce their operating costs, and expand their markets, and as regulators continue to resolve failed institutions.

Depository institutions are seeking economies of scale to fend off competition from nonbanks for deposits and loans.

Finally, this period has also seen a major reregulation brought about by the 1989 Financial Institutions Reform, Recovery, and Enforcement Act (FIRREA) and the Federal Deposit Insurance Corporation Improvement Act of 1991 (FDICIA), which provided additional capitalization to the FDIC's Bank Insurance Fund (BIF). These expanded regulatory powers reflect the increasing political and regulatory concern and scrutiny of the industry in the aftermath of the failure of hundreds of thrift and banking institutions.

Regulatory and Legislative

FIRREA.   FIRREA changed the way in which the savings and loan sector is regulated. In addition to increasing regulators' enforcement powers, FIRREA expanded the population of those held accountable for regulatory violations to include institution-affiliated parties. Institution-affiliated parties are defined to include accountants who are not otherwise participants in the affairs of a financial institution and who "knowingly or with reckless disregard participate in (a) any violation of any law or regulations; (b) any breach of fiduciary duty; or (c) any unsafe or unsound practice, which caused or is likely to cause more than a minimal financial loss to, or significant adverse effect on, the insured depository institution." As a result, regulators have increased the frequency of enforcement actions against professional advisors, including lawyers and accountants.

The Office of Thrift Supervision (OTS) is now the primary regulator for savings institutions; the FDIC is the secondary regulator for federally insured institutions and oversees the Savings Association Insurance Fund in addition to the BIF. As a result of FIRREA, capital requirements for thrift institutions were significantly increased, and restrictions were placed on permitted activities. Through the Resolution Trust Corporation, FIRREA provides partial funding for resolving failed institutions.

Many regulations were issued to implement FIRREA, some of which have since been superseded by FDICIA (discussed below). Among the regulations under FIRREA are growth limitations, restrictions on permitted types of investments and loans, and the required divestiture of certain investments. Savings institutions may not invest in noninvestment-grade corporate debt securities and equity investments. In addition, for federal savings and loan associations, nonresidential real estate loans may not exceed 400 percent of capital.

FDICIA.   Early in 1991, the General Accounting Office (GAO) warned Congress that the BIF would need more money as record numbers of banks failed, and reported that regulators needed timely information about the financial condition of banks. The GAO advocated tying funding of the BIF to an enhanced financial reporting system for federally insured depository institutions. The GAO's recommendations for strengthening the regulatory environment and recapitalizing the BIF became the basis for many of the reforms incorporated in FDICIA. Since its enactment, the federal banking and thrift regulatory agencies have undertaken a massive effort to develop implementing regulations. In addition to auditing and accounting provisions, FDICIA will result in changes to every major area of bank and thrift regulation. There are benchmark dates for the issuance of implementing regulations, and the extent of rule-making due process differs from provision to provision. Many regulations have been issued or proposed for comment, and others are still under development.

Many provisions of FDICIA are amendments or additions to the Federal Deposit Insurance Act (FDIA). Major provisions affecting auditors of depository institutions are summarized below. Other provisions affect operational and consumer compliance aspects of depository institutions.

Auditing Reforms. FDICIA adds Section 36 to the FDIA to provide early identification of needed improvement in financial management at insured depository institutions. These requirements apply to fiscal years ending December 31, 1993, and thereafter. The provisions do not apply to institutions with total assets of $500 million or less as of the beginning of the institution's fiscal year. The annual audit provision may be satisfied for consolidated subsidiaries by an independent audit of the holding company. Other provisions may be fulfilled by the holding company for subsidiaries having less than $5 billion in assets, or assets of between $5 and $9 billion and a regulatory CAMEL (or comparable) rating of 1 or 2.

New management responsibilities under regulations implementing Section 36 include the following:

- *Annual reporting.* Each institution must have an annual financial statement audit. Financial statements must be prepared in conformity with GAAP and any disclosure requirements regulators may establish. The financial statements must be accompanied by a written statement from management declaring its responsibility for financial statement preparation. Management must also report on its responsibility for and assessment of (a) the effectiveness of the institution's internal control structure over financial reporting and (b) the institution's compliance with laws and regulations relating to safety and soundness.

- *Communication with regulators.* Management must provide to federal and state regulators, within 15 days of receipt, a copy of any audit report, management letter, or other report from the institution's independent accountant. The institution also must notify regulators in writing of a change in auditors.

- *Communication with auditors.* Each institution must provide its independent accountant with copies of the institution's most recent reports of condition and examination, any supervisory memorandum of understanding or written agreement with any federal or state regulatory agency, and a report of any action initiated or taken by federal or state banking regulators.

- *Audit committee.* Each institution must have an audit committee composed of outside directors independent of management. Audit committees of institutions with $3 billion or more in assets must include members with relevant banking or financial expertise, have access to their own outside counsel, and exclude large customers.

Provisions affecting independent accountants under Section 36 include

- *Financial statement audits.* Mandated annual financial statement audits must be performed in accordance with generally accepted auditing standards (GAAS) and Section 37 of the FDIA.

- *Internal control and compliance attestation.* Using generally accepted standards for attestation engagements, the independent accountant must examine and report on management's assertions about the institution's internal control structure over financial reporting. The auditor must also, based on the performance of agreed-upon procedures, report on the institution's compliance with laws and regulations governing loans to insiders and dividend restrictions.

- *Other requirements.* Auditors must agree to provide related workpapers, policies, and procedures to federal and state banking regulators on request. Auditors also must undergo a peer or quality review following guidelines acceptable to the FDIC and must notify regulators if services to the institution cease.

Accounting Reforms.   FDICIA adds Section 37 to the FDIA to establish accounting objectives, standards, and requirements. Among other provisions, Section 37

- Requires regulatory financial reporting to be uniform and consistent with GAAP unless more stringent principles are considered necessary to reflect capital accurately, facilitate effective supervision, or permit prompt corrective action.

- Instructs relevant regulatory agencies to develop both a method for supplemental disclosures of market values of assets and liabilities and regulations to ensure adequate reporting of off-balance-sheet transactions, including contingent assets and liabilities. As of June 30, 1993 there are proposed regulations to require SFAS No. 107 disclosures as well as additional disclosures in call reports.

- Promotes uniformity of capital and accounting standards among federal regulatory agencies.

Prompt Corrective Action.   FDICIA adds Section 38 to the FDIA; this section focuses on changes in an institution's capital level. The regulation specifies five capital categories—well capitalized, adequately capitalized, undercapitalized, significantly undercapitalized, and critically undercapitalized. An institution is critically undercapitalized if its ratio of tangible equity to total assets is 2 percent or less, or if it otherwise fails to meet the critical capital level as defined. Institutions classified as undercapitalized or worse are subject to possible actions ranging from restriction or prohibition of certain activities to required submission of a capital plan for restoring an undercapitalized institution to an acceptable capital category. The plan must specify steps for becoming adequately capitalized, target capital levels for each year, how the institution intends to comply with other restrictions or requirements, and the types and levels of institution activities. Critically undercapitalized institutions are subject to regulatory seizure.

The regulation ties the five capital categories to total risk-based capital, Tier I risk-based capital, and Tier I leverage capital ratios, as defined by the relevant regulatory agencies. Section 38 permits the agencies to reclassify an institution between certain capital categories if an institution's activities or condition is deemed to be unsafe or unsound. Noncompliance or expected noncompliance with the capital requirements may be a condition that indicates substantial doubt about an entity's ability to continue as a going concern. This warrants attention by auditors when considering an institution's compliance with capital requirements.

Internal Control Standards.   New Section 39 of the FDIA requires federal agencies to prescribe safety and soundness standards for the management and operation of insured depository institutions, including standards for internal controls. Implementing regulations are effective no later than December 31, 1993.

Loan Loss Allowances.   In March 1992, the Office of the Comptroller of the Currency (OCC) revised Banking Circular 201 (BC 201), *Allowance for Loan and Lease Losses,* which requires that banks maintain an allowance sufficient to absorb estimated inherent losses in their loan portfolios. BC 201 also discusses the institution's responsibility for maintaining an effective loan review process; controls to identify, monitor, and address problem assets; and documentation of the process for determining the allowance, including analysis of collectibility factors affecting the portfolio. In January 1993, the OCC published a supplement to its Bank Accounting Advisory Series devoted to the interpretation of BC 201.

In October 1991, the U.S. Treasury, seeking to promote economic growth, announced plans to ease constraints on the availability of credit. The Treasury instructed examiners to assess income-producing property loans based on their income-producing capacity over time, taking into account liquidity and the cyclical nature of real estate markets. Examiners were also instructed to use the liquidation approach to valuing real estate only if a property was actually to be liquidated. In November 1991, the federal agencies issued an *Interagency Policy Statement on the Review and Classification of Commercial Real Estate Loans,* which reemphasized that real estate loans should not be valued on a liquidation basis. Other matters addressed included principles examiners follow in reviewing commercial real estate loans; indicators of troubled real estate markets and projects; factors examiners consider during loan review, including appraisal use; real estate valuation approaches; federal agencies' classification guidelines; and factors considered in evaluating an institution's allowance.

In March 1991, interagency statements were issued to clarify regulatory and accounting policies concerning loan loss allowances. The guidelines encouraged increased disclosure about loan portfolios, sought to mitigate a perceived credit crunch attributed to increased regulatory scrutiny, and sought to ensure proper valuation of real estate collateral. In July 1991, the OCC addressed these issues in Banking Circular 255, *Troubled Loan Workouts and Loans to Borrowers in Troubled Industries.*

Valuation of Securities.   An interagency policy issued in February 1992 addresses selection of securities dealers, policies and strategies for securities portfolios, unsuitable investment practices, and mortgage derivatives. The policy emphasizes that securities may be reported at amortized cost only if the institution has the intent and ability to hold the assets for long-term investment purposes and identifies factors for evaluating intent. High-risk securities, as defined, are prohibited from being recorded as investments under the presumption that they must be actively managed.

The SEC has recently emphasized that for an institution to qualify for amortized cost reporting, management's intent to hold securities must be clear. The SEC stated that intent to invest in securities to manage liquidity, interest rate, prepayment, or other such risks is inconsistent with an intent to hold. During 1992, the SEC required many institutions to reclassify certain securities from an investment to a held-for-sale category (i.e., from amortized cost to the lower of cost or market value). Registrants that do not choose early adoption of Statement of Financial Accounting Standards (SFAS) No. 115, *Accounting for Certain Investments in Debt and Equity Securities,* described later, and their auditors should be cognizant of the SEC's position.

SEC Staff Accounting Bulletin No. 59 (SAB 59) provides guidance for determining whether securities whose value is below cost should be written down and the amount charged to income. During 1992, the SEC emphasized that "other than temporary" is not equivalent to "permanent," that management must consider available evidence relating to the realization of securities, and that there may be specific factors that indicate an other-than-temporary decline. SAB 59 and related enforcement releases indicate the SEC's position that the extent of the market decline from cost and the duration of the decline are significant factors that may require a write-down. Evidence such as financial performance, near-term prospects, and subsequent recoveries were also identified as factors in determining whether a decline is other than temporary.

Loan Servicing Rights.   Normal servicing fee, discount, and prepayment assumptions for evaluating excess servicing fee receivables have been a subject of discussion by various regulatory agencies. In 1992, the SEC began reviewing registrants' policies for valuing excess and purchased servicing rights, particularly with regard to aggregation and discount rates. In 1993, the OTS issued Thrift Bulletin 60 on the valuation of purchased servicing rights. This bulletin contains guidance as to the components to be used in a discounted cash flow analysis of these rights, including prepayment and discount rate assumptions, and requirements for independent valuation appraisals.

Coordination Between Auditors and Examiners.   In July 1992, the federal agencies issued an *Interagency Policy Statement on Coordination and Communication Between External Auditors and Examiners.* The statement addresses information to be provided by institutions to external auditors, including information relating to FDICIA requirements. The statement encourages institutions to advise their external auditors promptly of the dates and scope of supervisory examinations so as to facilitate the auditors' planning and scheduling of work and to provide auditors with reports of actions undertaken by regulatory agencies. Auditors are encouraged to attend exit conferences and other meetings between examiners and management where examination findings are discussed. In addition, auditors may request a meeting with the federal regulators during or after examinations to inquire about relevant matters. Additional guidance is provided in AICPA Statement of Position 90-5, *Inquiries of Representatives of Financial Institution Regulatory*

Agencies, which states that auditors should request and review reports of bank examinations and related correspondence and encourages auditors to be present at exit conferences between the client and the examiner. The SOP also states that management's or the examiner's refusal of an auditor's request to review communications from the examiner would ordinarily constitute a scope limitation.

Other recent regulatory issues of importance to auditors of depository institutions include

- In June 1992, the FDIC issued a final rule restricting acceptance and renewal of brokered deposits, and the interest rates paid on such deposits, based on an institution's level of capitalization.

- In 1993, the federal agencies issued rules to revise limitations on intangible assets. The rules limit the amount of purchased mortgage-servicing rights (PMSR) and purchased credit-card relationships (PCCR) includible in Tier I capital to an aggregate limit of 50 percent of Tier I capital, with a further limit on PCCRs of 25 percent of Tier I capital.

- In December 1992, the Federal Financial Institutions Examination Council released an interagency statement restricting the allowable amount of deferred tax assets in capital to refundable taxes plus reversing temporary differences plus the lesser of (1) tax carryforwards that can be realized by shielding future taxable income within one year of the quarter-end report date, or (2) 10 percent of Tier I or core capital.

- In March 1992, the FDIC revised its rules to require an appraisal by a certified or licensed appraiser for real estate transactions, subject to certain exemptions, having a value of $100,000 or greater. In June 1993, the agencies jointly proposed to increase this limit to $250,000 and to expand and clarify exemptions.

- The OCC issued Banking Circular 272, *National Bank Appeals Process,* in June 1993. BC 272 outlines how reviews of examination decisions may be requested through the appropriate examination hierarchy. The other agencies are expected to issue similar guidance.

- In June 1992, the FRB issued changes to Regulation O. The revised regulation requires that loans to insiders be made with credit underwriting standards no less stringent than standards for other loans; creates a new limit on extensions of credit to all insiders as a class; applies the per-person lending limit to a bank's executive officers, directors, principal shareholders, and their related interests; and prohibits insiders from knowingly receiving an unauthorized extension of credit. In May 1992, the FDIC applied Regulation O limits to executives of FDIC-supervised banks.

- In February 1992, the OCC, FDIC, and FRB issued a joint statement of their intent to phase out the definition of highly leveraged transactions (HLTs) and discontinue reporting requirements. The agencies emphasized they would continue a thorough review of HLTs during examinations. The SEC staff has indicated that it will continue to review HLT disclosures in management discussion and analysis sections of reports.

- The OCC issued Banking Bulletin 92-38 in July 1992 regarding lender liability under the Comprehensive Environmental Response, Compensation, and Liability Act (also known as Superfund). This law exempts from liability those institutions who hold ownership in a property primarily to protect their security interest. However, the exemption does not apply to an institution that participates in managing the property. The key terms defining what constitutes such management are set forth in a final rule on lender liability issued by the U.S. Environmental Protection Agency in April 1992. The OCC suggests that national banks can protect themselves by not participating in the management of properties in which they have a security interest. The OCC bulletin states that its rule does not address institutions acting in a fiduciary capacity and suggests that such institutions ensure that they are properly addressing potential liability.

GAO Actions.   The GAO has been a persistent critic of the depository institution industry, its regulators, and its advisors. In September 1990, in its audit report on the BIF, the GAO concluded that the BIF's reserve levels might not be sufficient if bank failures occurred at a higher than anticipated rate. As a result, the FDIC raised bank assessments. Nevertheless, the GAO, in its April 1991 Report to Congressional Committees, *Failed Banks: Accounting and Auditing Reform Urgently Needed,* stated that "the Bank Insurance Fund reserves are dangerously low and the Fund needs to be recapitalized to avoid the need for taxpayer assistance." *Failed Banks* analyzed the call reports and regulators' examination reports for 39 commercial banks that had been examined and became insolvent in 1988 and 1989. The GAO's objective was to determine the effect of accounting and internal control weaknesses on those failures and to identify reform measures that might minimize future losses.

The GAO concluded that

- Call reports failed to give an early warning of impaired asset values.
- Pervasive internal control weaknesses were a major factor in the insolvencies.
- Many of the failed banks did not have independent audits.
- Independent audits, in combination with audit committees and management reporting on internal control, can lead to stronger internal controls.
- Large banks need to be closely scrutinized.

The GAO report contained a number of recommendations to Congress and accounting standard setters to address these findings, which, as noted earlier, formed the basis for FDICIA.

The December 1991 GAO report, *Market Value Accounting—Debt Investment Securities Held by Banks,* summarized the GAO's assessment of the effect market value accounting could have on bank financial statements. The GAO analysis of the effect of changes in interest rates on debt investment securities held by banks led to a hypothesis that a 1 percent increase in prevailing interest rates would decrease the value of U.S. banks' securities portfolios by 3 percent.

In June 1992, the GAO issued a report, *Depository Institutions: Flexible Accounting Rules Lead to Inflated Financial Reports,* that highlighted the GAO's disagreement with the FASB's loan impairment project. Also, the report was critical of regulatory agency efforts to revise accounting principles relative to loan losses, specifically the

Interagency Policy Statement on the Review and Classification of Commercial Real Estate Loans, mentioned earlier. The GAO believes that, unless corrective action is taken by the FASB and the regulatory agencies, Congress should consider holding hearings on the underlying issues and possibly legislating regulatory accounting principles for loan impairment that are more stringent than GAAP. The report essentially reasserts recommendations made in the April 1991 GAO report, *Failed Banks,* that GAAP be changed to lower the threshold for recognition of loan losses and require loan loss reserves to reflect the fair value of impaired loans and collateral based on known market conditions.

Accounting and Auditing

Noncompliance with regulatory requirements, such as failure to meet minimum capital requirements or participation in impermissible activities or investments, exposes depository institutions to regulatory action and is an important consideration in the audits of troubled institutions, particularly in view of the prompt corrective action provisions of FDICIA. Events of noncompliance may be brought to the auditor's attention during the application of normal auditing procedures, during the review of regulatory examination reports, or as a result of regulatory actions. Statement on Auditing Standards (SAS) No. 59, *The Auditor's Consideration of an Entity's Ability to Continue as a Going Concern* (AU Section 341), states that "the auditor has a responsibility to evaluate whether there is substantial doubt about the entity's ability to continue as a going concern for a reasonable period of time, not to exceed one year beyond the date of the financial statements being audited." As noted earlier, noncompliance or expected noncompliance with regulatory capital requirements is a condition, when considered with other factors, that could indicate substantial doubt about the entity's ability to continue as a going concern for a reasonable period of time.

In May 1993, the FASB issued SFAS No. 114, *Accounting by Creditors for Impairment of a Loan* (Accounting Standards Section I08). SFAS No. 114 applies to loans that are individually and specifically evaluated for impairment, whether collateralized or not, except loans accounted for at fair value or at the lower of cost or fair value. It requires impaired loans to be measured at the present value of expected future cash flows by discounting such cash flows using the loan's effective interest rate. Loans probable of foreclosure should be measured at the collateral's fair value. SFAS No. 114 amends SFAS No. 5, *Accounting for Contingencies,* to require a creditor to evaluate the collectibility of contractual interest and principal payments. In addition, SFAS No. 114 amends SFAS No. 15, *Accounting by Debtors and Creditors for Troubled Debt Restructurings,* to require a creditor to account for a troubled debt restructuring involving a modification of terms by discounting the loan's cash flows at the loan's original effective interest rate. SFAS No. 114 also amends SFAS No. 15 to eliminate in-substance foreclosure accounting for loans (that is, accounting for such loans as other real estate owned) unless the creditor receives physical possession of the debtor's assets. SFAS No. 114 applies to financial statements issued for fiscal years beginning after December 15, 1994, with early application encouraged.

Under SEC Financial Reporting Release (FRR) No. 28 and AICPA Practice Bulletin No. 7, a creditor is required to account for the operations of the collateral underlying some loans, even though the creditor has not taken possession of the collateral, as if foreclosure had occurred. SFAS No. 114 recognizes the practical problems of accounting for the operations of an asset the creditor does not possess and, therefore, requires that a loan for which foreclosure is probable should continue to be accounted for as a loan until the creditor receives physical possession of the debtor's assets. However, when a creditor determines that foreclosure is probable, the loan should be remeasured at the fair value of the collateral so that loss recognition is not delayed until actual foreclosure.

SFAS No. 114 and FRR No. 28 are in conflict. While FRR No. 28 specifies criteria for considering collateral as substantively repossessed and accounting for it as other real estate owned, SFAS No. 114 has essentially eliminated the notion of substantive repossession of collateral. Under SFAS No. 114, even though foreclosure may be probable, the receivable is accounted for as a loan until the creditor actually receives physical possession of the collateral. At the time of this writing, the SEC staff is considering whether to amend FRR No. 28 so as to make it consistent with SFAS No. 114.

SOP 92-3, *Accounting for Foreclosed Assets,* was issued in April 1992 and sets forth a rebuttable presumption that foreclosed assets are held for sale and requires them to be classified in the statement of financial position as assets held for sale and reported at the lower of fair value less estimated costs to sell, or cost. Foreclosed assets held for income production should be treated as if the assets were acquired in a manner other than through foreclosure. SOP 92-3 contains no guidance on accounting for foreclosed assets after acquisition. At the time of this writing, AcSEC is developing a proposed SOP to provide accounting guidance for foreclosed assets after acquisition.

An AcSEC task force is developing a proposed SOP to address accounting for acquisition, development, and construction (ADC) arrangements, including how lenders should report proportionate shares of income or loss on ADC projects, whether depreciation should be considered in determining income or loss, reporting of interest receipts, and the treatment of unrealized depreciation of the property.

In May 1993, the FASB issued SFAS No. 115, *Accounting for Certain Investments in Debt and Equity Securities* (Accounting Standards Section I80), discussed in Chapter 17 of this Supplement. SOP 90-11, *Disclosure of Certain Information by Financial Institutions About Debt Securities Held as Assets,* is discussed in Chapter 32 of this Supplement. During the recent recessionary period, depository institutions have revised investment strategies to earn higher yields, including the purchase of complex financial instruments. Auditors should be familiar with rules and regulations related to investments, some of which are discussed earlier in this chapter. Certain rules and regulations may affect classification and valuation of institutions' investments. Auditors should be aware of the risks involved in complex securities and should assess management's expertise in monitoring, evaluating, and accounting for the securities; consider whether the institution has established appropriate policies and procedures for investment in high-risk securities and whether there is adequate oversight by the board of directors; and involve specialists, when necessary, in valuing and auditing these investments.

In December 1991, the FASB issued SFAS No. 107, *Disclosures about Fair Value of Financial Instruments* (Accounting Standards Section F25), discussed in Chapter 21A of this Supplement. SFAS No. 107 is particularly relevant to depository institutions. Disclosures required under SFAS No. 107 entail many management estimates. Because no valuation methodology or format is specified for the variety of financial instruments that are likely to be encountered at depository institutions, the determination and presentation of disclosure amounts may be subjective, especially for infrequently traded instruments. When markets do not exist for an instrument, fair value might be estimated on the basis of appraisals, discounting of expected cash flows, or other methodologies that involve the use of subjective assumptions. Auditors should follow the guidance in SAS No. 57 when auditing these estimates.

Other recent accounting and auditing developments relevant to depository institution auditors include the following:

- In March 1992, the FASB issued Interpretation No. 39, *Offsetting of Amounts Related to Certain Contracts* (Accounting Standards Section B10). The interpretation defines "right of setoff" as used in Accounting Principles Board Opinion No. 10 and SFAS No. 105, and specifies conditions that must be met to have that right. It addresses the applicability of offsetting to forward rate swap, currency swap, option, and other conditional or exchange contracts and when it is appropriate to offset amounts recognized for those contracts in the balance sheet. In addition, it permits offsetting of fair values recognized for multiple-forward, swap, option, and other conditional or exchange contracts executed with the same counterparty under a master netting arrangement. The interpretation is effective for financial statements of years beginning after December 15, 1993.

- The EITF reached consensus on several recent issues that are specific to depository institutions, as follows:

  —Issue 90-21, *Balance Sheet Treatment of a Sale of Mortgage Servicing Rights with a Subservicing Agreement.*
  —Issue 92-2, *Measuring Loss Accruals by Transferors for Transfers of Receivables*
  —Issue 92-5, *Amortization Period for Net Deferred Credit Card Origination Costs*
  —Issue 92-10, *Table Funding Arrangements*
  —Issue 93-1, *Accounting for Individual Credit Card Acquisitions*

- SOP 90-6, *Directors' Examinations of Banks,* was issued, modifying the illustrative engagement letter and report in the industry audit guide, *Audits of Banks,* to include a statement identifying the omission, in a directors' examination, of certain procedures relating to high-risk accounts that are normally performed during an audit in accordance with GAAS. The SOP was issued because there had been confusion about the scope of the auditor's work in a directors' examination involving the application of agreed-upon procedures. Omitted procedures cited in the SOP are reviewing the collectibility of loans, the evaluation of collateral on loans, and the adequacy of the loan loss allowance.

- In November 1991, SAS No. 67, *The Confirmation Process* (AU Section 330), was issued to provide guidance on the confirmation process in audits performed in accordance with GAAS. SAS No. 67 specifically addresses the confirmation of loans, generally an important procedure in auditing depository institutions, and explicitly prohibits the use of negative confirmation requests except when the combined assessed level of inherent and control risk is low. This SAS is especially relevant to audits of depository institutions, which use confirmation procedures extensively for cash, investments, loans, and deposit balances. Chapter 12 of this Supplement includes further discussion of the provisions of SAS No. 67.

- In April 1992, SAS No. 70, *Reports on the Processing of Transactions by Service Organizations* (AU Section 324), was issued. The SAS provides guidance on the factors auditors should consider when auditing the financial statements of a service organization user, and guidance for auditors who issue reports on a service organization's processing of transactions. Depository institutions often use or serve as a service organization for processing significant information, such as general ledger and trial balances; loan, deposit, or credit card transactions; or investment information. Chapter 6 of this Supplement includes further discussion of the provisions of SAS No. 70.

- In September 1992, the Committee of Sponsoring Organizations of the Treadway Commission (COSO) issued its report, *Internal Control—Integrated Framework*. The report defines internal control and its elements, provides tools for assessing internal controls, and addresses management reporting on internal controls over financial reporting. The report has special significance for depository institutions, given the expanded management and auditor internal control reporting required by FDICIA and its implementing regulations. The COSO Report is discussed in more detail in Chapter 7 of this Supplement.

- The Auditing Standards Board issued Statement on Standards for Attestation Engagements (SSAE) No. 2, *Reporting on an Entity's Internal Control Structure Over Financial Reporting*. This statement, which supersedes SAS No. 30, *Reporting on Internal Accounting Control,* addresses engagements in which a CPA examines and reports on management's written assertion about the effectiveness of an entity's internal control structure for financial reporting. SSAE No. 2 is discussed in Chapter 24 of this Supplement. An SSAE dealing with reports on an entity's compliance with specified laws and regulations was exposed for comment in early 1993. As provided under FDICIA, these statements will be the basis for accountant reporting on management assertions about compliance with safety and soundness laws and regulations.

- In August 1991 and December 1992, respectively, the AICPA issued revised industry audit and accounting guides, *Audits of Savings Institutions* and *Audits of Credit Unions.* The AICPA is currently developing an industry accounting and audit guide for all depository institutions.

27

Auditing Colleges, Universities, and Independent Schools

RISK ASSESSMENT AND AUDIT STRATEGY

* **p. 797.** *Add at bottom of page:*

Standards of accounting and financial reporting practices for colleges, universities, and independent schools are continuing to change in response to the initiatives of various standard-setting bodies and the federal government. As discussed later, the FASB issued two major pronouncements affecting such organizations in 1993 and the AICPA Not-for-Profit Organizations Committee issued a major Statement of Position.

Congress and various federal commissions, agencies, and departments continue to focus on colleges and universities. The IRS, for example, announced several major initiatives in 1992. In addition to regulation, the economy is probably the key challenge facing colleges and universities. The economy affects sources of revenue, costs, and public demand for services. Other challenges facing colleges and universities include:

- *Decline in Charitable Giving.* According to a recent independent sector survey, "Giving and Volunteering in the United States, 1992," giving by Americans to nonprofit organizations declined from 1989 to 1991. Contributions to educational institutions dropped by 23 percent.

- *Reduction in Government Support.* Most colleges and universities receive federal and state grants and contracts. Given the reductions in federal and state budgets in 1993, support to these organizations has been cut once again. As a result, many colleges and universities have trimmed their staff and programs, and some institutions are considering closing their doors.

- *Increases in Costs.* Several universities have instituted hiring freezes or the more drastic measure of laying off some employees. These layoffs and hiring freezes are seen as an indication of how serious the economic problems are that confront universities. In addition, the health insurance costs of nonprofit organizations are increasing at a much more rapid rate than those of most business and government employers.

FASB and GASB Issues, AICPA Pronouncements, and IRS Guidelines

In June 1993, the FASB issued Statement of Financial Accounting Standards (SFAS) No. 116, *Accounting for Contributions Received and Contributions Made* (Accounting Standards Sections C67 and No5). In general, the statement requires that contributions received be recognized at their fair market value as revenues or gains, and, depending on the nature of the benefits received by the organization, as assets, decreases of liabilities, or expenses. Contributions received would be classified as unrestricted support or as temporarily or permanently restricted support. Unconditional promises to give (e.g., pledges) with payments due in future periods would be reported as restricted support unless the donor clearly intended the monies to be used to support current-period activities.

Although organizations must disclose certain information about their collections of works of art, historical treasures, and similar assets, they do not need to capitalize them or recognize contributed items as revenues or gains as long as the collections meet the following conditions:

- Are held for public exhibition, education, or research to further public service;
- Are protected, kept unencumbered, cared for, and preserved; and
- Are subject to an organizational policy that requires proceeds from sales of collection items to be used to acquire other collection items.

Contributed services would be recognized as revenues or gains only if they "create or enhance nonfinancial assets or require specialized skills, are provided by individuals possessing those skills, and would typically need to be purchased if not provided by donation."

In June 1993, the FASB issued SFAS No. 117, *Financial Statements of Not-for-Profit Organizations* (Accounting Standards Sections C25 and No5). The statement requires the financial statements of nonprofit organizations to focus on the entity as a whole, rather than reporting on several fund groups. Not-for-profit organizations are required, at a minimum, to present an aggregated statement of financial position, a statement of activities, and a statement of cash flows. The minimum requirements for each financial statement are as follows:

- The statement of financial position must include (1) total assets, (2) total liabilities, (3) amounts for three classes of net assets (unrestricted, temporarily restricted, and permanently restricted), and (4) total net assets.

- The statement of activities must include the amount of the increase or decrease in unrestricted, temporarily restricted, permanently restricted, and total net assets.
- The statement of cash flows must include the net cash used by operating, investing, and financing activities as well as the changes in cash and cash equivalents and a reconciliation of the change in net assets to the change in cash used by operating activities.

Both SFAS Nos. 116 and 117 are effective for annual financial statements issued for fiscal years beginning after December 15, 1994, except for not-for-profit organizations with less than $5 million in total assets and less than $1 million in annual expenses. For those organizations, the effective dates are extended by one year. Earlier application is encouraged. SFAS Nos. 116 and 117 provide detailed guidance on how the statements should be initially applied.

In addition, colleges and universities are affected by SFAS No. 106, *Employers' Accounting for Postretirement Benefits Other Than Pensions* (Accounting Standards Section P40), and SFAS No. 107, *Disclosures about Fair Value of Financial Instruments* (Accounting Standards Section F25). Educational organizations that generate taxable income are also affected by SFAS No. 109, *Accounting for Income Taxes,* which was issued in early 1992 and became effective for fiscal years beginning after December 15, 1992. Chapter 19 of this Supplement provides guidance on auditing income tax-related accounts under SFAS No. 109.

Because SFAS Nos. 116 and 117 establish standards for accounting for contributions and for reporting certain basic information in financial statements that are applicable to all not-for-profit organizations, provisions in AICPA Guides and Statements of Position that are inconsistent with these statements are no longer acceptable specialized accounting and reporting principles and practices.

Page 794 of the main volume notes that at the time of its writing, changes were taking place in the applicability of certain authoritative pronouncements to higher educational institutions. That was the result of a jurisdictional issue concerning which standard-setting body—the FASB or the GASB—had authority over colleges and universities. That issue was resolved by an agreement that government-owned entities would follow GASB standards, while other entities would follow FASB standards. Since that agreement was reached, the GASB has issued Statement No. 14, *The Financial Reporting Entity,* which became effective for periods beginning after December 15, 1992, and applies to public universities as well as municipal entities.

GASB Statement No. 15, *Governmental College and University Accounting and Financial Reporting Models,* requires governmental colleges and universities to use one of two accounting and financial reporting models.

1. The "AICPA College Guide Model." This is the accounting and financial reporting guidance recognized by the 1973 AICPA industry audit guide, *Audits of Colleges and Universities,* as amended by AICPA Statement of Position 74-8, *Financial Accounting and Reporting by Colleges and Universities,* and as modified by applicable FASB pronouncements issued through November 30, 1989 and all applicable GASB pronouncements.
2. The "Government Model." This model is the accounting and financial reporting standards established by National Council on Governmental Accounting

(NCGA) Statement 1, *Governmental Accounting and Financial Reporting Principles,* as modified by subsequent NCGA and GASB pronouncements.

The AICPA Not-for-Profit Organizations Committee (the Committee) is considering a number of issues at the time of this writing, including

1. *Applicability of Technical Pronouncements to Not-for-Profits.* In May 1993, the Committee issued an exposure draft of a Statement of Position on the applicability of the requirements of Accounting Research Bulletins (ARBs), Opinions of the Accounting Principles Board (APB), and Statements and Interpretations of the FASB to nonprofit organizations. The draft SOP states that such pronouncements should be applied by nonprofit organizations, unless the pronouncements specifically exclude nonprofit organizations.

2. *Reporting of Related Entities.* Also in May 1993, the Committee issued an exposure draft of a Statement of Position that provides guidance on consolidating investments in majority-owned, for-profit subsidiaries of nonprofit organizations as well as financially interrelated nonprofit organizations. Majority-owned subsidiaries should be accounted for under the guidance in ARB No. 51, as amended by SFAS No. 94. The equity method of accounting, in accordance with APB Opinion No. 18, should be used to report investments in for-profit entities in whose voting stock the investor has a 50 percent or less voting interest. (However, not-for-profit organizations that report investment portfolios at market value may continue to do so.) Not-for-profit subsidiaries of nonprofit organizations in which the organization has control or a beneficial economic interest should be consolidated. Depending on the degree of control and economic interest, there may be other reporting requirements.

3. *Accounting for the Costs of Joint Activities.* In 1993, the Committee issued an exposure draft of an SOP entitled *Accounting for Costs of Materials and Activities of Not-for-Profit Organizations and State and Local Governmental Entities That Include a Fund-Raising Appeal* that would clarify and revise SOP 87-2, *Accounting for Joint Costs of Informational Materials and Activities of Not-for-Profit Organizations That Include a Fund-Raising Appeal.* The Committee undertook this project in response to assertions by regulators, public oversight bodies, and the media that some nonprofit organizations were allocating too many fund-raising costs to program expenses, thereby abusing the guidance in SOP 87-2. In addition, some practitioners think that SOP 87-2 has not been interpreted and applied consistently.

4. *Compliance Auditing Under Government Standards.* The AICPA issued SOP 92-9, *Audits of Not-for-Profit Organizations Receiving Federal Awards,* in December 1992. The SOP provides guidance for auditing, under OMB Circular A-133, "Audits of Higher Education and Other Nonprofit Agencies," nonprofit organizations that receive federal financial assistance. Circular A-133 is discussed in Chapter 25 of this Supplement.

In December 1992, the IRS released proposed comprehensive college and university examination guidelines and is auditing all types of nonprofit organizations more thoroughly. The areas under scrutiny at nonprofit organizations include

- Unrelated business income.
- Corporate sponsorship.
- Compensation, including issues related to executive compensation and employees/independent contractors.
- Fund-raising, in particular, instances in which organizations mislead donors about the deductibility of their donations. (A case is pending in which the tax-exempt status of the United Cancer Council was revoked because it spent more than 90 percent of its income on fund-raising.)
- Political activity.
- Tax-exempt bond financing.

28

Auditing Construction Companies

* p. 809. *Add after third paragraph:*

RECENT DEVELOPMENTS

Industry and Economic

The construction industry is highly competitive, with companies typically operating at relatively low profit margins. The industry is also extremely sensitive to changes in economic conditions.

The impact of economic swings on the industry typically lags movements in other segments of the economy. During recessionary periods, construction budgets are generally the first to be cut as an entity's resources are focused on current operations. The effect of an economic downturn, however, is usually not immediately reflected in a construction company's financial statements. Instead, the effect is postponed because contracts in progress, some of which may extend over a number of years, are normally completed, providing revenues in the near-term. Moreover, decisions made at the start of periods of economic recovery to undertake new construction will typically not immediately be reflected in a construction company's results of operations because of the extended start-up period and the length of the contract period.

While the industry was performing well at the beginning of the recession that began around the fourth quarter of 1990 and did have the backlog that typically masks the slide, at the time of this writing the industry is in the doldrums and predictions are that it will be there for some time. Significant cuts in construction budgets by state and local governments and by entities in the private sector occurred during 1991 and continued through 1992; the number of housing starts fell drastically, although this was tempered by regional variations. In particular, in southern Florida home construction is expected to increase over the next several years as rebuilding takes place in the aftermath of hurricane Andrew.

During recessionary periods, construction companies are more likely to accept less profitable, riskier contracts as a means of utilizing fixed overhead and retaining experienced personnel. To win new work, costs may be underestimated—perhaps deliberately in the hope that the contractor will make up any profit shortfall after the project has started through opportunities for price revisions resulting from change orders that are likely to present themselves.

There is always the hope as well that costs can be cut below estimates as the work on a contract progresses. Despite the recession, however, many construction contractors are experiencing not lower, but higher, costs. Sometimes the cost increases are significant. There are three specific areas where costs appear to be rising significantly: insurance premiums for workers' compensation, so-called "impact fees" charged by some municipalities, and costs of obtaining environmental impact studies in connection with some projects. This suggests that construction contractors may experience negative cash flows, increased costs, and operating losses, both on specific contracts and on operations as a whole.

The AICPA Audit Risk Alert, *Construction Contractors Industry Developments—1992* notes some audit issues currently affecting the industry. First, construction contractors may find themselves responsible for significant amounts of clean-up costs under environmental laws and regulations. Second, in an economic downturn, contractors may be willing to deal with riskier subcontractors who offer lower bids than better established subcontractors. The auditor needs to determine that management has appropriately provided for and disclosed any contingencies arising from such situations, in accordance with Statement of Financial Accounting Standards No. 5, *Accounting for Contingencies.* Third, in an economy that has seen and continues to see high rates of business failures among contractors, going concern issues become particularly significant. Auditors of construction contractors should be cognizant of the possibility of conditions indicating the existence of substantial doubt about a client's ability to continue as a going concern.

Finally, reduced activity in the industry and higher costs (leading to lower profit margins) create a difficult audit environment. Even in good times, high inherent risk is associated with management judgments underlying the estimates of progress toward completion of a contract and of costs to complete, which can affect the amount of funds that can be drawn from owners or their lenders and the determination of recognized revenues, cost of revenues, accounts receivable, unbilled receivables, retentions receivable, and inventory. Contractor management is also typically optimistic when recording revenue from questionable change orders. In bad times, these tendencies are exacerbated, and the contractor's project evaluation and control procedures become even greater risk areas for the auditor.

In early 1992, the Financial Accounting Standards Board issued Statement of Financial Accounting Standards (SFAS) No. 109, *Accounting for Income Taxes,* which is effective for fiscal years beginning after December 15, 1992. Chapter 19 of this Supplement provides guidance on auditing income tax-related accounts under SFAS No. 109.

29

Auditing Emerging Businesses

p. 836. *Replace first two sentences and footnote 1 of first paragraph with:*
A 1988 report by the U.S. Small Business Administration[1] recognized the continuing need to encourage individual enterprise, independent business, and innovation. Significant legislation benefiting smaller business was enacted during the 1980s, including the Regulatory Flexibility Act, the Small Business Innovation Development Act, the Small Business Development Center Improvement Act, and the Tax Reform Act of 1986 (primarily in the potential tax benefits available under Subchapter S elections). The 1980s was a period of significant growth for small businesses. To continue that growth through the 1990s, entrepreneurs must be able to respond to new challenges—the need to streamline their labor force in order to remain competitive, increased international trade, and rapid technological changes.

p. 836. *Replace sections* **Characteristics of Emerging Businesses** *and* **Audit Strategies for Emerging Businesses** *with:*

CHARACTERISTICS OF GROWING AND EMERGING BUSINESSES

Small and growing businesses often experience common problems at similar stages of their development. Although Chapter 29 of the main volume refers

[1] U.S. Small Business Administration, *The Annual Report on Small Business and Competition* (Washington, DC: U.S. Government Printing Office, 1988).

to the companies described in the chapter as "emerging" companies, a more descriptive term, which is being used with increasing frequency, is *small and growing* companies. Considering the stage of a company's development facilitates an understanding of the company's nature, characteristics, and the problems it typically faces. The owners and management of small and growing businesses can enhance their understanding of current and future growth challenges, such as the need to attract and retain qualified people and to improve existing accounting and information systems and control procedures, by viewing issues in terms of typical stages of development.

A company's priorities change as its business grows and develops. An in-depth understanding of those priorities is needed by both owners and their business advisors and auditors. Because business issues have financial statement and auditing implications, an auditor cannot conduct an effective audit if he or she does not understand the client's business and related issues. Auditors of growing businesses must understand the characteristics unique to such businesses in order to develop the audit strategy, assess risk, and perform substantive procedures. These characteristics will vary in their significance to the entity and to the auditor's assessment of risk as entities move through various stages of growth. The more significant characteristics of growing companies are as follows:

- *Entrepreneurial management.* Growing entities reflect the drive, determination, and motivations of their entrepreneurial founder or chief executive. Business and organizational objectives are usually congruent with the personal objectives of the entrepreneur.

- *Owner-manager involvement.* The vast majority of growing and mid-sized businesses are closely held. Typically, the shareholder-owner(s) and family members also fill key managerial posts. In addition, an owner-manager usually has the authority to override prescribed procedures.

- *Limited financial expertise.* Many owner-managers are manufacturing, research, marketing, or sales oriented, but are not fully conversant with financial, accounting, cash flow, and administrative issues.

- *Limited middle management expertise.* Professional managers to serve in key technical and middle management positions are often not recruited until later in a company's life cycle, if at all. Thus, the objective analytical tools a professional manager would demand are not present in many small and growing entities.

- *Limited policy-making group.* The group above management, such as a board of directors, often consists of individuals who are not truly independent in thought and therefore are not an effective policy-making group.

- *Lack of supervision and segregation of duties.* With limited resources and thin middle management, separation of duties and supervision are often lacking. In addition, turnover can cause significant operating problems or excessive "stretching" of existing employees. These situations may be compensated for, in part, by watchful concern and involvement of the owner-manager.

- *Informal accounting and information systems.* The limited resources of growing businesses often result in their not having well-documented accounting and information systems. This may affect decisions on product profitability, customer retention and expansion, and other operational issues.

- *High leverage and undercapitalization.* The entrepreneur usually relies on banks, commercial finance companies, and vendors for financing. The owner's personal resources available for investment in the company, particularly in the early stages, frequently are limited. Therefore, growing businesses are often undercapitalized and highly leveraged.

- *Related party transactions.* Business transactions between the owner-manager and the company, or with entities under common ownership or owned by close relatives, are customary in entrepreneurial situations. Often these are motivated by income tax or estate tax considerations.

- *Economic dependence.* Growing businesses often cultivate one or more customers that represent a significant share of their revenues and profits. A loss of one or more of these major customers could be devastating to the business.

- *Loss of control over sales and inventory.* The business may be growing too quickly for management to properly analyze sales profitability, inventory control and quantities, and cash flow.

- *Maintenance of Subchapter S tax status.* Many small businesses elect to be taxed as a Subchapter S corporation to reduce taxes. However, they do not always have the expertise to monitor compliance with all the requirements necessary to maintain this tax advantage.

- *Potential exit strategies.* The entrepreneur may have established near-term deadlines to sell the business and consequently may exert pressure to inflate asset values and earnings.

The above factors clearly illustrate the need for owners and their business advisors/auditors to be responsive to developments affecting the company and its industry. Many owners and advisors wait until problems arise before addressing the need for changes. Success in a high growth company can be difficult to sustain and often temporary. Many of these companies experience erratic performance and crisis situations, which present a challenge to the auditor.

AUDIT STRATEGIES FOR GROWING AND EMERGING BUSINESSES

An audit strategy should always be designed to achieve maximum efficiency and timeliness without sacrificing audit effectiveness. Efficiency and timeliness are particularly important in auditing a growing business because

- Generally the company's accounting staff is limited.
- Credit grantors often have tight deadlines for receipt of financial statements.
- The cost of professional services is an important concern.
- The owner-manager often makes certain operating decisions based on the audited financial statements.

To design an effective and efficient audit strategy and provide the services the owner-manager expects, the auditor must be knowledgeable about the operation of the business, including the products or services the company sells, how it manufactures or obtains its products, the market it serves, its competitive position, and the way it markets its products or services. The auditor must also understand the control structure, which consists of the control environment (particularly management's objectives, plans, operating style, and philosophy), the accounting system, and control procedures. Finally, the auditor must assess the risks associated with the company's operations and control structure. Chapter 8 of the main volume discusses the various means of obtaining insight into a company's business and its control structure.

Risk Assessment

The following factors are relevant to the auditor's consideration of inherent risk in the growing company business environment:

- Owner-managed companies often depend on outside financing, and credit grantors typically impose stringent financial requirements and covenants, such as maintaining a minimum equity, working capital, or current ratio, or limiting dividends and capital expenditures.

- Continued or increased financing may be dependent on the company maintaining its financial position or achieving certain levels of current operating results.

- The management of a small business enterprise may adopt accounting practices based solely or primarily on their income tax effects.

- The business may be dependent on one or a few products that, in a rapidly changing technological environment, may suddenly become obsolete, or on a key supplier or one key customer.

- As noted earlier, family-owned businesses may engage in related party transactions like leasing arrangements, loans, and sales to or purchases from affiliated persons or companies.

- Particularly in recessionary times, substantial doubt may exist concerning a highly leveraged entity's ability to continue in existence.

The auditor should consider a range of matters affecting the industry the company operates in, the company's present and planned operations, and its financial condition. For example, the auditor should inquire about possible adverse trends in the industry and should compare the company's operating results with the industry average. Many operational characteristics are indicative of the various types of risks faced by an enterprise, like the possibility of technological changes making the company's products obsolete, its dependence on only a few suppliers or customers, substantial dependence on the success of a particular project, unusual transactions with related parties, a significant decline in sales or gross margins, or a recent easing of credit policies. While these matters are of importance in entities of all sizes, they may be of particular importance in small and growing businesses.

The risk of errors or irregularities occurring in the financial statements of small and growing businesses is often concentrated in the areas of revenues and receivables, or inventory, depending on the nature of the business. The major risk for smaller service companies tends to be in the area of revenues and receivables, especially if the company recognizes service revenue in stages, such as on a proportional performance basis or, if appropriate, on a straight-line time basis. A major audit concern is that revenue recognized reflects work actually performed. Other principal concerns for service companies are billed and unbilled receivables, and the allowance for uncollectible accounts, since those accounts are often subject to considerable judgment and estimations, and are likely to be subject to increased owner-manager control. The auditor should be particularly alert to ascertaining that a proper revenue cutoff was achieved and that the allowance for uncollectible accounts appears adequate, since there may be limited past experience to go by. For smaller manufacturing or distribution companies, inventories are a high-risk area because owner-managers may try to minimize income taxes by understating ending inventories and gross margins. Also, growing companies, which generally have limited product lines and distribution channels, encounter net realizable value and obsolescence issues more frequently. The auditor's attention should be directed particularly to determining that proper receiving and shipping cutoffs were achieved, along with the other usual auditing procedures for inventories (described in Chapter 14 of the main volume).

Small and growing businesses generally do not have the internal resources to keep current and comply with the ever-increasing tax regulations. Two tax areas of particular importance to small and growing businesses are monitoring the amount of earnings retained in the business (i.e., not paid out as taxable dividends) and compliance with Subchapter S regulations. Loss of Subchapter S status could lead to significant tax liabilities.

In assessing control risk in a small and growing business, the auditor should be aware of the frequent lack of segregation of duties in accounting functions. This results from limited staff, easy accessibility to financial records and assets by clerical and administrative personnel, and informal and undocumented authorization and supervisory procedures. The involvement of the owner-manager can compensate for a lack of formal control procedures, provided the level of involvement is ongoing. The owner-manager, however, typically has the authority to override the control procedures that may exist in a growing business. The auditor's assessment of that risk should influence the audit strategy.

Selecting the Audit Strategy

The auditor's procedures in obtaining and evaluating audit evidence are basically the same for a small and growing business as for any other business enterprise, although the mix of procedures may vary from that used in large entities. The procedures consist of tests of controls, substantive tests of details, and analytical procedures, and are explained in detail and illustrated in the chapters in Part 3 of the main volume on auditing transactions and account balances. Materiality considerations, which enter into the choice of an audit strategy as well, are also the same for a small and growing business as for an established one.

*   Because owner-managed businesses typically have small accounting staffs, low transaction volume, and limited segregation of duties and supervision, the most efficient strategy is often one that emphasizes substantive tests of year-end account balances. Nonetheless, on each engagement the auditor must understand the internal control structure. In many cases, there are strong management control methods exercised by the owner-manager. Based on this understanding, the auditor determines whether performing tests of controls may be effective and efficient, and the nature, timing, and extent of specific substantive tests.

Auditing Research Monograph No. 5, *Audit Problems Encountered in Small Business Engagements*, indicated that many auditors of smaller businesses "at least occasionally accept management's representations as audit evidence when completeness of recorded transactions cannot otherwise be substantiated."[4] The auditor must be careful not to place undue reliance on uncorroborated representations, especially when faced with deficiencies in the control structure.

Chapter 7 of the main volume indicates some of the effects of inadequate completeness control procedures on the conduct of an audit. If those control procedures are not effective, substantive testing may have to be changed or increased through analytical procedures, substantive tests of details of related populations, and other substantive tests that are available but are not ordinarily performed. An example of a substantive test of a related population would be testing cash disbursements in the subsequent period to search for liabilities that were unrecorded at the balance sheet date. Confirming accounts payable, including those with known vendors with zero balances, for the same purpose, is an example of a substantive test that is not ordinarily performed, except in poor control structures. If sufficient competent evidence cannot be obtained, a scope limitation may result, and the auditor should consider the effect on the audit opinion.

[4] D. D. Raiborn, *Audit Problems Encountered in Small Business Engagements,* Auditing Research Monograph No. 5 (New York: AICPA, 1982), p. 74.

30

Auditing Health Care Institutions

* p. 847. *Add after first paragraph:*

RECENT DEVELOPMENTS

Industry and Economic

The health care industry continues to face significant pressures from both the revenue and the cost side of its business. These pressures are evident in the (a) continued reductions in federal reimbursement for Medicare and Medicaid beneficiaries; (b) growth of managed care and direct contracting arrangements, which create even greater pressure on health care providers to manage costs so that they can be profitable in fixed fee (capitation) or per diem arrangements; (c) shift to outpatient settings, which entails providing appropriate outpatient facilities as well as reconfiguring unused inpatient space; and (d) growth of the uninsured and underinsured portion of the population, which has resulted in a greater commitment of hospital resources for the provision of charity care. Generally, health care providers are operating in an environment of rapidly escalating costs driven by (a) costly labor and benefits packages that have become necessary to attract and retain staff; (b) rising costs associated with medical malpractice claims (the median medical malpractice award rose to over $600,000 in 1992); and (c) the increasing difficulty in obtaining capital.

In addition, the health care environment has been further altered by a number of social issues. For example, the U.S. population of individuals over 80 years of age continues to increase, with an increase of 24 percent projected between 1992 and 2000, compared with a total population increase of approximately 8 percent. Furthermore, it is estimated that approximately 30 percent of Medicare spending is for care in the final year of life. The cost of care rendered to AIDS and HIV-positive patients is projected to rise to $15 billion by 1995. The cost pressures of these social issues have added to the burdens on an industry whose revenues have not kept pace with costs.

Regulatory and Legislative

From the regulatory perspective, numerous federal and state initiatives have attempted to control the rapid rise of health care costs. Significant federal regulations include:

- A *prospective payment system for capital expenditures* was instituted in 1992, with a 10-year transition, which will phase out cost-based reimbursement for health care capital expenditures.
- The *Medicare Resource Based Relative Value Scale* (RBRVS) was implemented effective January 1992 in an effort to reform the payment mechanism for physicians. It is designed to decrease reimbursement to specialists in favor of primary care physicians in an effort to encourage more preventive care.
- A *Medicare Geographic Classification* review was completed in 1992, which reclassified 1,158 rural hospitals to their neighboring urban community, resulting in increased Medicare reimbursements. The reclassification was intended to be budget neutral, and nearly $500 million of Medicare funds shifted from urban hospitals to their rural competitors.
- *Safe harbor rules* were published in July 1992 outlining 11 areas relating to referral, investment, and payment methods in which health care providers can operate safely, without concern for infringement of Medicare fraud and abuse regulations.
- *IRS scrutiny* of the tax-exempt status of health care providers has increased under pressure to increase tax revenue and public questioning of hospitals' charitable intent. The IRS's focus has broadened to include examination of physician relationships, senior executives' compensation, and adherence to a community benefit standard.

Several state initiatives have responded to rising Medicaid expenditures. For example, Hawaii has had a single payer system since 1985, whereby all employers are required to provide at least a minimum health benefit package to their employees. The results have been impressive, with administrative costs low and only 3 percent of the population uninsured. The Department of Health and Human Services recently granted Oregon a waiver in order to implement a Medicaid system of prioritizing acute care services for the poor. The Oregon plan provides universal access, but only for care that maximizes the benefit to the total population.

Health Care Reform

The 1992 presidential campaign highlighted the nation's concern regarding its health care system. Concern on the part of business leaders that U.S. global competitiveness is being hurt by rising employee benefit costs, coupled with a consensus among industry groups and politicians that real reform is needed, has prompted tremendous debate on health care reform during 1993. Due in part to sharply increasing costs, the nation's health care expenditures (13 percent of the gross national product in 1992) are projected to reach 16 percent by the year 2000. That projection, together with the fact that approximately 36 million people are uninsured or underinsured, makes it no surprise that health care reform has emerged as a critical national issue.

Shortly after his inauguration, President Clinton appointed Hillary Rodham Clinton to chair a Health Care Task Force. The task force, which included more than 500 members, was charged with the task of defining the steps necessary to reform the American health care system in order to accomplish universal access and cost control.

A fundamental concept that has served as a foundation for the task force's reform strategy is *managed competition*. As defined, managed competition seeks to link consumers to informed groups who will help direct them to the highest quality, lowest cost, most appropriate health care delivery. The managed competition model has three major components:

1. *Health Alliances* (HAs), which comprise individuals and small businesses that pool their resources (in the form of health care premiums) to purchase care from an accountable health plan.
2. *Accountable Health Plans* (AHPs), which represent groups of physicians, hospitals, and insurers who form plans to provide medical services. AHPs will compete with each other for business from large employers and HAs.
3. A *National Health Board*, which will be responsible for determining the standard set of benefits to be offered by each AHP, establishing uniform billing procedures, and collecting and disseminating data on quality and cost.

While details of the Health Care Task Force's recommendations are not fully known at the time of this writing, it is anticipated that the following components will be included in the health care reform proposal:

- Universal coverage will be mandated, with a government-established standard benefit package that will include inpatient and outpatient hospitalization, physician services, dental care, outpatient prescription drugs, diagnostic services, and mental health coverage.
- Cost controls are likely to be established in the short term through either mandatory price controls or negotiated voluntary price restraints. Over the long term, states would use global budgets to keep cost increases within the rate of inflation.
- At least one HA per state will be formed that will include all employers of fewer than 1,000 employees, individuals currently eligible for Medicaid, and all other uninsured people. The HA would have the regulatory authority to collect premiums, approve AHPs, and set premium plan rates.
- Employers and employees would pay payroll taxes of approximately 7.0–7.5 percent and 2.0–2.5 percent, respectively, to fund the HA. The tax would

replace current health care premiums and would include a surcharge to cover uninsured people. The HA would collect the premiums and allocate the monies to the AHPs. Additional funds to support the health care reform package may be raised through taxes on alcohol, tobacco, and possibly guns; provider taxes; and tax caps on insurance premiums.

The reform proposal is expected to be introduced in Congress in Fall 1993, with a lengthy congressional debate anticipated, leading to modifications to the task force's recommendations. Although the details of both the proposal and the final law to be enacted are uncertain at the time of this writing, the result could be the most sweeping change in the financing and delivery of health care since the passage of legislation in 1963 enacting Medicare and Medicaid.

Accounting and Auditing

In July 1990, the AICPA issued an audit and accounting guide entitled *Audits of Providers of Health Care Services* (the Guide), which became effective for fiscal years beginning on or after July 15, 1990. The Guide replaced the AICPA industry audit guide, *Hospital Audit Guide,* and five AICPA Statements of Position (SOPs) that subsequently amended it. This Guide was one of the most significant auditing and accounting events affecting health care entities in recent years.

Substantive changes in accounting and reporting are contained in the Guide, including the following:

1. The scope of the Guide has been expanded to include substantially all entities that deliver health care services to patients.
2. Separate fund reporting is permitted but not required.
3. Patient revenue should be reported net, with deductions disclosed if deemed necessary.
4. Bad debts are required to be reported as an operating expense.
5. Charity care is not considered to be revenue and accordingly should be excluded from both accounts receivable and revenue. Disclosure is permissible.
6. A cash flow statement is considered a basic financial statement for health care entities, in accordance with SFAS No. 95.
7. The caption "nonoperating revenue," used to report transactions that are peripheral or incidental to operations and are the result of events largely beyond management's control, has been changed to "nonoperating gains and losses."

Implementation of the Guide's provisions requires management and perhaps board decisions relating to the health care entity's charity care policy and its definition of operating, as opposed to nonoperating, activities.

In November 1990, the AICPA issued SOP 90-8 entitled *Financial Accounting and Reporting by Continuing Care Retirement Communities* (CCRCs). The SOP provides guidance to CCRCs on accounting for and reporting fees, the obligation to provide future services to and the use of facilities by current residents, and costs of acquiring initial continuing care contracts.

In June 1993, the FASB issued Statement of Financial Accounting Standards (SFAS) No. 116, *Accounting for Contributions Received and Contributions Made* (Accounting Standards Sections C67 and No5). Of particular interest to the health care industry are the provisions addressing the recording of pledges received, contributed services, and receipt of both donor-restricted and unrestricted contributions. In general, the statement requires that contributions received be recognized at their fair market value as revenues or gains, and, depending on the nature of the benefits received by the organization, as assets, decreases of liabilities, or expenses. Contributions received would be classified as unrestricted support or as temporarily or permanently restricted support. Unconditional promises to give (e.g., pledges) with payments due in future periods would be reported as restricted support unless the donor clearly intended the monies to be used to support current-period activities. SFAS No. 116 is discussed in more detail in Chapter 27 of this Supplement.

SFAS No. 116 is effective for annual financial statements issued for fiscal years beginning after December 15, 1994, except for not-for-profit organizations with less than $5 million in total assets and less than $1 million in annual expenses. For those organizations, the effective date is extended by one year. Earlier application is encouraged.

In addition, certain health care providers are affected by the provisions of SFAS No. 106, *Employers' Accounting for Postretirement Benefits,* and SFAS No. 112, *Employers' Accounting for Postemployment Benefits.* See Chapter 16 of this Supplement for further discussion of SFAS Nos. 106 and 112.

31

Auditing High Technology Companies

RISK ASSESSMENT AND RELATED AUDIT CONSIDERATIONS

* p. 875. *Add after second full paragraph:*

Hardware (New)

The issues facing high technology companies that develop computers and other hardware components necessary to run software applications are similar to those facing technology companies in general. The business environment is competitive and is characterized by efforts to improve price performance ratios through R&D and by markets that continually demand new products. This results in significant technology investments with shorter product life cycles. Audit issues of concern are the valuation of current and long-term assets, excess or obsolete inventory, and order cancellations or reschedulings.

In attempts to ensure their future viability, many companies have undertaken restructurings, or right-sizing as it has been termed, over the past few years. Among the actions associated with right-sizing have been outplacement of personnel, reduction in overhead by selling or leasing excess space, and elimination of specific product lines or divisions. The focus of the auditor's attention should be on the impact of reductions in personnel on operations and the internal control structure, and the adequacy of reserves relating to current restructuring plans.

Transferring developed technology between companies through strategic alliances or acquisitions helps to decrease development time and supplement available technology. Many companies have developed "new ventures" groups to manage the transfer to other companies of technology they have developed but that does not fit into their current product architecture. Alternatively, obtaining technology through licensing arrangements or acquisitions is a way of supplementing a company's development efforts. The auditor's key concerns over such arrangements include the terms of licenses, the accounting for equity investments, and the valuation of intangible assets.

* **p. 876.** *Replace section* **Computer Software Sales** *with:*

Computer Software Sales

Many high technology companies sell software, generally by means of a license for its use in perpetuity or for a fixed term. The earning process may vary substantially because software may be standard or customized, or may necessitate significant installation support. In addition, customer acceptance may be uncertain, and the selling agreement may provide for extended payment terms, trial periods, or liberal termination features.

In December 1991, the AICPA Accounting Standards Executive Committee issued Statement of Position (SOP) 91-1, *Software Revenue Recognition.* SOP 91-1 was precipitated by the lack of specific guidance on revenue recognition for computer software, as well as a wide range of current accounting practices among companies that sell software, including recognition based on contract signing, delivery, percentage of completion, completed contract, and lease-type accounting methods. In recent years, the SEC has required several major publicly held software companies to change their revenue recognition policies and restate prior-year financial statements.

SOP 91-1 states that revenue from software transactions should be recognized on delivery of the software, provided that collectibility is probable, the vendor has no significant remaining obligations after delivery, and significant uncertainty does not exist regarding customer acceptance of the software. If a significant uncertainty exists about customer acceptance of the software after it has been delivered, revenue should not be recognized until the uncertainty becomes insignificant.

The SOP also provides guidance in the following circumstances:

- The vendor has insignificant obligations after delivery under the sales or licensing agreement;
- The vendor has significant obligations after delivery;
- The software transaction has been structured as a lease;
- No reasonable basis exists for estimating the degree of collectibility of receivables arising from software transactions; and
- The vendor provides services or the right to receive product enhancements (postcontract customer support [PCS]) during or after the initial license period.

SOP 91-1 also contains guidance on accounting for software service contracts and applying contract accounting to software transactions. In addition, it includes disclosure requirements.

Considerable judgment is needed in applying the provisions of the SOP. The auditor must ensure that he or she is familiar with the customer contract, especially if it includes nonstandard terms and conditions. The auditor should be particularly sensitive to software transactions with cancellation privileges, vendor duplication of software, exchange rights, and deferred payment terms, all of which are discussed in detail in the SOP. Adequate audit evidence should be obtained to support prices used when unbundling PCS or service transaction revenues from software product license fees.

Subsequent to the issuance of SOP 91-1, a number of implementation issues have surfaced regarding the guidance in the SOP. In March 1993, the AICPA commenced a project to develop a practice bulletin to provide interpretive guidance with respect to implementing the SOP. The practice bulletin, which was scheduled to be issued at the end of 1993, is expected to provide guidance on

- How software "keys" that can restrict the operation of programs, affect the SOP delivery requirements.
- Accounting for the costs of PCS arrangements and determining prices for unbundling of license and PCS fees.
- Fiscal funding clauses in software contracts.
- Applying contract accounting when off-the-shelf software or output measurements are used.

SFAS No. 86, *Accounting for the Costs of Computer Software to be Sold, Leased, or Otherwise Marketed* (Accounting Standards Section Co2), specifies the accounting for the costs of internally developed and purchased software. The costs of research and development-related activities, which must be expensed in the period incurred, are differentiated from the costs of production activities, which are capitalized. The difference between these two activities is based on the concept of "technological feasibility." To qualify for capitalization, costs must be incurred subsequent to establishing technological feasibility. Software rights purchased or leased for resale must also meet the requirements for technological feasibility to be capitalized.

The auditor must make a judgment regarding technological feasibility. To do this, he or she reviews the product plan and software development methodologies. The auditor must ensure that software is not carried in excess of net realizable value and that revenue forecasts, if amortization is based on revenue, are reasonably constructed, adequately documented, and realistic in view of a company's established channels of distribution and financial resources. (Comparing the costs capitalized under SFAS No. 86 with total company research and development spending for a particular period may be helpful in identifying changes in a company's methodologies, establishing the reasonableness of amounts capitalized, and comparing a company's costs with industry norms.) The auditor must also ensure that the product lives, which typically range from three to five years, are reasonable. The amortization of these costs should not be included in research and development costs, but should be charged to costs of goods sold or a similar expense category.

* **p. 880.**   *Add after first full paragraph:*

In recent years, a number of software companies have reported business combinations in which a substantial portion of the purchase price was allocated to software to be used in a research and development project and that did not have an alternative future use. The amounts allocated to software were immediately expensed in accordance with FASB Interpretation No. 4, *Applicability of FASB Statement No. 2 to Business Combinations Accounted for by the Purchase Method* (Accounting Standards Section B50).

The auditor should evaluate the reasonableness of the purchase price allocation to the assets acquired and should ensure that there is adequate supporting evidence for the valuation of the acquired software to be used in research and development. The auditor should also consider the nature and stage of development of the software acquired, as well as its expected use by the acquirer. The purchase price allocated to software acquired as part of a business combination, for which the acquirer has met the technological feasibility criteria of SFAS No. 86 and that no longer is considered to be in the research and development stage, should not be immediately expensed.

32

Auditing Insurance Companies

* **p. 882.** *Add after fourth paragraph:*

RECENT DEVELOPMENTS

Industry and Economic

The U.S. insurance industry accounts for approximately $2.2 trillion of the nation's assets.[1] It provides financial protection against catastrophic events such as death and property loss, as well as a large share of the nation's health, welfare, and other financial benefits, making it one of the most important financial services industries of the U.S. economy.

Insurance and other financial institutions have, for many years, been considered virtually invulnerable. They have typically been characterized as conservative investors and well-regulated entities. The collapse of the savings and loan industry, and the failure or near failure of a number of U.S. banks and several large insurers, however, have raised questions about the solvency of other financial institutions.

Property and Liability Companies. Property and liability (also known as property and casualty) companies reported capital and surplus of over $160 billion as of December 31, 1992.[2] Over the past decade, property and liability insurers as a group

---

[1] Estimate as of December 31, 1992 derived from preliminary results published by "Best Insurance Management Reports" (Property/Casualty Supplement, Release 8, March 25, 1993, and Life/Health Supplement, Release 9, April 8, 1993), Oldwick, NJ: A.M. Best Company.

[2] See footnote 1.

experienced underwriting losses (before investment income and realized investment gains and losses) in every year. In each of those years, however, the industry had net income after investment returns.

Property and liability insurers undergo what analysts and other observers have identified as distinct underwriting cycles, which recur every several years.[3] During periods of industry profitability, downward pressure on prices occurs as new companies enter the market and existing companies seek to expand and maintain their market share. This phase of the cycle is often characterized by the practice of pricing and risk acceptance by companies that is referred to as *cash flow underwriting*. Companies may be inclined to accept additional underwriting risk in profitable times in anticipation of investment earnings on premiums collected. Under the cycle theory, this underwriting trend eventually leads to depressed earnings as lower prices result in higher underwriting losses. Companies react by firming prices and being more selective in accepting risks, thus causing a turn in the cycle.

Property and liability insurers had record losses in 1992 due to catastrophes, including hurricanes Andrew and Iniki, other major storms, the Chicago flood, and riots in Los Angeles. Industry-wide catastrophe losses, after reinsurance recoveries, have been estimated at record levels of more than $20 billion for 1992 and have continued to mount in 1993. The first half of 1993 saw catastrophes resulting in billions of dollars of losses, including major winter storms along the east coast of the United States and the bombing of the World Trade Center in New York. These events and the problems being experienced at Lloyds of London, a major reinsurer in the world markets, have created significant pressure on market capacity and availability of reinsurance. In addition, several industry observers have predicted a firming of premium rates and reversal of the prolonged downcycle the industry has been in.

Higher losses and loss adjustment expenses have generally been experienced across several lines of business in recent years, particularly in automobile, worker's compensation, and liability lines. In many cases rising costs can be attributed to the increased ability and willingness of claimants to litigate. Together with underwriting and distribution expenses, costs have been rising faster than premiums. Increasing numbers of new entrants in the market and regulatory measures inhibit the ability to increase premiums to meet rising costs. Initiatives such as California's Proposition 103, which called for mandatory rollbacks of insurance premiums to lower rates for certain lines of business, demonstrate the attitudes of some consumers and legislators about increasing insurance premiums.

Another real, but as yet uncertain, exposure that the industry faces is presented by environmental pollution. Environmental losses and liabilities are already significant for many companies. Reports by several observers estimate nationwide pollution clean-up costs in the range of $500 billion to $1 trillion or more. The insurance industry's potential share of this cost is still largely unknown

---

[3] The most severe downcycle experienced by the industry since the identification of this phenomenon concluded in 1984. According to many observers, property and liability companies are currently in a protracted downcycle that began approximately in 1988. However, with recent and significant new capital entering the market amidst the industry's perceived continuing soft pricing, some observers are questioning whether a significant change in the cycle has occurred or is in process.

and dependent on future legislation and court decisions. Chapter 16 of this Supplement discusses environmental liabilities in detail.

Life and Health Companies.   Life and health insurers are also facing significant profitability issues. Newer interest-sensitive products such as universal life and investment-type contracts typically promise higher investment returns to policyholders than do traditional products. Interest-sensitive product premiums have increased to become a significant portion of total life premiums, and this trend is expected to continue.

To meet increasing costs and commitments to higher returns for policyholders, many life companies held significant investments in real estate and mortgage loans in addition to bonds and equity securities. Some life insurers acquired significant investments in high-yield, noninvestment grade (junk) securities. These investments typically provided substantial returns to investors in the past, but recently have proven to be relatively risky assets. Declines in value and liquidity issues regarding these investments have emerged largely because of the sluggish state of the economy. As a result, the importance of asset quality and asset–liability matching by companies has become evident to management, investors, policyholders, and others.

Health insurers are facing some unique challenges and potentially major market-related changes. Traditional insurance products are being supplemented or replaced with administrative services only (ASO) contracts and managed care programs such as health maintenance organizations (HMOs) and preferred provider organizations (PPOs). These plans attempt to minimize the effects of rising costs by establishing contracts with health care providers to provide reduced rates and incentives for more efficient care.

Despite these trends, health care costs continue to grow at a faster pace than other costs and have become a major economic and political issue. As costs have continued to increase, group health plan enrollments have declined. Major employers are turning more to self-insurance of employee medical benefits. The nation's health insurers of last resort, most notably Blue Cross and Blue Shield plans, have come under increasing scrutiny as financial problems are believed to exist in perhaps many of the plans.

The number of Americans with no health care benefits, over 30 million by most estimates, has become a major issue as well. As a result, the current administration has set health care reform as a national priority. While still uncertain, such reforms, including a proposed national network based on managed competition, are expected to have substantial effects on health insurers, including possibly providers of automobile and worker's compensation medical benefits in the property/liability industry. Health care reform is discussed in more detail in Chapter 30 of this Supplement.

Regulatory and Legislative

Congressional Activities and Industry Oversight.   Insurance industry issues have been investigated and addressed by several congressional committees following financial difficulties experienced by some companies. The U.S. General Accounting Office (GAO) has conducted several studies, including special investigations into specific troubled or failed companies, the adequacy of state regulation, and the current system of state guaranty funds. A number of additional studies, particularly related to life insurers, are in progress.

In 1992, Congressman John Dingell (D-Michigan) introduced the Federal Insurance Solvency Act of 1992. The proposed legislation would allow companies meeting proposed standards to obtain a federal certificate and to be regulated for solvency by a newly created Federal Insurance Solvency Commission. Certain larger insurers writing commercial policies for large buyers would be exempt from rate and form regulation by the states as well. The proposed bill would also establish the National Insurance Protection Corporation (a federal guaranty fund), federal regulation of reinsurers, and a national registry of agents and brokers.

The bill was reintroduced as the Federal Insurance Solvency Act of 1993 (H.R. 1290) during the first part of 1993. In the meantime, Congressmen Henry Gonzalez (D-Texas) and Joseph Kennedy (D-Massachusetts) introduced another comprehensive bill (H.R. 1257) that would establish a federal agency to deal with insurance regulation. H.R. 1257 addresses other matters as well, including prohibitions again "redlining," a practice whereby companies seek to reduce exposure by electing not to renew or write new business in specific (usually high-risk) geographic areas.

The McCarran Ferguson Act provides certain antitrust immunities to the insurance industry, which allow companies, through organizations such as the Insurance Services Office, to obtain industry data in order to prevent inadequate pricing of products. This practice, which is often associated with price fixing in other industries, is considered important by the insurance industry since insurers must bill and collect premiums before actual costs are known. A bill was introduced in Congress during 1991 that would have eliminated this exemption, but failed to pass. However, revisions to the McCarran Ferguson Act, including limitations on antitrust immunities enjoyed by the industry, are still under consideration by some in Congress. The McCarran Ferguson Act also delegates regulatory authority over the insurance industry to the individual states.

Many close to the industry speculate that some form of federal oversight of the insurance industry will occur in the future. Areas believed most probable for a federal role are regulation of reinsurance, particularly foreign reinsurers who assume risks in U.S. markets; prevention and prosecution of illegal acts and fraud; and solvency regulation.

State Regulation and the NAIC.   State regulators and the National Association of Insurance Commissioners (NAIC) have actively responded to industry issues and congressional activities. In 1989, the NAIC adopted a solvency policy agenda that includes several initiatives aimed at preserving industry solvency and protecting consumers. These initiatives include, among others, development of an accreditation program and financial regulatory standards, evaluation of the insurance company examination and solvency analysis processes, and standards leading to the uniform evaluation of reinsurance.

Financial Regulatory Standards and State Accreditation.   In a report delivered to Congress based on a study of the NAIC, the GAO has criticized the current system of insurance regulation by the individual states and the effectiveness of the NAIC in that process.[4] Other GAO reports have tended to result in similar criticisms. One of the major criticisms is the NAIC's lack of authority to enforce or to compel states to adopt its model legislation and rules. Advocates of state regulation, however, deny the need for federal regulation and cite, among other reasons, the relatively successful results under the current system as compared with the regulation of other financial institutions.

Under the NAIC's formal accreditation program for states, standards have been established for state insurance departments to apply for and, on approval, receive formal certification by the NAIC attesting to the quality of their regulation of insurers. Among these standards are some 21 model laws and regulations that a state must adopt to become and/or remain accredited. As of March 1993, 18 states were accredited (19 including New York, which was suspended in March for failing to enact certain designated legislation), with some 20 or more states in varying stages of the accreditation process. The NAIC had originally predicted that substantially all states would receive accreditation by January 1, 1994; however, at the time of this writing this does not appear likely.

Asset Valuation and Interest Maintenance Reserves (AVR/IMR). Beginning with the 1992 NAIC annual statement form for life/health companies, the mandatory securities valuation reserve (MSVR), discussed on p. 887 of the main volume, was replaced by the AVR and IMR. The AVR is basically an expanded version of the MSVR, comprising default (bonds and mortgage loans) and equity (equity securities and real estate) components. The new IMR was created to prevent companies from "cherry picking" their portfolios to generate realized gains. It is designed to defer interest-related gains and losses or sales of securities and to amortize them over the remaining life of the underlying securities.

Risk-Based Capital Standards. Many regulators and industry observers have questioned whether fixed minimum capital and surplus requirements adequately ensure the solvency of all insurers.[5] Several states have increased minimum capital and surplus requirements for licensed insurers. In December 1992, the NAIC adopted risk-based capital (RBC) standards for life and health insurance companies, including a model act. The NAIC has also undertaken a project to develop risk-based capital standards for property and casualty companies. A draft of the P&C RBC formula and model act has been exposed by the NAIC and is expected to be finalized in time for application beginning with disclosure in 1994 annual statements.

The concept of risk-based capital was developed to provide a mechanism that can be applied to an individual company to ascertain whether it has a minimum acceptable level of surplus. For life companies, individual risks related to assets,

---

[4] U.S. General Accounting Office, Report to the Chairman, Subcommittee on Oversight and Investigations, Committee on Energy and Commerce, House of Representatives, *Insurance Regulation: Assessment of the National Association of Insurance Commissioners,* May 1991.

[5] In the past, minimum capital and surplus amounts were generally established by states in fixed amounts. In recent years, some states have adopted new minimums expressed in terms of the greater of (1) a specified fixed amount(s) or (2) a specified percentage of a company's reserves or total liabilities. Additionally, most states limit the amount of property/casualty premiums written to a specified multiple of total capital and surplus.

insurance (liabilities), interest rates, and business risks (C1 through C4-type risks) are quantified into a composite index to determine risk-based capital for a company. Several companies and rating agencies have developed risk-based capital or similar models for internal use, and some state insurance departments use them to monitor solvency.

The Life/Health RBC Model Act, once it has been adopted by the individual states, will require companies whose "total adjusted capital" (reported policyholders' surplus, *plus* the asset valuation reserve, voluntary reserves, and one-half of policyholder dividend liabilities) falls below *company action level* or *regulatory action level* RBC to submit detailed RBC plans, undergo regulatory examination or analysis, and/or implement corrective orders, if applicable. Companies whose total adjusted capital falls below *authorized control level* RBC may be placed under regulatory control. If total adjusted capital falls below the *mandatory control level,* a company must be placed under regulatory control. Total adjusted capital and "authorized control level risk-based capital" have been included in the 1993 NAIC annual statement form for life and health companies.

Annual Audit Requirements.   Before 1986, only a few states required audited financial statements to be filed by insurers. Today, many states have solvency legislation in place that includes a requirement for companies to file audited financial statements annually.

In June 1991, the NAIC adopted a new instruction to its 1991 annual statement that required insurers to file statutory financial statements audited by an independent certified public accountant by June 1, 1992. Since then, the NAIC has revised its model regulation, Annual Audited Financial Reports, and added it to the list of models required to be enacted by the states to receive accreditation.

NAIC audit rules also require, among other things, that companies file reports received from independent auditors pointing out reportable conditions in their internal control structure, if any, noted during the audit, as well as material errors in the financial statements and failure by companies to meet minimum capital and surplus requirements. In addition, the new NAIC rules mandate rotation of independent CPAs or the partner in charge of the engagement every seven years.

Investment Regulations.   The near collapse of the junk bond market and increasing risk of defaults have heightened concerns about insurance industry investments. The takeovers and financial difficulties of several large life insurers, in particular, have been attributed largely to excessive holdings of noninvestment grade securities and nonperforming real estate and mortgage loans.

In response to these events, the NAIC is considering a model regulation that would limit investments in noninvestment grade securities. The limitations under the proposed regulation are established in terms of the investment classifications used by the NAIC's Standard Valuation Office. The proposed model regulation currently under consideration would limit aggregate holdings in security categories considered noninvestment grade to 20 percent of an insurer's admitted assets, with further limitations within subsets of those categories. Some states have also established investment limitations; in certain instances, states have passed legislation more restrictive than that currently proposed by the NAIC. In addition to traditional investments, the scope of the NAIC's proposed Investments

Model Act has been expanded to address complex investments such as collateralized mortgage obligations (CMOs) and derivative investments that recently have subjected insurers to significant prepayment and valuation risks.

Statements of Actuarial Opinion. The extensive underwriting losses experienced by property and liability insurers in the mid-1980s raised many questions about the industry's loss reserve practices. States began to require companies to have their loss and loss adjustment expense liabilities examined by qualified loss reserve specialists. In 1990, the NAIC adopted an annual statement instruction requiring certification of loss reserves. Life insurers had previously been required to file statements of actuarial opinion with respect to their reserves and other actuarially determined liabilities.

The NAIC annual statement instruction and most state rules currently allow statements of actuarial opinion to be made by qualified loss reserve specialists or actuaries who are employed by or otherwise not independent of the companies whose reserves are being evaluated. Certain states are considering requiring independent certification of reserves, in some cases in addition to the annual certifications currently required.

Several states have adopted the NAIC's "valuation actuary" amendments to the Standard Valuation Law for life and health insurers. The amendments require opining actuaries to address in their reports whether a company's reserves, when considered together with assets held to support those reserves, are adequate to meet the company's policy and contract obligations, unless a company meets certain requirements for exemption. An accompanying NAIC model regulation, Actuarial Opinion and Memorandum Regulation, contains additional requirements, including that the actuary be appointed by the authority of the board of directors.

Reinsurance. The complexities and quality of reinsurance ceded and assumed by companies continue to receive attention by regulators. Four major property and liability insurance company failures and two near failures in the 1980s were investigated by the House Subcommittee on Oversight and Investigations. The subcommittee issued a landmark report, *Failed Promises—Insurance Company Insolvencies,* in February 1990, which projected that the ultimate cost to the public of the insolvencies investigated would be more than $5 billion. Among the reasons cited in the report for the insolvencies were extensive and complex reinsurance transactions. Many of the concerns expressed about reinsurance have focused on (1) the lack of regulation and oversight of reinsurance markets, particularly foreign reinsurers; (2) the complexities and ambiguities of contracts and programs; (3) the extensive use of reinsurance as a mechanism to provide only temporary surplus relief; and (4) alleged fraud and misrepresentation believed by some regulators to be a significant risk among companies, intermediaries, brokers, and others in the market.

In response to these concerns, states have adopted many new and stringent laws and regulations. These have been aimed largely toward giving states more authority to disallow credit to companies for reinsurance deemed to lack a bona fide transfer of insurance risk among the parties and to be only for the purpose of providing surplus relief. In 1991, California adopted regulations (revised in 1992) essentially banning coinsurance/modified coinsurance (Mod-co) arrangements entered into for surplus relief.

The NAIC has been actively addressing reinsurance issues as well. In 1989, the NAIC substantially modified Schedule F of the property and casualty annual statement, requiring more detailed reinsurance data and providing a penalty for overdue reinsurance. In December 1991, the NAIC amended Chapter 22, "Reinsurance," of its *Accounting Practices and Procedures Manual—Property/ Casualty Insurance Companies* to adopt guidance regarding risk transfer in reinsurance contracts. The NAIC guidance is substantially similar to (and taken directly from) rules proposed by the American Institute of Certified Public Accountants in the exposure draft of its proposed Statement of Position, *Guidance for Assessing Risk Transfer in Property and Liability Reinsurance Contracts*.[6]

The NAIC is continuing to consider model rules and regulations aimed toward uniformity of reinsurance contracts and the use of reinsurance as surplus relief. In 1992, the NAIC developed the Life and Health Reinsurance Agreements Model Regulation, which, upon adoption by individual states, will increase restrictions regarding risk transfer in life and health reinsurance contracts. The NAIC model is similar to the regulations adopted in California (mentioned above). In addition, the NAIC has adopted a new model regulation, Credit for Reinsurance, that imposes solvency standards and other regulatory requirements on reinsurers in order for ceding companies to receive credit in their annual statements. The NAIC is also nearing completion of new model regulations regarding fronting arrangements and assumption reinsurance.

Statutory Accounting Practices.   Statutory accounting practices have traditionally been viewed as conservative. Supplemented by minimum capital and surplus requirements of individual states and other financial regulations, these measures have served as one of the primary means by which regulators monitor industry solvency. However, in recent years, certain financial regulations and statutory accounting rules—for instance, the use of surplus notes[7] and other transactions entered into by companies solely to increase surplus—have been perceived as loopholes and criticized by regulators and Congress as "accounting gimmicks." Statutory accounting also does not clearly provide in all cases for the establishment of economic-based allowances for losses in the value of assets, such as those required by GAAP.

Some recent insurance company failures have been linked to alleged weaknesses in statutory accounting and disclosure, regulatory, and audit practices. As a result, many state insurance departments and examiners have begun to more actively challenge transactions that enhance surplus, especially when the underlying economic

---

[6] The AICPA Insurance Companies Committee formally withdrew this exposure draft in early 1993 following the issuance of Statement of Financial Accounting Standards (SFAS) No. 113, *Accounting and Reporting for Reinsurance of Short-Duration and Long-Duration Contracts* (discussed later). The NAIC is in the process of considering further amendments to conform Chapter 22 of its accounting manual with the risk transfer accounting guidance contained in SFAS No. 113.

[7] Surplus notes represent loans to insurers that, on meeting certain criteria, may qualify under statutory accounting practices to be accounted for as surplus (equity) rather than as a liability. Surplus notes typically bear interest and are repayable (without special consent) only upon certain conditions and from defined excess surplus funds available.

purpose of the transaction is not otherwise apparent or appears questionable. In addition, the accounting profession is considering guidance for auditors regarding communication with insurance regulators to determine whether transactions for which statutory accounting practices are not otherwise prescribed will be permitted by those regulators.

The NAIC currently has projects underway to develop a codification of statutory accounting practices beginning with the guidance contained in the *Accounting Practices and Procedures Manuals* (life/health and property/casualty). The overall objective of these projects is to promote uniformity of statutory accounting practices among the individual states. In a recent development, the AICPA delivered a white paper to the NAIC that, among other things, pointed out certain perceived weaknesses in statutory accounting practices as a comprehensive basis of accounting other than GAAP and recommended that the NAIC consider codifying statutory accounting practices, beginning with GAAP as a foundation for such practices.

Federal Taxation.   A few significant changes have occurred since the passage of the 1984 and 1986 tax acts discussed on page 888 of the main volume. One was a requirement enacted in 1990 that property and casualty insurers account for salvage and subrogation on the accrual basis for tax purposes. A permanent forgiveness of income (fresh start) was granted for 87 percent of the discounted amount of salvage recoverable at the close of the last tax year beginning before January 1, 1990. The remaining 13 percent generally will be taken into income ratably over a period not to exceed four tax years. For companies that previously accrued salvage and subrogation for tax purposes, 87 percent of the discounted estimated salvage recoverable as of the end of the tax year beginning before January 1, 1990 is deductible ratably over the four tax years beginning after December 31, 1989.

Historically, for tax purposes life insurance companies deducted agents' commissions and other selling expenses in the year the expenses were incurred. A 1990 provision requires the capitalization and amortization of policy acquisition expenses for purposes of determining taxable income. The amount to be capitalized is determined using a "proxy method," which specifies percentages of net premiums to be considered as policy acquisition expenses. The percentages are 1.75 percent for annuity contracts, 2.05 percent for group life contracts, and 7.7 percent for all other "specified insurance contracts." "Specified insurance contracts" are defined as annuities, group life, and other life business, including noncancellable and guaranteed renewable accident and health insurance contracts. The specified acquisition expenses may not exceed the company's general deductions for the taxable year. The capitalized amounts are amortized over a 120-month period (60-month period for small companies).

Accounting and Auditing

In 1990, the AICPA published an industry audit and accounting guide, *Audits of Property and Liability Insurance Companies*. The guide superseded its predecessor, *Audits of Fire and Casualty Insurance Companies,* and includes the requirements of Statement of Financial Accounting Standards No. 60, *Accounting and Reporting by Insurance Enterprises* (Accounting Standards Section In6), and statements of position previously issued by the AICPA, including *Auditing Property and Liability Reinsurance.*

Statement of Position (SOP) 90-10, *Reports on Audited Financial Statements of Property and Liability Insurance Companies,* contains guidance regarding how auditors should apply Statements on Auditing Standards Nos. 58 and 62 when issuing opinions on statutory financial statements of property and liability insurance companies.

SOP 90-11, *Disclosure of Certain Information by Financial Institutions About Securities Held as Assets,* amends six industry audit guides, including both the property and liability and stock life insurance guides. The SOP provides guidance for disclosure by financial institutions of certain information about debt securities carried either at historical cost or at the lower of cost or market. The SOP provides guidance, which will be superseded by SFAS No. 115 when it becomes effective (see below), for disclosure by financial institutions of certain information about debt securities carried either at historical cost or at the lower of cost or market. The SOP requires an explanation of accounting policies used, including the basis for classification of securities as investment or trading.

SOP 90-11 also requires disclosure of the amortized cost, estimated market values, and gross unrealized gains and losses for each category (U.S. Treasury, government and political subdivisions, corporate, and others) of debt securities held as assets. The aggregate amortized cost and estimated market values summarized by maturities, and, for each income statement presented, proceeds from securities sales and gross realized gains and losses must also be disclosed.

SOP 92-3, *Accounting for Foreclosed Assets,* requires that foreclosed assets held for sale be accounted for at the lower of fair value less estimated costs to sell, or cost. All foreclosed assets are presumed to be held for sale; however, this presumption is rebuttable (except for in-substance foreclosures) by a preponderance of evidence. A valuation allowance is established and changes in the allowance are recorded in income. Foreclosed assets held for production of income are accounted for as though acquired in a manner other than foreclosure. An exposure draft of a proposed SOP, *Accounting for the Results of Operations of Foreclosed Assets Held for Sale,* has also been issued.

SOP 92-4, *Auditing Insurance Entities' Loss Reserves,* contains comprehensive guidance for independent auditors regarding auditing loss reserves, including situations where a company employs or does not employ a qualified loss reserve specialist. It provides, among other things, that the absence of a qualified loss reserve specialist (other than one employed by the independent auditor) may be a reportable condition or material weakness.

SOP 92-5, *Accounting for Foreign Property and Liability Reinsurance,* requires use of the periodic method, which is essentially the equivalent of U.S. GAAP, to account for reinsurance assumed from foreign companies unless the amounts cannot be reasonably determined. When the amounts cannot be reasonably determined due to differing accounting practices used by foreign ceding companies, and there is lack of information to estimate the differences, the open-year method should be used (recording the transactions as underwriting balances and excluding them from the income statement until adequate information is obtained). A zero balance, or cost recovery, method should not be used.

The NAIC amended the instructions to its annual statement form for property/casualty insurance companies to require companies to instruct their independent auditors to extend the auditing procedures applied to the basic financial statements to include tests of certain loss and loss adjustment expense data contained in Schedule P – Part 1. SOP 92-8, *Auditing Property/Casualty Insurance Entities' Statutory Financial Statements—Applying Certain Requirements of the NAIC Annual Statement Instructions,* provides guidance in applying such auditing procedures and for issuing reports that may be required.

A Notice to Practitioners, *Auditors' Responsibilities Concerning Statement of Actuarial Opinion Required by Insurance Regulators,* provides guidance by the AICPA Insurance Companies Committee in the form of questions and answers concerning an auditor's responsibilities when the actuary rendering an actuarial opinion on the client's reserves (1) assumes responsibility for examination of the underlying data, or (2) states in the actuarial opinion that he or she relied on the auditor for the accuracy of the underlying data. The notice also contains guidance for auditors when providing assistance to independent actuaries in their examination of data underlying reserves and discusses circumstances where the actuary is an employee of the audit firm. It states that an auditor should not consent to actuaries expressing, in their statement of opinion, reliance on the auditor's work regarding the accuracy of data underlying a company's reserves.

In December 1991, the AICPA adopted an interpretation of SAS No. 62, *Special Reports,* entitled "Evaluation of Appropriateness of Informative Disclosures in Statutory-Basis Financial Statements of Insurance Enterprises" (AU Section 9623). The interpretation requires that the independent auditor determine whether disclosures similar to those required in financial statements prepared in conformity with GAAP are appropriately included in the audited statutory-basis financial statements of insurance enterprises, including mutual life insurers, for the same or similar types of items, in order to prevent those financial statements from being misleading.

Practice Bulletin 8, *Application of FASB Statement No. 97,* Accounting and Reporting by Insurance Enterprises for Certain Long-Duration Contracts and for Realized Gains and Losses From the Sale of Investments, *to Insurance Enterprises,* contains implementation guidance in the form of 15 questions and answers about SFAS No. 97.

At the time of this writing, the AICPA Insurance Companies Committee has several additional projects underway. Among these are an exposure draft of a proposed industry accounting guide entitled *Insurance Agents and Brokers,* a proposed SOP that would require disclosures about certain risks and uncertainties unique to the insurance industry; a project to develop guidance on accounting for guaranty fund and certain other assessments; and a project to develop GAAP for mutual life insurance enterprises following the issuance of FASB Interpretation No. 40 (see below). The committee is also developing a comprehensive revision of the industry audit guide, *Audits of Stock Life Insurance Companies,* which, among other things, will be expanded to cover both stock and mutual life insurance enterprises.

SFAS No. 105, *Disclosure of Information about Financial Instruments with Off-Balance-Sheet Risk and Financial Instruments with Concentrations of Credit Risk,* the first statement of the FASB's financial instruments project, requires disclosures about financial instruments that have off-balance-sheet risk or concentrations of credit risks among issuers or holders. SFAS No. 107, *Disclosures about Fair Value of Financial Instruments,* became effective for financial statements issued for fiscal years ending after December 15, 1992 (December 15, 1995 for companies with less than $150 million in assets) and requires fair value disclosures for financial instruments. Insurance contracts, other than investment and financial guarantee contracts as defined under SFAS Nos. 60 and 97, are exempt from the disclosures. SFAS Nos. 105 and 107 are discussed in Chapter 21A of this Supplement.

SFAS No. 113, *Accounting and Reporting for Reinsurance of Short-Duration and Long-Duration Contracts,* establishes conditions under which contracts may be considered reinsurance as opposed to financing-type contracts (e.g., risk transfer) and provides accounting guidance, including the requirement for gross reporting of reinsurance assets and the deferral of gains on retroactive contracts. It also provides disclosure guidance, including the application of SFAS No. 105 to reinsurance contracts. The new reinsurance accounting standard applies to contracts between insurance enterprises that report under SFAS No. 60, whether or not specifically referred to as reinsurance; such contracts include intercompany pooling agreements, fronting arrangements, and servicing carrier agreements. Financing-type contracts are not accounted for as reinsurance, but by the deposit method as required under SFAS No. 60. SFAS No. 113 became effective for financial statements issued for fiscal years beginning after December 15, 1992, and contains special transition rules for the various sections, as well as provisions regarding application to existing contracts.

SFAS No. 114, *Accounting by Creditors for Impairments of Loans,* was issued in June 1993. It will require creditors to write down loans, excluding certain high-volume, small retail loans, when it is expected that borrowers will not meet the terms of their loan agreements. The amount to be written down ordinarily is determined by the difference between the present value of the expected cash flows and the carrying value of the loan (two alternative measurements are provided for expediency). The discount rate to be used is the effective interest rate of the loan. SFAS No. 114 will become effective for financial statements issued for fiscal years beginning on or after December 15, 1993.

SFAS No. 115, *Accounting for Certain Investments in Debt and Equity Securities,* was also issued in June 1993. It will amend SFAS No. 60, which now requires insurers to carry investments at amortized cost when companies have both the ability and intent to hold them to maturity, and at market in the absence of ability and intent to hold and when the company is a trader in bonds. SFAS No. 115 will require all companies to classify investments into three categories: *held-to-maturity, available-for-sale,* and *trading.* Only held-to-maturity investments, which will be determined using stricter criteria under SFAS No. 115, will be carried at amortized cost. Available-for-sale securities and trading securities will be carried at market. Unrealized gains and losses on available-for-sale securities will be recorded directly as a component of equity, while holding gains and losses on trading securities will be recorded in income. Transfers of securities among the categories will be treated essentially like sales, with resulting gains and losses recorded in income. SFAS No. 115 will become effective for financial statements for fiscal years beginning on or after December 15, 1994. The statement is discussed further in Chapter 17 of this Supplement.

FASB Interpretation No. 40, *Application of Generally Accepted Accounting Principles to Mutual Life Insurance and Other Enterprises,* issued in April 1993, will preclude statutory accounting practices from being considered GAAP for mutual life insurers effective for financial statements issued for years beginning after December 15, 1994. Interpretation No. 40 requires companies to disclose the impending change in financial statements issued for years beginning after December 15, 1992.

The FASB Emerging Issues Task Force has discussed two agenda items specifically applicable to the insurance industry: EITF Issue 92-9, *Accounting for the Present Value of Future Profits Resulting from the Acquisition of a Life Insurance Company,* and EITF Issue 93-6, *Accounting for Multiple-Year Retrospectively Rated Contracts by Ceding and Assuming Enterprises.*

33

Auditing Investment Companies

* p. 908. *Add after first paragraph:*

RECENT DEVELOPMENTS

Industry and Economic

At the end of 1992, management investment companies—both open-end or mutual and closed-end funds—had assets in excess of $1.6 trillion invested in approximately 3,850 different funds. Significant growth continues in this industry, fueled in particular by a growing distribution network of bank-affiliated fund products, the trend in corporate America away from defined benefit retirement plans and toward defined contribution arrangements organized around a variety of mutual fund products, and the growing globalization of investment products and markets.

The growing focus on innovative marketing strategies is evidenced by an increasing use of multiple class funds. Shareholders in these funds may select among several (generally three) sales commission structures: a traditional "front-end" load; a deferred "back-end" sales charge tied to an annual 12b-1 fee (asset-based distribution charge), and a so-called "level load" charge (generally 1%) annually for as long as the shares are held. The deferral of sales loads may also require a significant pool of capital to fund commission payments to brokers until the 12b-1 or contingent deferred sales charge payments materialize. This has led to distributors seeking arrangements with banks or other funding agents and to new forms of 12b-1 plans (discussed later in this chapter).

Another approach to segmenting the market, while at the same time centralizing assets, is the "hub-and-spoke" fund structure, which groups similar shareholders in a "spoke" that in turn invests in a central "hub." This approach enables marketers to develop specific fee structures for particular markets, for example, institutional and retail, while collecting assets into one central pool for investment management purposes.

The Securities and Exchange Commission (SEC), as part of its 50th Anniversary review of the Investment Company Act of 1940, has suggested a number of possible amendments. While they have not yet been finalized into specific regulations, the amendments would permit existing closed-end funds to redeem shares at periodic intervals, for example, quarterly, or enable open-end funds to sell foreign investor-specific fund products that would facilitate tax compliance while enhancing foreigners' ability to invest in U.S. products.

Regulatory

While there have not been any major amendments to the underlying regulatory structure of investment companies, several long-term projects have recently been finalized.

The SEC has revised the annual reporting requirements for both open-end and closed-end funds on Form N-1A and Form N-2, respectively. The changes are aimed at clarifying specific matters considered by the SEC to be important to shareholders, for example, financial highlights of per share information, specific information concerning the portfolio investment manager, and management's discussion of fund performance as compared with portfolio benchmarking. The information may be presented in the annual report or the prospectus (registration statement).

Regulations of the National Association of Securities Dealers (NASD) affecting the 12b-1 fees paid by funds became effective on July 7, 1993. These regulations ensure that most fund shareholders will not pay more than the current maximum front-end sales commission (8.5% at the time of this writing), no matter what pricing structure they choose. Both an annual cap of 0.75 percent and a cumulative cap of 6.25 percent (7.25% if no service fee is charged) are in place for 12b-1 fees.

Several amendments and clarifications have been undertaken by the Internal Revenue Service, with effects on regulated investment companies. In particular, the regulations covering "passive foreign investment companies" have been clarified to facilitate a fund's "marking-to-market" such instruments at year-end (or upon discovery) to avoid an unexpected tax liability.

Other amendments, for example, a proposal to change the 30 percent requirement regarding short-term gains or to require funds to offer shareholders a summary of the tax cost of their shares, are presently under consideration by Congress.

Accounting and Auditing

A number of Statements of Position (SOPs) have been developed by the AICPA Investment Companies Committee, including:

- 93-1, *Financial Accounting and Reporting for High-Yield Debt Securities by Investment Companies*
- 93-2, *Determination, Disclosure, and Financial Statement Presentation of Income, Capital Gain, and Return of Capital Distributions by Investment Companies*
- 93-4, *Foreign Currency Accounting and Financial Statement Presentation for Investment Companies*

Each of the SOPs aims at clarifying specific issues that in the past led to a diversity of financial reporting practices. SOPs 93-1 and 93-2 become effective for years ending after December 15, 1993 (including the interim periods of such years), while SOP 93-4 will take effect for years ending after December 15, 1994. In approving SOP 93-4 for issuance, the Financial Accounting Standards Board agreed to the AICPA Investment Companies Committee's request to be allowed to form a subcommittee to study further the question of bifurcating foreign currency gains/losses from market appreciation/depreciation. This subcommittee's task will be to consider whether such disclosure is useful and, if so, how such a goal might be effectively attained.

The issuance of SAS No. 70, *Reports on the Processing of Transactions by Service Organizations* (AU Section 324), also has a direct impact on the investment company industry, where service agents (fund custody, transfer agency, and administration) often play a critical role. This SAS specifically affects custodian and transfer agent third-party internal control reports, as well as multiple class fund design/operation reporting on expense allocation and the calculation of net asset value (NAV) per share and distributions. Thus, the requirements of this standard should be carefully considered as auditors plan their third-party control procedures. (Statement on Standards for Attestation Engagements No. 2, *Reporting on an Entity's Internal Control Structure Over Financial Reporting*, which was issued in May 1993 and superseded SAS No. 30, *Reporting on Internal Accounting Control*, does not apply to the auditor's report on internal controls included in Form N-SAR.)

Another area of significance auditors must focus on is multiple class funds. Specific reports on the design and functioning of a fund's systems of expense measurement and allocation to particular classes, as well as the daily NAV per share and distributions, must be submitted to the SEC. Tax compliance issues are extensive, and failure to comply can result in a "disproportionate dividend" disqualifying the fund from RIC status (discussed on page 905 of the main volume). Financial statement presentation of information that is fund or class specific may be complex. The Investment Company Institute's Accounting Policy Subcommittee has issued a white paper entitled *Multiple Class Accounting and Reporting* (ICI Accounting/Treasurers Members White Paper No. 18-92, March 31, 1992) to help fund accountants and auditors understand the various issues surrounding multiple class operational and financial presentation issues. A second white paper, published by the ICI, addresses accounting, tax, and operational issues for mortgage-backed securities.

Other issues currently under consideration by the AICPA include so-called "enhanced" 12b-1 plans, under which a fund enters into an agreement to reimburse the fund's distributor for any unreimbursed 12b-1 costs even if the 12b-1 plan is terminated; unregistered investment partnership financial statement issues, including presentation of the investment portfolio and performance fees; and revision and updating of the investment company audit guide.

The variety of fund products whose objectives extend from global to ultra-specific, modern-derivative investment strategies continuously challenge the investment company auditor. Issues relating to security valuation, portfolio custody (particularly foreign securities held by foreign subcustodians or foreign central depositories), and a fund's overall internal control structure continue to be important matters for consideration. Careful attention to a fund's prospectus, registration statement, and operational arrangements is essential.

34

Auditing Mining Companies

OVERVIEW OF THE INDUSTRY

* **p. 922.** *Add after second full paragraph:*
   Solvent extraction-electrowinning (SX-EW) is a method often used in processing oxide ore, a less common type of ore found in the United States. The SX-EW process involves extracting metal from mined ore through leaching and then removing it from the solvent using electrochemical refining techniques. The final product of the SX-EW process is refined metal.

RECENT DEVELOPMENTS

Environmental Issues

Mining companies are facing increased legislation and prosecution relating to environmental violations; as a result, the area of contingent liabilities often is the key focal point in the auditing process. Two federal laws provide the primary basis for regulation of hazardous waste disposal and clean-up. They are the Resource Conservation and Recovery Act of 1976, referred to as RCRA, and the Comprehensive Environmental Response, Compensation and Liability Act of 1980, referred to as CERCLA and also known as Superfund. Both laws, which are administered by the Environmental Protection Agency (EPA) and by similar state agencies, established regulatory controls over the generation, transportation, and disposal of hazardous wastes. Chapter 16 of this Supplement presents a summary of recent developments in the area of environmental liabilities, including related accounting implications and auditing considerations. That discussion is particularly relevant to auditing a mining company's accounting for and disclosure of environmental liabilities.

RISK ASSESSMENT AND AUDIT STRATEGY

* **p. 926.** *Add after first full paragraph:*
Collectibility of receivables traditionally has not been a major concern in the industry, since sales historically have been to customers who are relatively strong financially. However, economic conditions are not static, and the auditor must be cognizant of the company's customers and the industries in which they operate. For instance, suppliers of copper may experience declining demand from end users in the construction industry who are negatively affected by a slump in residential and commercial real estate markets. In the current economic environment, collectibility of receivables has become a troubling issue. Confronted with long-outstanding balances, the auditor must determine the extent (if any) to which assets have been impaired.

Additionally, in light of SFAS No. 105, *Disclosure of Information about Financial Instruments with Off-Balance-Sheet Risk and Financial Instruments with Concentrations of Credit Risk,* the auditor should determine the extent to which group concentrations of credit risk exist. SFAS No. 105 states that "group concentrations of credit risk exist if a number of counterparties are engaged in similar activities and have similar characteristics that would cause their ability to meet contractual obligations to be similarly affected by changes in economic or other conditions." In other words, concentrations of credit risk may exist where a producer sells a product (e.g., copper) to a small number of large customers who operate in one industry (e.g., construction). In situations where concentrations of credit risk exist, the auditor should ensure that the disclosure requirements of SFAS No. 105 are met. (See the more detailed discussion of SFAS No. 105 in Chapter 21A of this Supplement.)

TYPICAL TRANSACTIONS, CONTROL STRUCTURE POLICIES AND PROCEDURES, AND AUDIT TESTS

The Expenditure Cycle

* **p. 932.** *Insert at end of third full paragraph:*
In the case of leach operations, generally the mineral content of the ore is estimated and costs are inventoried. However, practice varies and some companies do not inventory costs until the leached product is introduced into the electrochemical refinery cells.

Income Taxes

* **p. 937.** *Replace last line through first full paragraph on page 938 with:*
A credit for minimum tax paid (minimum tax credit, or MTC) is allowed to offset regular tax liability in future years. However, the MTC may not reduce the

regular tax below the tentative minimum tax for the taxable year in which the credit is utilized. For tax years beginning after December 31, 1989, all AMT paid results in MTC. An extremely important issue for the mining industry relates to the interplay of percentage depletion and net operating loss carryforwards in calculating the MTC.

In early 1992, the Financial Accounting Standards Board issued Statement of Financial Accounting Standards (SFAS) No. 109, *Accounting for Income Taxes,* which is effective for fiscal years beginning after December 15, 1992. Chapter 19 of this Supplement provides guidance on auditing income tax-related accounts under SFAS No. 109.

35

Auditing Oil and Gas Producing Activities

ACCOUNTING PRINCIPLES

Gas Accounting Issues

* **p. 950.** *Add at the end of fourth paragraph in section:*
COPAS Bulletin No. 24, *Producer Gas Imbalances,* issued in 1991, further explains gas imbalance accounting.

RISK ASSESSMENT AND AUDIT STRATEGY

Inherent Risk

p. 953. *Replace third bullet with:*

- *Complex Income Tax Considerations.* Income tax provisions, proved reserve quantities, and the standardized measure may be affected by income tax deductions and tax credits peculiar to the oil and gas and similar industries. Examples of tax matters unique to these industries are percentage depletion, tax credits for nonconventional fuel production, and tax credits for enhanced oil recovery. Virtually every oil and gas company is faced with a variety of transactions that either must or may be treated differently for tax purposes than for financial reporting purposes. Furthermore, most independent oil and gas producers pay the alternative minimum tax rather than the regular federal income tax, which makes the income tax computation particularly complex. The auditor should have an adequate understanding of the principal income tax considerations affecting oil and gas companies.

* • *Hedging.* Some oil and gas producers from time to time hedge or speculate with energy futures or options on such futures. Normally, the following year's production, rather than existing inventory, is hedged. Any contracts treated as hedges for financial statement purposes, proved reserve determinations, or calculations of the Standardized Measure disclosure must meet the high correlation criteria of SFAS No. 80, *Accounting for Futures Contracts* (Accounting Standards Section F80). Some futures contracts, particularly for natural gas, may not meet those criteria for natural gas delivered in certain regions of the country.

SUBSTANTIVE TESTS: AUDIT OBJECTIVES AND PROCEDURES

Oil and Gas Property Costs

p. 957.   *Replace second and third paragraphs with:*

Full Cost Method.   Under the full cost method of accounting for oil and gas producing activities, the major audit issues relate to determining which oil and gas property costs are capitalizable, the appropriate realizable value or "ceiling" for those costs, and how they should be amortized. S-X Rule 4-10 prescribes how a public company should make those determinations.

For many companies, the greatest risk that the financial statements will be materially misstated arises from misapplication of the full cost ceiling test. The largest component of the ceiling is the present value, at a 10 percent annual discount rate, of the future net revenues of the company's proved oil and gas reserves, using prices that are current as of the applicable balance sheet date. The SEC staff has informally expressed the view that oil and gas companies should make ceiling tests quarterly based on spot prices and fixed and determinable contract prices as of the end of each quarter. This means that seasonally low gas prices at the end of a quarter may necessitate an irreversible write-off of capitalized costs, even though the impairment that has occurred is not irreversible.

Supplementary Financial Disclosures

p. 966.   *Add after the carryover paragraph:*

For financial reporting purposes, SFAS No. 25 specifies that the definition of "proved reserves" is that developed by the Department of Energy and adopted by the SEC. In applying for credit and for other purposes, however, oil and gas companies often use proved reserve estimates based on the definition of proved reserves adopted by the Society of Petroleum Engineers (SPE) and Society of Petroleum Evaluation Engineers (SPEE), which is broader than the SEC definition.

Income Tax Accounting

* **p. 967.** *Replace text with:*
In early 1992, the Financial Accounting Standards Board (FASB) issued Statement of Financial Accounting Standards No. 109, *Accounting for Income Taxes,* which is effective for fiscal years beginning after December 15, 1992. Chapter 19 of this Supplement provides guidance on auditing income tax-related accounts under SFAS No. 109.

36

Auditing Pension Plans

p. 971. *Add at beginning of chapter:*

RECENT DEVELOPMENTS

Industry and Economic

Some pension administrators and investment managers in recent years directed an increasing portion of plan investments into higher yielding and, in many cases, higher risk investments, including junk bonds, real estate, foreign securities, and guaranteed investment contracts issued by insurance companies and other financial institutions. With the weakening of the economy and the decline of certain investment markets (junk bonds and real estate in particular), the quality and value of investments of some plans have been called into question. Auditors should carefully consider the valuation of and disclosures related to

* plan investments in light of the volatility of financial markets, and may want to consider whether plans' policies and procedures for identifying market value changes are adequate in light of current conditions. For plans with investments in contracts with financial institutions with significant holdings in high-risk investments, auditors also need to consider the financial stability of the issuing company and its ability to fulfill its contractual obligations.

Regulatory and Legislative

Concerned with the quality and value of plan assets, as well as responding to pressure from Congress, the Department of Labor (DOL) has intensified its review of ERISA audits and its pension-related enforcement activities. Following its 1990 review, the DOL proposed various legislative changes, including proposals to repeal the limited-scope exemption (discussed on pages 1001-1002 of the main volume), require that ERISA audits be included in peer review programs, provide incentives for plan participants to exercise their rights to bring private litigation under ERISA, and strengthen deterrents to unlawful behavior.

During 1991, the DOL initiated a new quality review program, under which it performs selected on-site reviews of independent auditors' working papers. If the DOL determines that substandard audit work or deficient reporting has occurred, it can request correction in future audits or appoint another auditor. The DOL can also assess civil penalties, reject the report, or refer the auditor to the state licensing board or the AICPA's Professional Ethics Division.

The DOL has also increased its application of ERISA penalty provisions to plans filing deficient annual reports. The penalties vary according to the severity of the deficiency, and can be as much as $1,000 a day, starting the date the annual filing was due. Common deficiencies have included incomplete financial statements and footnote disclosures, omission of an auditor's report or the filing of a report that failed to cover required supplemental schedules, and limited-scope audit reports for plans that did not qualify for the exemption.

* In 1992, the U.S. General Accounting Office (GAO) issued a report to Congress entitled *Improved Plan Reporting and CPA Audits Can Increase Protection Under ERISA,* which recommended to the AICPA a number of ways the quality of audits under ERISA could be improved. It also recommended to Congress that ERISA regulations be amended to eliminate the provision permitting limited-scope audits, and that the DOL require plan administrators to report on the effectiveness of plan internal controls, with auditor involvement in the reporting process. Additionally, it recommended requirements for auditors' reporting of fraud and serious ERISA violations to the DOL if plan administrators fail to do so, for participation in a peer review program, and for addressing audit reports to both plan administrators and participants.

* The IRS has announced a Voluntary Compliance Resolution (VCR) program designed to permit plan sponsors to correct operational defects under their qualified retirement plans. Under this experimental program, which extends through 1994, the IRS will not pursue plan disqualification and related penalties against plan sponsors that voluntarily identify and correct operational defects. Plan sponsors may use this window of opportunity to evaluate whether there are potential operational defects that could be revealed as a result of an IRS examination, and consider the advantages and disadvantages of participating in the VCR program.

Accounting and Auditing

A number of standards and governmental reports affecting pension plans have been issued, including

- The DOL's *Trouble Shooters' Guide to Filing the ERISA Annual Reports,* which describes the DOL's processing procedures and how to avoid certain filing errors and penalties.
- Revised Form 5500 instructions relating to, among other things, the computation of realized and unrealized gains and losses. Since 1991, the DOL has

been enforcing the requirement that realized and unrealized gains and losses reported on Form 5500 must be determined using revalued cost, that is, the current value of plan assets at the beginning of the plan year. Previously, many plans used historical cost as the basis of calculating realized and unrealized gains and losses. Although not required by SFAS No. 35, some plans also report realized and unrealized gains and losses in their GAAP financial statements. Because GAAP requires the use of historical cost in computing realized and unrealized gains and losses, a discrepancy may exist between the amounts reported in the financial statements and in Form 5500. ERISA regulations require that such discrepancies be reconciled in the notes to the financial statements.

- SFAS No. 102, *Statement of Cash Flows—Exemption of Certain Enterprises and Classification of Cash Flows from Certain Securities Acquired for Resale* (Accounting Standards Section Pe5), provides an exemption from presenting a statement of cash flows for defined benefit pension plans and certain other employee benefit plans. This statement formalized what had been generally followed in practice.

- SFAS No. 105, *Disclosure of Information about Financial Instruments with Off-Balance-Sheet Credit Risk and Financial Instruments with Concentrations of Credit Risk,* establishes requirements for entities to disclose information about financial instruments with off-balance-sheet risk of loss and concentrations of risk.

* - SFAS No. 110, *Reporting by Defined Benefit Pension Plans of Investment Contracts* (Accounting Standards Section Pe5), requires defined benefit pension plans to report all investment contracts, whether issued by an insurance enterprise or other entity, at fair value. This Statement amends SFAS No. 35, *Accounting and Reporting by Defined Benefit Pension Plans,* to permit defined benefit pension plans to report at contract value only contracts that incorporate mortality or morbidity risk (as well as deposit administration and immediate participation guarantee contracts entered into before March 20, 1990).

* - Revisions of the AICPA Audit and Accounting Guide, *Audits of Employee Benefit Plans.* The guide was revised twice (in 1991 and 1992) to incorporate applicable accounting and auditing standards issued since the previous edition. Guidance added in 1991 includes the auditor's responsibility to read financial information contained in the plan's Form 5500 and the auditor's responsibility if he or she concludes that the plan has entered into a prohibited transaction.

*   Guidance added in 1992 highlights DOL requirements for certifications by trustees in limited-scope audits, emphasizing that in order for plan administrators to elect to request auditors to limit the scope of their audit with respect to certain information prepared and certified by banks and similar institutions, or insurance carriers, that act as trustees or custodians, the trustee must certify both the accuracy and completeness of the information submitted. Failure to obtain both these certifications will disqualify plan administrators for the exemption.

* - Statement on Auditing Standards (SAS) No. 70, *Reports on Processing of Transactions by Service Organizations* (AU Section 324). The SAS provides guidance to a plan auditor when the plan uses a service organization. The SAS supersedes SAS No. 44. This topic is discussed in more detail in Chapters 6 and 23 of this Supplement.

* Among pending changes in accounting and auditing standards is a proposed statement of position on reporting of investment contracts held by defined contribution pension plans (and health and welfare benefit plans), addressing issues similar to those covered by SFAS No. 110.

37

Auditing Public Utilities

* p. 1005. *Add after third paragraph:*

RECENT DEVELOPMENTS

Industry and Economic

Electric Utilities. The generating sector of the electric utility industry has become increasingly competitive as independent and affiliated nonutility power developers provide a growing percentage of the nation's new capacity. Utilities' increasing reliance on buying power from outside sources has raised questions about operational reliability, because nonutility generators (NUGs) have no statutory obligation to serve and because most are much more highly leveraged than utilities. The rates that utilities pay for NUG power are usually market-based, often determined through a competitive bidding process. There are also concerns about possible increases in the purchasing utilities' cost of capital because of the nature of the take-or-pay contracts that utilities usually sign with NUGs.

The passage of legislation providing open wholesale transmission access has increased pressures on utilities to provide retail transmission access. Under retail access, large industrial end-users could shop for inexpensive power and have it transmitted to them over their former retail suppliers' lines. This causes concern to utilities whose remaining customers would have to bear a greater portion of the fixed costs. Many believe, however, that the forces favoring retail access will prevail sooner or later.

Possible health effects related to radiation from electric and magnetic fields (EMF) are an environmental concern, which utilities are addressing through research and customer and employee communications. If EMF radiation is found to be hazardous, the cost of rectification could be enormous. Many utilities are already dealing with litigation costs related to real estate, siting, and personal injury suits.

Gas Utilities.   The impact of deregulation has been felt in all areas of the natural gas industry, including producers, interstate pipelines, and local distribution companies (LDCs). Interstate pipelines have been directly affected through a series of regulatory orders issued by the Federal Energy Regulatory Commission (FERC) designed to promote greater competition in wellhead and downstream gas markets through "open access transportation" and "unbundling of services" for all users of the U.S. natural gas transmission system. Although this has led to much greater flexibility in the number of users and choices in the natural gas market, it has also resulted in difficult transitional issues with which the industry has had to deal, such as the sharing among pipelines and their customers (including LDCs, industrials, and shippers) of take-or-pay liabilities and stranded investment or transition costs resulting from the unbundling of various services formerly provided almost solely by interstate pipelines.

LDCs, while remaining under state rate-making regulation, have also felt the impact of deregulation as costs and issues flow downstream to be dealt with separately by each state commission. LDCs have been uniquely affected by industrial customers "bypassing" their systems and purchasing gas directly from producers or pipelines, potentially shrinking their customer base and limiting their ability to allocate and recover costs, both fixed and transitional.

One result of increased competition within the industry and the favor natural gas is enjoying compared with other forms of energy, has been a tremendous expansion in pipeline construction, particularly in the western (primarily California) and northeastern markets. A number of these expansions and new systems were approved based on greater assumptions of risk on the part of their owners, another aspect of competition endorsed by FERC. Potential transmission overcapacity, bypass, and the impact of interfuel competition with other forms of energy are all issues that will be of strategic importance to companies and their regulators as competition increasingly pervades the natural gas industry.

Regulatory and Legislative

Electric Utilities.   The National Energy Policy Act of 1992 is expected to cause sweeping changes in the electric industry. Title VII of the Act seeks to increase competition in electric generation by revising the Public Utility Holding Company Act (PUHCA) so that it is no longer an impediment to the development of nonrate-based power plants, and by granting FERC broad new authority to open up the electric utility transmission grid.

A new class of power providers, exempt wholesale generators (EWGs), has been created. EWGs are exempt from the substantial and pervasive regulation by the Securities and Exchange Commission (SEC) under PUHCA, and thus do not have to assume convoluted business structures to avoid such regulation. EWGs are allowed to own eligible generating facilities, including those located abroad. The law also includes a foreign utility exemption that allows EWGs to own foreign facilities that sell electricity at retail. States were directed to perform evaluations of the effect of wholesale power purchases on utility cost of capital, the effect of leveraged capital structures on reliability, the adequacy of fuel supply, and whether to provide advance approval of long-term power purchases.

Any utility, federal power marketing agency, or other entity generating power may apply to FERC for an order requiring a transmitting utility to provide transmission services, including any enlargement necessary. The law sets forth pricing requirements that are unclear but leave ample room for an appropriate pricing policy to be developed by FERC. FERC-mandated retail wheeling (providing transmission of electric energy directly to an ultimate consumer) is prohibited.

The Clean Air Act of 1990 contains provisions for the reduction of sulfur dioxide and nitrogen oxide emissions, which are thought to be primary sources of acid rain. The legislation focuses on emissions from electric utility coal- and oil-fired generating facilities. It is historic in its unprecedented cost—$4 to $9 billion a year—and in its reliance on market forces. The Act allows affected generators substantial flexibility in selecting compliance approaches by creating an entirely new market for emission allowances. (An emission allowance is a license to emit one ton of sulfur dioxide during a calendar year.) Since this legislation mandates compliance on a system-wide basis, rather than on the basis of individual facilities, a utility can overcomply at one site and undercomply at another. Regulators, who must approve utilities' compliance expenditures before their costs can be included in rates, will scrutinize the allocation of these significant costs among jurisdictions. Furthermore, the regulators can be expected to examine the total cost of compliance to ensure that the most cost-effective approach was adopted.

Gas Utilities.   To resolve the take-or-pay liabilities resulting from the move to open-access transportation on interstate pipelines and in response to various court actions, in the late 1980s FERC issued a series of regulations to provide for a cost-sharing approach among the various parties affected, including pipelines, industrials, and LDCs. FERC also encouraged state commissions to require LDCs to absorb a share of such costs passed to them by pipelines rather than directly passing through all such costs to their customers. Although most take-or-pay contracts were restructured in response to these initiatives, the recovery of these costs by pipelines and LDCs from their customers is still a significant issue for the industry.

In what was characterized as the final stage in the move to a competitive environment in the natural gas industry, in 1992 FERC issued a new series of orders (the "restructuring rules") designed to ensure comparability of transportation service such that both pipeline and nonpipeline gas sellers "compete for gas purchasers on an equal footing." These rules provide for, among other things, the unbundling and separate pricing of various services such as gathering, sales, and storage and the recovery by the pipelines of various "transition costs" such as unrecovered purchase gas costs remaining from regulated gas sales activities, gas supply contract realignment costs, and stranded costs of facilities that cannot be directly allocated to customers of unbundled services. Most observers of the industry agree that costs, as well as operational issues, resulting from these latest FERC regulations will be substantial and that significant litigation and regulatory proceedings will be necessary to resolve them.

Communications Companies. In October 1990, the Federal Communications Commission (FCC) initiated a system of price caps for local exchange carriers (LECs). In effect, this is a modified form of regulation, which retains some aspects of traditional regulation in that it is tied to a rate of return measure and requires prospective refunds (i.e., sharing of earnings) if earnings exceed specified levels. However, the price cap rules are based on an incentive structure that is more closely tied to the general economy than traditional regulatory measures were and on a competitive market model. The FCC's Report and Order (in Docket No. 87-313) states that "LECs that can outperform the productivity level embedded in the annual adjustment mechanism are rewarded with the ability to retain reasonably higher earnings than would be available under the former regulatory system" (para. 2). The price cap rules are mandatory only for the Bell Operating Companies and GTE; smaller LECs have the option of continuing to use traditional rate of return regulation and most have chosen to do so. (AT&T, the dominant interexchange carrier, also operates under price cap regulation, with no sharing requirements and a different productivity offset.)

The price cap mechanism has three elements: a measure of inflation, a productivity offset, and exogenous costs, that is, cost changes beyond the control of the carrier. The measure of inflation is the 45-day estimate of the Gross National Product Price Index (GNP-PI); it is adjusted by an allowance for exogenous costs. The productivity offset is designed to reflect the degree to which LEC operations are more efficient than the general economy. Identifying and justifying exogenous costs is complex and involves determining that a cost is outside the control of the carrier and that it is unique to carriers (i.e., not already reflected in the GNP-PI) and is not an ongoing industry occurrence.

Accounting and Auditing

Emerging accounting and auditing issues for electric and gas utilities are largely driven by environmental concerns, including the disposition of materials containing polychlorinated biphenyle (PCB), the disposition of high and low levels of radioactive waste, the reduction of sulfur dioxide emissions, and asbestos removal.

Identifying and quantifying risks and liabilities for asbestos and PCB treatment are often difficult. The Clean Air Act of 1990, which becomes effective January 1, 1995, has set sulfur dioxide emissions limits of 2.5 pounds per million BTUs. The Nuclear Regulatory Commission has defined the minimum funding requirements for nuclear facility decommissioning but has yet to establish a permanent repository for high-level radioactive waste.

The Emerging Issues Task Force (EITF) has addressed two accounting issues dealing with environmental concerns. On EITF Issue 89-13, *Accounting for the Cost of Asbestos Removal,* the consensus of the task force was that costs incurred to treat asbestos within a reasonable time period after a property with a known asbestos problem is acquired should be capitalized as part of the cost of the acquired property, subject to an impairment test. The task force also reached a consensus that in other instances costs incurred to treat asbestos may be capitalized as a betterment, subject to an impairment test. When costs are incurred in anticipation of a sale of property, they should be deferred and recognized in the period of the sale, to the extent they can be recovered from the estimated sales price.

EITF Issue 90-8, *Capitalization of Costs to Treat Environmental Contamination,* deals with whether environmental contamination treatment costs should be capitalized or charged to expense. The task force reached a consensus that, in general, environmental contamination treatment costs should be charged to expense. Those costs may be capitalized (if they are recoverable) only if any one of the following criteria is met: The costs extend the life, increase the capacity, or improve the safety or efficiency of property owned by the company; the costs mitigate or prevent environmental contamination that has yet to occur and that might otherwise result from future operations or activities and the costs improve the property compared with its condition when constructed or acquired, if later; or the costs are incurred in preparing for sale property currently held. For costs of treating environmental contamination to be capitalized by public utilities, the costs must also meet the requirements of SFAS No. 71, *Accounting for the Effects of Certain Types of Regulation,* as amended, for probability of recovery through rates, as discussed on pages 1012–1013 of the main volume. Chapter 16 of this Supplement presents a summary of recent developments in the area of environmental liabilities, including related accounting implications and auditing considerations. That discussion is particularly relevant to auditing a public utility's accounting for and disclosure of environmental liabilities.

The EITF has recently addressed two accounting issues affecting rate-regulated industries. On EITF Issue 92-7, *Accounting by Rate-Regulated Utilities for the Effects of Certain Alternative Revenue Programs,* the consensus of the task force was that once specified events occur that permit billing of additional revenues due to weather abnormalities or to compensate the utility for demand-side management initiatives or reward the utility for achieving certain objectives, the regulated utility should recognize the additional revenues if all of the following conditions are met:

1. The program is established by an order from the utility's regulatory commission that allows for automatic adjustment of future rates. Verification of the adjustment to future rates by the regulator would not preclude the adjustment from being considered automatic.
2. The amount of additional revenues for the period is objectively determinable and is probable of recovery.
3. The additional revenues will be collected within 24 months following the end of the annual period in which they are recognized.

On EITF Issue 92-12, *Accounting for OPEB Costs by Rate-Regulated Enterprises,* the task force reached several consensuses. For continuing OPEB plans, the task force reached a consensus that a regulatory asset related to Statement of Financial Accounting Standards (SFAS) No. 106 costs should not be recorded if the regulator continues to include OPEB costs in rates on a pay-as-you-go basis. For a continuing plan a rate-regulated enterprise should recognize a regulatory asset for the difference between SFAS No. 106 costs and OPEB costs included in the enterprise's rates if the enterprise (1) determines that it is probable that future revenue in an amount at least equal to the deferred cost (regulatory asset) will be recovered in rates, and (2) meets all of the following criteria:

1. The rate-regulated enterprise's regulator has issued a rate order or a policy statement or generic order applicable to enterprises within the regulator's jurisdiction that allows for both the deferral of SFAS No. 106 costs and the subsequent inclusion of those deferred costs in the enterprise's rates.

2. The annual SFAS No. 106 costs (including amortization of the transition obligation) will be included in rates within approximately five years from the date of adoption of SFAS No. 106. The change to full accrual accounting may take place in steps, but the period for deferring additional amounts should not exceed approximately five years.

3. The combined deferral-recovery period authorized by the regulator for the regulatory asset should not exceed approximately 20 years from the date of adoption of SFAS No. 106. To the extent that the regulator imposes a deferral-recovery period for SFAS No. 106 costs greater than approximately 20 years, any proportionate amount of such costs not recoverable within approximately 20 years should not be recognized as a regulatory asset.

4. The percentage increase in rates scheduled under the regulatory recovery plan for each future year should be no greater than the percentage increase in rates scheduled under the plan for each immediately preceding year. This criterion is similar to that required for phase-in plans in paragraph 5(d) of SFAS No. 92, *Regulated Enterprises—Accounting for Phase-in Plans*. The task force observed that recovery of the regulatory asset in rates on a straight-line basis would meet this criterion.

For discontinued plans (those that have no current service costs), the task force reached a consensus that a regulatory asset related to SFAS No. 106 costs should be recorded if it is probable that future revenue in an amount at least equal to any deferred SFAS No. 106 costs will be recovered in rates within approximately 20 years following the adoption of SFAS No. 106. Rate recovery during that period may continue on a pay-as-you-go basis.

The task force also reached a consensus that a rate-regulated enterprise should disclose in its financial statements the regulatory treatment of OPEB costs, the status of any pending regulatory action, the amount of any SFAS No. 106 costs deferred as a regulatory asset at the balance sheet date, and the period over which the deferred amounts are expected to be recovered in rates.

Additionally, the task force concluded in Issue No. 93-4 that if a rate-regulated enterprise initially fails to meet the regulatory asset recognition requirements of the consensus developed in Issue No. 92-12, but meets those requirements in a subsequent period, then a regulatory asset for the cumulative difference between SFAS No. 106 costs and OPEB costs included in rates since the date of adoption of SFAS No. 106 should be recognized in the period the requirements are met. The task force also reached a consensus that a cost that does not meet the asset recognition criteria in paragraph 9 of SFAS No. 71 at the date the cost is incurred should be recognized as a regulatory asset when it does meet those criteria at a later date. Additionally, the task force reached a consensus that the carrying amount of a regulatory asset recognized pursuant to the criteria in paragraph 9 of SFAS No. 71 should be reduced to the extent that the asset has been impaired. Impairment of a regulatory asset should be judged in the same manner as for assets of enterprises in general. SFAS No. 71 is discussed in the main volume beginning on page 1012.

38

Auditing Real Estate Companies

* p. 1031. *Add after third full paragraph:*

RECENT DEVELOPMENTS

Industry and Economic

After suffering its most severe slump in more than two decades, the U.S. real estate industry is showing signs of recovery in some markets and property types, with further deterioration in others.

Residential real estate prices, which were driven down by a recessionary slowdown in household formation and overbuilding in the single-family market, have begun to stabilize. Home sales and new construction of single-family homes are rising gradually in response to favorable interest rates and increasing consumer confidence. The aging of the baby boom population, now in their 30s and 40s, will contribute to sustained improvement in this market. Although demographic changes appear to be working against the multi-family market, the sharp reduction in multi-family construction—initiated by the Tax Reform Act of 1986 and fueled by credit shortages and restrictive zoning in some areas—is pushing apartment vacancy rates down and should eventually translate into higher rents.

On the commercial side, the country continues to face an oversupply of space in almost all markets, following significant overbuilding in the 1980s. The office market is in the weakest condition, with existing supplies expected to last more than ten years in some cities. The addition of over two billion square feet of office space since 1980 has pushed vacancy rates to almost 20 percent, more than three times traditional levels. Both weakness in the service sector and corporate downsizing will slow the office market recovery, and turnover of high-rent leases written in the late 1980s will threaten the stability of even the most successful office properties, as companies relinquish underutilized space and negotiate better lease terms.

The industrial and retail sectors have fared better than the office market, and are expected to regain normal occupancy levels within three years. Their relative stability is due in part to the predominance of build-to-suit construction, especially industrial space. Retail formats targeting value-oriented shoppers continue to outperform traditional shopping centers, although prime location is important for capturing scarce consumer dollars.

Value-oriented hotels will lead the recovery of the lodging industry, as cost-conscious consumers take advantage of the lower rates offered by limited services facilities. The outlook for the industry as a whole is favorable, despite high hotel loan delinquency rates over the past several years, which are due largely to over-financing associated with the 40 percent increase in hotel room supply that occurred during the 1980s. Low construction rates, coupled with moderate increases in demand over the next three years, are expected to raise hotel occupancy rates.

The dearth of new construction will assist the real estate recovery in general, allowing even moderate increases in demand to translate into lower vacancy rates. Severe credit shortages continue to limit additions to supply, as lending institutions take large loan write-downs and struggle to comply with increasingly strict capital reserve requirements. Banks and life insurance companies, the real estate industry's traditional lending sources, must also contend with mortgage rollover risk. *The Wall Street Journal* reported in November 1992 that almost half a trillion dollars in bullet mortgages are scheduled to expire within the next five years, most without alternate financing arrangements.

With little new financing available from traditional sources, the real estate industry is exploring alternative sources of capital. Real estate securities, notably real estate investment trusts and collateralized mortgage obligations, are gaining favor as vehicles for raising capital and increasing the liquidity of real estate investments. The National Association of Real Estate Investment Trusts (NAREIT) reported that together these two types of instruments raised $6.5 billion in 1992, a nearly three-fold increase over the previous year. The Resolution Trust Corporation, the agency charged with disposing of the portfolios of failed savings and loan institutions, has been a leading issuer of pooled mortgages and should lead to the creation of a broader investor base and a more liquid commercial mortgage securities market, benefiting other potential issuers.

Many observers believe that the real estate industry emerging from the current crisis will be fundamentally different from its 1980s counterpart. They argue that the country is now experiencing a structural change in how real estate is viewed, a change that may have long-lasting ramifications. Investors and lenders will place greater emphasis on current cash flows as expectations of appreciation in value are scaled back in a low inflationary environment with slow anticipated increases in rental rates. Profits will be earned from value-oriented, management-intensive real estate, where success depends on basics like better market research and tenant services.

39

Auditing Securities and Commodities Broker-Dealers

THE CHANGING ENVIRONMENT

* p. 1052. *Add after first full paragraph:*
    The securities and commodities industry has been affected in a variety of ways by recent industry and economic developments and changes. The auditor should be aware of these developments and consider the effects on clients' operations.

Increased Competition from Banks

Banks are likely to continue to be formidable competitors to securities firms, with or without changes in the legal and regulatory framework. The sizable fees that securities firms earn from investment banking activities, and the profits derived from trading activities, ensure that banks will continue to enter these arenas. In addition, as restrictions on the types of securities that banks may underwrite ease, the securities industry faces competition in what traditionally has been one of the most profitable lines of business. Capital requirements for banks give them a competitive advantage, as they take advantage of leveraging their vast capital bases.

Market Globalization

As a result of worldwide ideological transformations and the anticipated changes in the European community, the move toward globalization of the securities and commodities industry continues. Many broker-dealers have placed an emphasis on accessing new markets, such as the Commonwealth of Independent States, the

Eastern European Community, and China. U.S. Securities Exchange and Commission (SEC) registration requirements, however, are considered restrictive and limit participation in the market expansion by some foreign companies. U.S. institutions currently are requesting modification of the SEC registration requirements for those companies.

Streamlining of Operations

The ramifications of the October 1987 market crash, the leveraged buy-out excesses of the 1980s, and the uncertain outlook for economic recovery in the early 1990s have caused many broker-dealers to reduce long-term debt and re-engineer operations in order to operate more efficiently and competitively. Retrenchment and cost containment measures have become the rule, not the exception. Common buzzwords are downsizing, right-sizing, re-engineering, and outsourcing. Outsourcing of operations finds its fullest expression in the practice of correspondent clearing. Several firms have been quite successful in developing this business, often clearing for dozens or even hundreds of other firms.

Expansion of the Derivative Products Market

Recently, the industry has witnessed an expansion of the derivative products market, in number of transactions, types of products, and number of derivative product players. Many broker-dealers, as well as insurance companies, have established divisions or subsidiaries solely for this business purpose. The innovative and complex nature of the products themselves, coupled with the rapid expansion of the market and limited authoritative accounting literature related to these entities and products, significantly increases audit risk.

THE REGULATORY FRAMEWORK FOR SECURITIES BROKER-DEALERS

Net Capital (Rule 15c3-1)

* **p. 1054.** *Replace last sentence of carryover paragraph with:*
In December 1992, the SEC issued amendments to the net capital rule. The amendments changed the minimum net capital requirements for all broker-dealers, certain securities haircuts (including the undue concentration and contractual commitment charges), and charges relating to aggregate indebtedness. The new net capital requirements will be phased in over a period of 18 months, with intermediate requirements scheduled to become effective June 30, 1993 and December 30, 1993, and full compliance by June 30, 1994. At the time of this writing, the SEC has proposed additional amendments to the net capital rule; if enacted, they would alter the minimum net capital requirements for certain other broker-dealers and the capital maintenance requirements of market makers.

Other Rules and Regulations

* **p. 1059.** *Add after carryover paragraph:*

During 1992, the SEC issued final risk-assessment rules 17h-1T and 17h-2T. These rules require that broker-dealers maintain and preserve records and other financial information and that they report, on a quarterly basis, certain information to the SEC regarding the financial activities of Material Associated Persons (MAPs). MAPs are affiliates or other associated persons that could have a material impact on the financial or operational condition of a broker-dealer. Broker-dealers who clear customer accounts and have less than $250,000 in capital, including subordinated debt, as well as broker-dealers who do not clear customer accounts and are exempt from Rule 15c3-3, and have less than $20,000,000 in capital, including subordinated debt, are exempt from these new rules. Rule 15c3-3 is discussed on page 1054 of the main volume. The rules became effective for periods ended December 31, 1992. Although independent auditors are not required to report on compliance with these rules, the auditor should assess clients' need to comply and their compliance with the new rules as part of the other procedures performed on regulatory matters.

THE REGULATORY FRAMEWORK FOR COMMODITIES BROKER-DEALERS

* **p. 1059.** *Add at bottom of page:*

On October 5, 1992 the CFTC finalized amendments to the net capital rules for FCMs and introducing brokers. The new rules contain two additional factors that must be considered by FCMs when determining the minimum amount of required capital and raise the minimum capital requirements for introducing brokers not guaranteed by an FCM. The new rules became effective as of December 31, 1992.

40

Auditing State and Local Governmental Entities

OVERVIEW OF THE STATE AND LOCAL GOVERNMENTAL ENVIRONMENT

p. 1091. *Replace fourth paragraph with:*

Auditing guidelines and regulations established by federal, state, and local governments do not supersede generally accepted auditing standards, but may prescribe additional requirements with which the auditor should comply. Generally accepted governmental auditing standards (GAGAS) for federally assisted programs are set forth in *Government Auditing Standards,* popularly referred to as the "Yellow Book," first published by the U.S. General Accounting Office (GAO) in
* 1972 and most recently revised in 1988. (A major revision of *Government Auditing Standards* was exposed for comment in July 1993.)

The AICPA has provided guidance to the auditor in its 1992 audit guide, *Audits of State and Local Governmental Units,* as amended by Statement of Position 92-7, which presents examples of auditors' reports. In addition, when auditing a state or local governmental unit that receives federal financial assistance, the auditor must comply with the requirements of the Single Audit Act of 1984 (the Act) as described in Circular A-128, "Audits of State and Local Governments," issued by the U.S. Office of Management and Budget (OMB).

In 1991, Statement on Auditing Standards (SAS) No. 68, *Compliance Auditing Applicable to Governmental Entities and Other Recipients of Governmental Financial Assistance* (AU Section 801), was issued, which explains the relationship among generally accepted auditing standards (GAAS), the Yellow Book, and the Act. SAS No. 68 also clarifies certain reporting issues and incorporates the requirements for audits of certain nonprofit organizations receiving federal grants. SAS No. 68, which superseded SAS No. 63, is discussed further in Chapter 25 of this Supplement.

GOVERNMENTAL ACCOUNTING AND REPORTING PRINCIPLES

Fund Accounting

p. 1093. *Replace second item in list in first paragraph with:*

Special Revenue Funds—Account for the proceeds of specific revenue sources (other than expendable trusts or for major capital projects) that are legally restricted to expenditures for specified purposes.

p. 1093. *Replace second sentence in last paragraph with:*
The general fixed assets account group reflects a governmental unit's fixed assets, except those used in enterprise, internal service, or nonexpendable trust fund activities and therefore recorded in those funds.

Modified Accrual Basis Accounting

p. 1094. *Replace third full paragraph with:*
    In May 1990, the GASB issued Statement No. 11 entitled *Measurement Focus and Basis of Accounting—Governmental Fund Operating Statements,* which applies to governmental and expendable trust fund operating statements and requires the use of the flow-of-financial-resources measurement focus and the accrual basis of accounting. This statement, which will modify many revenue and expenditure concepts described in Chapter 40 of the main volume, was originally to be effective for financial statements for periods beginning after June 15, 1994 (with early application not permitted). However, in June 1993, the GASB issued Statement No. 17, *Measurement Focus and Basis of Accounting—Governmental Fund Operating Statements: An Amendment of the Effective Dates of GASB Statement No. 11 and Related Statements.* Statement No. 17 defers the effective date of Statement No. 11 to periods beginning approximately two years after an implementation standard for Statement No. 11 has been issued.

Standard Setting for Governmental Accounting

* **p. 1095.** *Replace last three sentences of first paragraph in section with:*
Those statements and interpretations, as well as GASB statements, interpretations, and technical bulletins issued as of June 30, 1992, are included in the GASB's *Codification of Governmental Accounting and Financial Reporting Standards as of June 30, 1993.* GASB pronouncements issued after that date have not yet been included in the *Codification.* The AICPA has designated the GASB as the body to establish financial accounting principles for state and local governmental entities under Rules 202 and 203 of the AICPA Code of Professional Conduct. Since its formation, the GASB has issued 17 accounting standards, one interpretation, one concepts statement, and three technical bulletins.

* **p. 1095.** *Add after second paragraph in section:*

As noted in Chapter 22 of this Supplement, in January 1992 SAS No. 69, *The Meaning of* Present Fairly in Conformity With Generally Accepted Accounting Principles *in the Independent Auditor's Report* (AU Section 411), was issued. Under the hierarchy established by SAS No. 69, Financial Accounting Standards Board (FASB) pronouncements will not be a source of established accounting principles for state and local governments unless the GASB issues a standard incorporating them into GAAP for state and local governments. SAS No. 69 is effective for audits of financial statements for periods ended after March 15, 1992.

Financial Reporting

* **p. 1095.** *Replace last bullet on page with:*

- Combined statement of cash flows—all proprietary fund types and similar trust funds.

In June 1991 the GASB issued Statement No. 14, *The Financial Reporting Entity,* which establishes standards for defining and reporting on the financial reporting entity. The financial reporting entity consists of (a) the primary government, (b) organizations for which the primary government is financially accountable, and (c) other organizations, the nature and significance of whose relationship with the primary government are such that exclusion would cause the reporting entity's financial statements to be misleading or incomplete. In addition, Statement No. 14 provides for discrete presentation of components as well as blending of component units, depending on the relationship with the primary government.

SUBSTANTIVE TESTS

Balance Sheet Accounts

* **p. 1103.** *Replace first two sentences of first paragraph with:*

Receivables from Taxes. As noted in Chapter 40 of the main volume, governmental fund-type revenue presently is recognized under the modified accrual basis of accounting, that is, when it becomes measurable and available. (This will change when GASB Statement No. 11 is implemented, the date of which is currently unknown.)

p. 1103. *Replace last sentence of second paragraph with:*
Amounts that are not currently available should be accounted for as reserves.

Comparisons of Budget and Actual and Other Operating Statements

p. 1105. *Delete next to last sentence of first full paragraph.*

Cumulative Index

Pages in **boldface** refer to the page on which the term is defined or to a block of pages that includes the definition of the term. The **"S"** preceding page numbers refers to Supplement pages.